THE KING
OVER THE WATER

Michael Pye

Holt, Rinehart and Winston
New York

For my parents,
who wanted to know

Library of Congress Cataloging in Publication Data
Pye, Michael, 1946–
The king over the water.
Bibliography: p.
1. Edward VIII, King of Great Britain, 1894–1972.
2. Windsor, Wallis Warfield, Duchess of, 1896–.
3. Oakes, Harry, Sir, Bart., 1874–1943. 4. Bahamas—
Governors—Biography. I. Title.
DA580.P9   941.084'092'4 [B]   81-617
ISBN: 0-03-057551-6

First American Edition

Printed in the United States of America
1 3 5 7 9 10 8 6 4 2

AUTHOR'S NOTE

This book would have been impossible without the careful, painstaking and sometimes ingenious help of archivists. I especially thank John Taylor and other staff members of the National Archives in Washington; Ronald Mellor and the staff of the Public Records Office in London; and Gail Saunders and the staff at the Archives in Nassau, Bahamas. I am also grateful for the help of Edna Rolle and the staff at the Nassau Public Library. Those dozens of people who helped by giving interviews and writing letters are listed and thanked in the sources, where it is possible to thank them by name. During my work on this book, I was grateful for the support of Celia Haddon, Isabel Hilton, Ronald Payne, Neal Ascherson, Michael Klein, Swythin and Sharon Wilmott and, as always, John Holm. My agents, Anthea Morton Saner and James Brown, were rock-like supports, and I am thankful for the help of my editors, Jennifer Josephy and Trent Duffy at Holt, Rinehart and Winston, and James Cochrane and Sue Hogg at Hutchinson.

Village Road, Nassau
June 1980

CONTENTS

Part One   TREASON   13

Part Two   RIOT   133

Part Three   MURDER   211

Part Four   REFLECTION   245

The Sources   263
Notes   269
Bibliography   278

Twelve pages of photographs follow page 152.

PHOTOGRAPHIC ACKNOWLEDGEMENTS

[i] (*above*) Bahamas Archives, Nassau; (*below*) Wide World Photos
[ii] Wide World Photos
[iii] (*above*) Wide World Photos; (*below*) Stanley Toogood for *Nassau Magazine*, New York Public Library
[iv] *Nassau Magazine*, New York Public Library
[v] Stanley Toogood for *Nassau Magazine*, New York Public Library
[vi] (*above*) Wide World Photos; (*below left and right*) Bahamas Archives, Nassau
[vii] (*above*) *Nassau Magazine*, New York Public Library; (*below*) Wide World Photos
[viii] (*above*) *Nassau Magazine*, New York Public Library; (*below*) Stanley Toogood, *Nassau Magazine*, New York Public Library
[ix] Wide World Photos
[x] (*above*) Stanley Toogood, *Nassau Magazine*, New York Public Library; (*below*) Wide World Photos
[xi] Wide World Photos
[xii] Wide World Photos

We acknowledge the help of the Bahamas Archives, Nassau, and their picture collections; the New York Public Library (Astor, Tilden and Lennox Foundations); Stanley Toogood, Nassau, Bahamas

PART ONE

TREASON

A faint August wind came from the shore, stifling and lifeless and hot. It was barely dawn, and the island already breathed heat. At the harbour mouth, the escort destroyer slipped away to the open sea, and left the SS *Lady Somers* to come into Nassau at a stately, ceremonial rate. The journey was finished. The exile had begun.

The most distinguished passengers had climbed to the bridge, to watch their new home slip into view. The captain pointed out the landmarks of Nassau, a tight little settlement on a ridge, facing the eastern trade winds. A pink mansion stood high on the hill, all jalousies and verandahs, sprawling among tall palms.

'Darling,' said the Duke of Windsor to his Duchess, 'there it is. Our home for the duration.'

The Duchess saw a house like a plantation mansion from her childhood. It seemed familiar. It would be a home at last, even if they had not chosen it, and the Duke would at last have a job. From 9 July 1940 he had been the Governor Designate of the Bahama Islands, a minimal outpost of the British Empire which London long ago had decided was beyond its control. Their tattered life could begin to reassemble itself among the pink houses and the splashy flowers.

They came in 1940, still glowing from a legend: the King who left his throne for love, the woman who was worth the disruption of a monarchy. They were famous lovers, touched with royal magic. They would leave the islands, in a bare five years, in utter disgrace. Instead of the lovely legend, there would be a bickering middle-aged couple, furiously beating back age and boredom in a shallow little world of rich people, trivial times. Instead of royal dignity, there

15

would be a Duke disqualified from any public position except that of mourner or celebrant at great family occasions. In Nassau, the main settlement of the Bahamas, their legend would die away, and their chances of public life would finally be wrecked.

For in Nassau, the Windsors brushed too close to treason, riot and murder. Their refuge from the endless running, so bright and gaudy in the humid morning light, would be a trap for them.

The town was waiting, nervously. Bunting spread like vines along the main streets and the waterfront. The police band, crisp in white with broad helmets, tuned their instruments. In the official buildings, draped for the day in purple and palmetto leaves, the powers of Nassau spread themselves on wooden chairs and waited. Big ladies powdered their faces pancake brown to cover the wear of the sun. A little plane landed at the seaplane dock and spilled out two bustling men: Harold Christie, real estate dealer, the man who sold the Bahamas to the rich; and Harry Oakes, gold millionaire, his most spectacular customer. They rushed to cars and their homes to put on the formal clothes proper for welcoming such unexpected royalty to the islands.

For the Windsors were wholly unexpected. They had not seemed likely replacements for the last Governor, Sir Charles Dundas, who had planned to end his career in the Bahamas. Dundas had not been liked by the rich residents – Americans had petitioned for his removal – but he had fancied himself a proper figure for Nassau. Abruptly, he was told to go to Uganda, close to the firing lines, an uncomfortable post for an ageing colonial civil servant. He was not allowed to say who would be his replacement. He could only drop hints – that the appointment would be 'big news'. He told a newspaperman in Nassau: 'I don't know why I should be pushed out to make room for him.'

Dundas was moved in order to open a place of exile for the Windsors. London had watched the royal couple in Lisbon with a growing anxiety about what they might do next. Nassau was a place to park them, to take them away from danger and temptation. Nothing much, London thought, could happen there. Even the general unrest of the Caribbean islands in wartime had not spread so far north.

The House of Assembly of the Bahamas – the lordly, ponderous cabal of merchants and lawyers known as the Bay Street Boys from the main commercial street – granted the town a one-hour holiday for the welcome, and began to organize its flags. Balconies on official buildings were shored up, cutting the cables to the warning siren which was the sum of Nassau's defences. Cameras were allowed in the House of Assembly but were 'liable to confiscation if necessary'. 'It was agreed,' said Executive Council minutes, 'that the reception should be arranged on the lines of previous receptions for Governors and that no very special arrangements were required, except perhaps in regard to the control of the Press.'

But the morning was special. Nassau was a little town, dominated by the rich men on Bay Street and the rich transient winter residents. Its rulers were white and insular; hidden over the hill, beyond the ridge on which stood the Windsors' new home, was a black majority who had not yet learned their power or their rights. The islands had a history of lawlessness, of wrecking and piracy, gun-running for the South during the American Civil War and rum-running during Prohibition. Their basic asset was land – not for growing crops or mining minerals, but for selling to rich men who wanted winter homes or a haven from taxation. Their main glory was a sparkling, emerald sea that brought the tourists south. For those tourists, the Windsors proved a magnet. Already, despite the cruel August sun, the SS *Arcadia* had sailed from New York with not a cabin free. Tourists, in those days rich and substantial persons, shared the general Bahamian curiosity about the Duke and Duchess. They wanted to see for themselves the King who had left his throne, the woman who had made it worthwhile.

To be Governor of the Bahamas was no great thing. Previous Governors had been forced to bombard the House of Assembly with artillery fire to get their way; Speakers of the House had been known to fire pistols at Governors, even to beat them over the head with muskets. Governors ruled at the whim of the House, which alone could raise taxes. The merchants of Bay Street almost alone could fill seats in the House. Bay Street had the power.

The Governor was the nominal ruler of islands with terrible problems of hunger, a kind of king with constitutional limits on his power. David Windsor, once King Edward VIII, was sent over the water like the Stuart pretenders because he represented risk to the ruling house. He was wilful, compassionate, stupid, brave, and egocentric, all at once. He was capable of absurdly petty private dishonour with ugly consequences, and of grand, public courage. In the soft, amoral islands, he was free to show both his capacity for caring, and his capacity for squalid tricks.

He was supposed to be safe from harm in the Bahamas – the harm the Nazis might do him, the harm he might do Britain in wartime. He was not. The Windsors seemed trivial counters in a world war, but they remained dangerous – because their legend, their charisma, their royal status still commanded attention. They were still stars. What might have been acceptable private views of appeasement, surrender, negotiated peace, became downright scandals when the man proposing them was an ex-King of England. What might have been the common sort of rich man's money deal – even Laval in Vichy France was protected financially throughout the war by an American officer ranked so high that even Roosevelt could not dismiss him – became tinged with treason when a one-time monarch was defying British law for his own profit. In Nassau, Windsor came too close to schemes of treason and even of murder, and far too close to the people involved. The curtain between royal persons and brute reality no longer protected him. He became a player in a game that sometimes turned to scandal.

He also had to rule – to play at politics, to translate his ideas into practice while respecting constitutional limits. He was the representative of the King. Some still thought he should not have abdicated, that he was needed. He was 'The King over the water' – the King's surrogate who still trailed the glory of having once been King.

This book is about how he used – and abused – his power.

Far from Nassau, a Swedish multi-millionaire called Axel Wenner-Gren received a letter from contacts in Rio. Wenner-Gren had made his Bahamas home on Hog Island, in a mansion he called Shangri-la, among exotic birds and flowers and trees. He had good friends in Germany, and he fancied himself something of a diplomat. His pushy, hard-drinking wife encouraged that illusion; he liked to humour her.

In any case, the politics were a logical development of Wenner-Gren's economic powers. George C. Messersmith, a senior American diplomat in Mexico, warned the State Department in 1942: 'I recall hearing Goering say, some time in 1933, that Wenner-Gren was one of the most powerful instruments which the Nazis would be able to use in their economic operations with important people in England, France and the United States.'

Wenner-Gren's letter from Rio said this:

> You will soon find there [that is, Nassau] a new and interesting family with which I assume you will at once become very friendly. I have met an old acquaintance who formerly lived in the same street as your brother and he states that family hold sympathetic understanding for totalitarian ideas. This acquaintance and his fellow-countrymen have much consideration for people of that family. This should be of great significance for forthcoming development of events. They will gladly talk with you and furthermore these people have been prepared for talks.

British Intelligence had already seen that letter and they would hand it to the Americans when it suited them. They omitted the name of the contact in Rio. They left the text as evidence of Wenner-Gren's curious and sinister contacts.

The family was the Windsors. The preparation had taken place in Spain and Portugal. Wenner-Gren would return in autumn to Nassau and offer the Windsors a dazzling, dangerous escape.

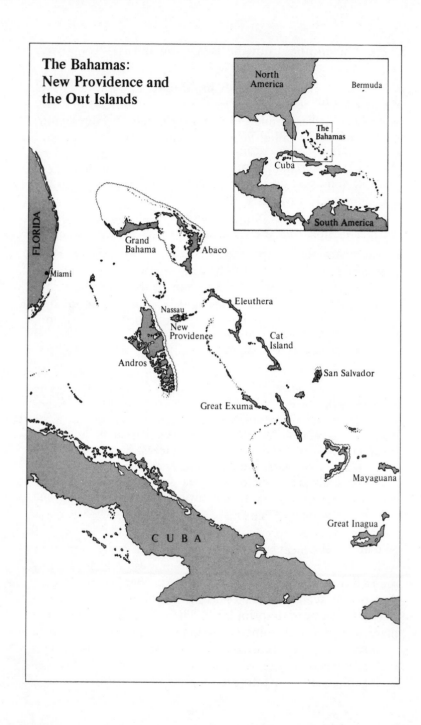

The Bahamas:
New Providence and
the Out Islands

North America

Bermuda

The Bahamas

Cuba

South America

FLORIDA

Miami

Grand Bahama

Abaco

Eleuthera

Nassau

New Providence

Cat Island

Andros

San Salvador

Great Exuma

Mayaguana

Great Inagua

C U B A

The Duchess knew from the first hours in Nassau that she would need an escape. She waited a few moments before following the Duke down the gangway. She could see sweat standing on his face, beginning to seep through the khaki of his uniform. She hated the heat, hated the way it cracked open elegance and decorum.

By the time he had stood to swear the oath of loyalty – 'I, Edward Albert Christian George Andrew Patrick David, Duke of Windsor, do swear that I will be faithful and bear allegiance to His Majesty King George, his Heirs and Successors, according to law' – she saw that sweat was running down him, smearing the signatures to a vague black wash.

They made official conversation. The Duke in particular talked with the American consul and asked if he was a consul general, a privileged conversation that John Dye was quick to report to Washington. They drove past a bland white statue of Queen Victoria flanked by captured German field-guns from the First World War and turned into Bay Street. They saw the scarlet and coral-pink of poinciana, sheets of summer colours; and the stores that Nassau boasted, the Jaeger shop, the perfume shops, the grocery store with separate sides for whites and blacks, and the warehouses on the seaward side where the high tides still gurgled under the old floorboards; and they turned up the hill to their official home. Crowds cheered and clapped and sang. It was a welcome to the Windsors, loudest from starry-eyed blacks.

Colonial ladies had filled Government House with summer flowers – hibiscus, ixora, frangipani, their strong colours and strong, heavy scents. The Duchess was not fooled. 'I'm afraid you won't find this very comfortable after the houses you are used to in France,' said Mrs Heape, wife of the Colonial Secretary who would act as Windsor's deputy. The Duchess saw heavy mahogany, bad paintings presented by the dealer Duveen, some royal images and a distinct lack of recent paint. She saw the imprint of a dozen governors on tables, chairs, sofas. 'It is absolutely lovely,' she lied. She determined that she could not live there.

That afternoon, the Windsors drove to the cabana that Governors used, down to the west by the wide arc of Cable

Beach. They swam, and washed away the day. On Sunday morning, the Duchess was prostrate with heat and excused herself from cathedral services. The Duke stood awkwardly, shifting from foot to foot, in the cathedral pews. He had no great faith, and ceremonial religion was only interesting when it came with colour and drama and saints. He felt out of place as an official worshipper, without Wallis, after so many years. And he suffered the special agony of a patch of prickly heat that had started in Bermuda and was now lodged, like a little purgatory, between his shoulder blades.

Heat overwhelmed the island. Sudden lightning that rolled along horizons, thunder that spoke from unpredictable corners of the sky, sheeting rain and high winds were the only breaks in the hot days and nights. Wallis Windsor, cool, strong lady, was terrified of thunder. That, and the scuttling of the landcrabs that scratched along the sidewalks, would be her special horrors in the Bahamas.

She took paper headed Government House, and she crossed out the address. In its place, she wrote: 'Elba'.

Their way to the Bahamas had been long and curious, a skein of melodramas and panics and dreams. Now that David Windsor was to govern, his old training and formation was once again important. His attitudes to race, to politics, to social life would be exposed – anything from his drinking to his skills at meetings. He would have a detailed political job as well as a ceremonial role.

He was an unknown man, for all the public appearances and the drama of love and abdication. Think of the Duke of Windsor, and you think of a fantasy – 'We didn't have movie heroes or aviators in uniform to worship,' the writer Adela Rogers St John remembered of her American girlhood. 'Most of us concentrated on His Royal Highness the Prince of Wales. I had his picture in a silver frame on my dressing table. The dream of every American girl was to dance with him.' He was 'pretty and engaging' to Lady Diana Cooper, 'a faded but once great beauty' to Christopher Isherwood. He was blond and boyish, open, simple and fair. He said himself that he had been 'trained in the manners and maxims

22

of the nineteenth century for a life that had all but disappeared by the end of my youth.' He was a hero-prince, used to homage but resisting it, wanting a job to do. In the First World War he bitterly resented the fact that he was worth more as a trophy, if captured, than he ever could be as a fighting man.

He was born into a monarchy which did not have any certainty of survival. He once told Mabell, Countess of Airlie and lady-in-waiting to his mother, Mary: 'I shall have to work to keep my job. I don't mind that, but the trouble is they won't give me a free hand.' Despite the sentimentality which was growing around it, monarchy was an institution which could still be blown away. The Duke's grandfather, Edward VII, had once sat with friends as Windsor passed: 'There,' said Edward, 'goes the last King of England.'

Kings had to work to prove their usefulness. Windsor, while still Prince of Wales, became a grand political symbol. Lloyd George would send him out, like a star on tour before a movie, to sell the *status quo* across the Empire. Windsor would appear, dapper and uniformed and charming, wherever there was trouble that only charisma could resolve. In India, Windsor was sent to counteract the influence of Gandhi, to keep the streets full even when Gandhi declared hartal, and be a focus for loyalists. If the Québécois were restive in Canada, Edward went; if Australia had labour trouble and strikes, Edward went; if the Boers and British were too obviously jarring against each other in South Africa, Edward went. He was genuinely popular, genuinely loved; he could hold a crowd, and in the moment that they worshipped him, they reaffirmed loyalty to the whole machine of British Empire.

Edward was made to carry this huge role despite his early shyness. He claimed he had the tastes of a gentleman farmer; 'I like,' he once said, 'what we in England call "the simple life".' He was vulnerable and, as often as not, that vulnerability appeared in public as wilfulness, a defence against what he had to do. He was reluctant to be hustled into any course of action, but his rebellion could only be on minor matters. The rest was stage-managed. He always had advisors. He

23

could rebel, certain that the advisors would prevent any disastrous consequences; and his revolts were often no more than being late for diplomatic parties, wearing dress less formal than the invitation demanded, drinking too much or else abandoning himself to one of his violent enthusiasms – golf, hunting, flying. Each was an obsession for a while; all were dispensable. He knew the gap between the short, brisk figure that met the crowds and the rather unformed man he was in private life. By 1919 he was called in America, 'one of the great democratic figures of the world'; privately, he said that 'often I remain retired within myself'.

There was one point at which the private man and the glorious prince did overlap, often to the consternation of his political managers. Edward cried. He had no sense of a political system or how it worked, but he did have a sudden, wrenching pity. In Glasgow in 1921 he met a man who had lost both arms in wartime, and he wept; he told a crowded hall that 'we cannot have happy peace until all sections of the community are satisfied' and that 'the present horrible epidemic of unemployment and the tragedy of the suffering that it brings in its train worries me a great deal'. He was remembered in the First World War for his bravery, and also for his insistence that he see the most badly wounded men in a field hospital, and his tears when he saw them. He would become notorious later for telling South Wales miners that 'something must be done' about their conditions. His sympathy was real and graceful, but it was also a quality which could be exploited. Edward gave humanity to the established system, and helped defuse political reaction to the growing misery of the 1930s and the brute depression. He was coldly used as, in the boast of his supporters, 'a symbol against Socialism'.

Although he had great symbolic value to politicians – at home among the unemployed, abroad in Empire or as salesman for things British – he was never allowed time to absorb the peculiar and subtle skills that a constitutional monarch needs. The Court knew that, and some members of it saw the danger. He saw the world from the viewpoint of a prince; triumphal arches were hung with animal skins in Nepal to

24

welcome 'Britain's Sporting Prince' and, at Bhopal, thrones of turquoise and gold were set out for the Emperor. He saw only welcoming faces – simple old Gambia chiefs' huts in Barbados covered in bright paper, a carnival welcome for the 'King Piccinin', the throngs of Canadians pushing to greet him and leaving his hands crushed and bleeding from too many eager handshakes. The Empire still had durbars, ceremonies at which the subject population literally offered worship to the monarch. Edward's power seemed at once limitless and unreal – worship but no influence. Managing that frustration and that tension is the essence of a constitutional monarchy, where kings must not claim too much nor damage their magic too much. Edward never learned.

His politics were of his class and time – instinctual, usually conservative, often with a stain of unconsidered racism. When he toured the West Indies, his supporters reckoned that he 'revived those feelings of solidarity with Great Britain which have sometimes been strained by the preachings of race prejudice from which no people situated as these can ever be completely exempt, be the white administration never so tactful.' In Australia he blustered to a dinner audience about the dream of a continent for a nation, a nation for a continent; and no Greeks, orientals, blacks or dagoes in either. 'Now see,' he said, 'with what a faith and force the Australian people have taken that ideal to their hearts. You are determined that this nation shall be pure of race and that all your citizens shall have an equal chance. . . .' In South Africa, the 'races' he wished to reconcile were the Boers and the British. When he was still a child, he had waited for his parents to return from some great Imperial progress, and he always remembered, with horror, his growing fear that they would return scorched black by the sun.

But 'subject races' played no great part in his thinking. His world was centred on Europe. Like a true nineteenth-century man, he still thought in terms of a continent divided between France and Germany, the two great languages and cultures and political powers. He felt comfortable with German; he later took to calling it *'meine Muttersprache'*. He remembered a bullying French governess, disliked the French

25

language and had little taste for French people; his Riviera exile was lived out, in the 1930s, among British and American friends, and Italian servants. He loved his German background – 'those vigorous people whose blood flows so strongly in my veins'. When Weimar fell and Hitler came to power, it was no more in Windsor's mind than an internal trouble in his beloved Germany. People and nation were still the same. He hated the carnage of world war, and wanted to avoid any new conflagration. He would speak for friendship between the old soldiers of Britain and Germany, to the horror of the veterans' organization he addressed. In his world, chic people thought it absurd to be 'pro-Semitic' and reckoned Germany should have a little more room to live in Europe, perhaps some of those obscure Balkan states of which smart London knew little. The Prince of Wales was openly reported to have Nazi sympathies, and Ribbentrop reported the rumours to Berlin with glee. Hitler even seemed to share Windsor's comfortable faith in old empires and kingdoms; there were rumours that the Nazis planned to restore the Hohenzollerns as Kaisers of Germany. Windsor, still personally angry at the Bolshevik treatment of his uncle Czar Nicholas, approved very much.

Perhaps a more sophisticated or a more trained man would have seen the dangers in all this, for Windsor's sympathies were assumed to be political factors of great moment. His public statements could always embarrass governments. For as long as he was Prince of Wales and King, he could never be ignored. He imagined that England and Germany could amicably divide the world, that the cut-out cartoon capitalists might be routed, that the working man would be less cold, less hungry, less battered. In this view of the world no great subtlety is possible. Politics exists either in the great chancelleries of Europe, where historic friendships and alliances counted far more than the growing evidence of the true nature of Nazism, or else in the streets, where the Prince showed an unformed compassion. Nobody told him how to think, carefully, about the actions that his strong feelings should produce. His father and mother were remote and imperious, and he had little chance to learn his trade by

26

osmosis; his Empire tours prevented formal training or regular contact with political reality. He came to the throne as he came to the Bahamas later – a sheltered, none-too-clever man with no political sense, who cared deeply but who carried with him a binding load of prejudices and half-thought fears.

He had one other enthusiasm which was awkward in a prince. He loved women. He had glamour, and his title alone made him a figure from dreams. John McMullin of *Vogue* shrewdly called him 'God's gift to women', not because of any particular sexual expertise but because 'he adores them and simply has no interest whatever in any man'. He was easily influenced in love. Thelma Furness, Wallis Simpson's predecessor, was thought to have Americanized him – 'making him over-democratic, casual and a little common', according to one diarist, Chips Channon. He began to sound vaguely American, a fault which Channon said would not be great 'since all the Royal Family except the Duke of Kent have German voices'. He needed the warmth of his women, not least because his own family had been so icily careless in his childhood. He was also used to being dominated by his women – from his arm-twisting governess to his later mistresses.

Women are a fine avocation for a Prince, but love can present problems. Wallis Simpson was the nemesis of David Windsor.

She was a woman with a past, like any woman who had not perfected her life to meet the exacting standards of the British Court. She had wit and grace, and a sure sense of how to present herself. She was foreign, which Edward had been told in 1920 was an unacceptable condition for his future Queen; she was already in her second marriage, which was swiftly cooling; she was an admirable mistress and an impossible Queen. Sentiment could not override the ways in which she demystified the throne. It was fine the King should have his 'cutie' but Noel Coward was probably right that Britain did not want a Queen Cutie; certainly, it would be hard to attribute magic to a Queen whose two living husbands would be able to say they had slept with Her Royal Highness. The monarchy was not on the most sure of grounds as it was. The possibility of moral objections to a divorcee, or scandal in the past of the Queen, or general talk about the circle of the King would undermine the ability of the Court to present a monarchy at once magical in authority and bourgeois at home.

But she was remarkable, all the same. She knew how to hold a room. 'She is a jolly, plain, intelligent, quiet, unpretentious and unprepossessing little woman,' Channon wrote, 'but . . . she has already the air of a personage who walks into a room as though she almost expected to be curtsied to.' Her face needed the life and animation of talk to be beautiful; at rest, in photographs, it was not obviously handsome. 'In repose,' Cecil Beaton wrote, 'her expression is wistful, but the grave effect is shattered by the sudden explosion of her broad firework laughter.' Even on casual meeting she left a distinct impression. E. Berry Wall, the American dandy who in Paris exile was known as King of the Dudes, met her once in the Hotel Meurice in Paris and thought her a 'slender, effectively dressed, young-looking woman, with a faintly whimsical smile edging a wide, generous mouth that you were especially conscious of because of the dead white of her face.' She had wit and a formidable social skill; she was 'never embarrassed, ill at ease, and would in her engaging drawl charm anyone,' Channon said. The drawl began to take an English edge as the Duke's American intonations became more noticeable. At dinner with Somerset Maugham, Harold Nicolson noticed that 'her voice was also changed. It now mingles the accents of Virginia with that of a Duchess in one of Pinero's plays.'

She showed no signs of wanting to be a queen. To the very moment of the abdication, she was ready to renounce marriage and her prince. All the confusion and the passion came from the silly uxorious instincts of the Prince of Wales once he had become King. He wanted to marry; he wanted to marry Wallis. He would give up his throne for the warmth, the strength of his woman. Faced with that sacrifice, her scope for escape was limited. She may not even, wholly, have

28

wanted to share the rest of her life with a dull, sandy-haired boy of forty. His obsessive, devoted form of worship, all fawning eyes and constant, jealous interest, was never matched by similar symptoms of passion on her side. Yet she knew, because she had carefully practised twice, the duties of a wife. She would support him and give him what she could. After the melodrama of the abdication, and the long painful separation while her divorce became final, she would always have to carry a terrible burden of expectation. At no time could she be ordinary. Married to the ex-King of England, she could neither take on the duties and title of a royal spouse nor fully escape the judgements of others. She would have all the hurt of a public figure with none of the supports that Court or conventions offer.

As a private woman, her friendships with German diplomats – casual, sympathetic – would not have been scandals. As it was, Roosevelt was told by his London Ambassador in 1937 that Mrs Simpson had long been rumoured to be in German pay; and since the Prince of Wales was said to have Nazi sympathies, the scandal was born. As a private person, and an American, her later sympathies would have been wholly understandable. But the fact of her marriage made those sympathies exploitable, and so unforgivable. Marriage, cruelly, limited her right to public opinions.

Her divorce was scandalous – 'KING'S MOLL RENO'D IN WOLSEY'S HOME TOWN', read one American headline. Queen Mary admitted that 'it is no ordinary love he has for her', but she also spluttered, when the whole apparatus of political battle and scandal had come close to abdication: 'Really! This might be Roumania!'

There was already one pointer to their later career, which might have surprised those who thought Mrs Simpson ambitious and trivial and greedy. At the moment of the abdication, it was she who had a clear idea of the King's duty. She knew how to settle for less than perfect circumstances because she had already known them. King Edward VIII would brook no opposition, would have his way. He had never learned the limits of his power. He never did grasp what duty means. But she did, and in the Bahamas exile that would become a very important fact.

Once abdicated, and sent out of England on a night boat, Edward VIII was merely David Windsor, Duke without role or job. Out of the Court's protection, he was uncertain and buffeted, ignorant of how to deal with money since he had never had to handle it, and barely able to cope with the mechanics of his new life. And his exile was complete. Queen Mary told Lord Queensborough in 1939 precisely when he could return to Britain: 'Not until he comes to my funeral.'

David Windsor was a rich man who simply did not know it. At the time of his abdication, he was personal owner of the great royal estates of Balmoral and Sandringham; while Prince of Wales, he had drawn the revenues of the Duchy of Cornwall, which can hardly have been worth less than £250,000 ($1,000,000) a year; he had received a £1,200,000 ($5,000,000) bequest from his grandmother, Queen Alexandra. The Cornwall income also gave him £31,850 ($125,000) a year for life, and the Civil List, the Treasury's roster of payments to its royal clients, included a decent income for Windsor, its precise amount camouflaged by royal discretion.

But this affluence was nothing like the indivisible net of royal credit, royal privilege, royal standing. A prince conventionally does not pay bills when out to dinner; an equerry settles them. Some princes, like Edward VII in his younger days, repaid the equerries and some, like David Windsor, did not. Such etiquette divorces a man from his real financial standing. He does not have to take the simplest responsibility for what he wants. Windsor never managed money nor considered it. His homes and property were entwined with his position – palaces, servants, planes and cars, pictures and jewels which could be enjoyed without any deep thought about whether they were the property of David Windsor as an individual or David Windsor in his capacity as King. At the abdication, Windsor had to consider what was personally his.

He resented the doubts about what he really owned; it

was thought wrong for him to give to Wallis the jewels he had inherited from Queen Alexandra, since they were a kind of trust for the royal family, and once given to Wallis Windsor they passed outside the family's control. He tried to take his father's £1,250,000 ($5,000,000) postage stamp collection, but discovered that it had been entrusted to keepers paid by the state and had therefore become a public trust, not private property. He threatened to lease Balmoral to exotic New Yorkers, a horrid threat since the Scottish estates were peculiarly associated with the still-revered Queen Victoria; he settled for £125,000 ($500,000) and selling them to the royal family. When he left Britain he had no land except for a ranch in Canada, the EP Ranch in Alberta; during his tour of 1919, he had bought 1600 acres, leased another 2400 and put in ponies and cattle. It was his only certain, personal asset. Much of the rest depended on the goodwill of the Treasury – how much would be paid as annual allowance – and the disentangling of a complex financial settlement made between the lawyers of Windsor and his brother's lawyers. He was simply not used to the idea of personal wealth, as opposed to the financial privilege of a royal career; and the surprises and negotiations and quibbles about what he could take, what he could sell, what he could do, all added to his financial insecurity.

He resented the limits which governments put on his money, even, it seems, the limits imposed in wartime by exchange control to keep British money available to the British war effort. By any rational criteria, he was extremely comfortable, with the possibility of informal royal subsidies if he needed them; he had the financial advice of the shrewdest money men on both sides of the Atlantic; he cannot, simply on the basis of the deals made public at the time of the abdication, have been less than a dollar millionaire who also had additional income from the Civil List. But he was a titled man without the security of estates or a home, and with a fortune that seemed uncertain. He feared political change which might take away what privileges were left to him. The fact that he could not appreciate his wealth because it seemed so different from easy privilege, his political fears

31

and his inexperience with money left him peculiarly open to the over-clever schemes of financial operators.

By law, the wife and children of the Duke of Windsor were excluded from royal titles. It was a miserable snub, and Windsor always resented it. He would sometimes call the Duchess by the title he thought she should have had – Harold Nicolson remembered the frisson when 'the Duke called her Her (gasp) Royal (shudder) Highness (and not one eye dared meet another).' He would present her, to Americans especially, as 'My wife, Her Royal Highness the Duchess of Windsor.' He never lost his anger at the Court's attitude. 'This cold-blooded act,' he wrote in the 1960s, 'represented a kind of Berlin wall alienating us from my family.'

After the abdication he was again in pursuit of a job. He could always live for style, of course. The *Vogue* people, like John McMullin, reckoned: 'The Duke and Duchess of Windsor – once they have had time to get together – will undoubtedly create a glamorous life somewhere into which I can again pop and perhaps write about from the housemaid's angle.' *Vogue* owed Wallis Windsor a favour; she had fixed for them a special photo sitting of the King in his coronation robes. But style did not satisfy him. Since London would offer no serious posts, he was vulnerable to anyone's suggestions. Charles Bédaux used him – first by providing the château where the Windsors married, then by arranging and financing a tour of Nazi Germany, then by attempting to plan a tour of America which was fiercely resisted by labour unions. Bédaux was a Fascist sympathizer whose main achievement was the invention of the time and motion study and the Bédaux clock for workers to punch time cards and 'clock in'. American diplomats considered the Windsor links with Bédaux disastrous, and the Duchess always thought that the British intelligence service had been remiss in failing to warn them of Bédaux's sympathies. But for the moment a fact-finding tour of Germany allowed the Duke to pursue his proclaimed interest in low-cost housing, although it was unclear what would happen with the facts he found when the tour was over. The American tour seemed attractive and the Windsors resented the flurry of diplomatic activity which ended in its cancellation. They were often naive about their contacts, and inclined to value the kindness of associates above any political danger. She had a fine instinct for social politics, but little for a wider sort of political risk; he had never learned. They remained loyal to Bédaux after his arrest in 1942 as a collaborationist, until his suicide in Allied hands in 1944.

In the last months before world war, Windsor desperately wanted to make some intervention to stop the war, to restore the natural friendship he imagined must lie between Germans and Britons. His position was not absurd. The rhetoric of the coming war had to do with the defence of Empire and glory; moral opposition to the racism and the genocide of Nazism had not yet developed, nor was there a certain definition of the threat to 'freedom', nor would that be the mainspring of war. When Chamberlain announced, finally, that there would be no more appeasement, Windsor must have felt that he had lost a personal struggle – for the moment. He would persist, though; and by any means he could.

On 13 September 1939, he returned to Britain as a suppliant, the Duchess on his arm. War had been declared ten days before and he wanted a part in it. He came in great secrecy and found no warmth or welcome – not even a place to stay. His friends the Metcalfes had to throw dustsheets off their country house to give the Windsors a bed. The barriers he faced were political and personal. He had broadcast from Verdun, a message banned by the British Broadcasting Corporation but widely reported in America. He had chosen an emotive battleground for his speech, and he spoke passionately, pleading that 'such cruel and destructive madness shall never again overtake mankind.' He looked a fool. The broadcast was ineffectual but highly embarrassing. For King George, the quiet, stuttering introvert who had been pushed to the throne by Edward's defection, the problem was acute: he had loved and worshipped his brother, but he could not tolerate his brother in the country for long. Edward would be popular, glamorous, attractive in ways

33

that George could not; and George feared the dominance of his elder brother. He foresaw 'difficulties'. He offered at first two positions – Windsor could be a staff member of the Regional Commission for Civil Defence in Wales, well away from London; or else he could opt for Paris, as a Major General in the British Mission. Windsor decided that he wanted the Welsh job; but after their talk, George had reconsidered. Windsor was told, coldly, that: 'The conclusion reached by His Majesty is that His Royal Highness would be most suitably employed as a member of the Military Mission to France.' It was a cruel appointment: Windsor would be junior in rank to his own younger brother Gloucester, Chief Liaison Officer to the British Expeditionary Force.

Windsor knew the feeling inside the Court. He knew that it would be hard for George's wife, Queen Elizabeth – Wallis called her the 'Dowdy Duchess' – ever to forgive the strain and prominence which Edward had bequeathed to George. But still he felt betrayed. 'I had been given a promise,' he said later, 'that if I abdicated I would serve the King, my brother George VI, as I had served the King, our father, George V.'

They had no great objection to the Paris exile on other grounds. It was already their city, their style, a little international coterie with good food and taste. Parisians thought their city impregnable and the war, in any case, seemed to consist entirely of shouting and posturing. The Duchess joined the Red Cross and made trips to the front with supplies three times a week; the front was not yet active, and the war was still 'phony'. The Duke wrote worthy reports, notably about the real weakness of the Maginot Line, which won him neither credit nor attention. They worked hard, but the work seemed unreal. The Maginot Line was not yet threatened. Real, shooting war seemed so distant that it was hard to keep enthusiastic.

And then the Nazis were advancing on Paris, and the weaknesses in the Maginot Line were of more than theoretical interest. Without leave, Windsor headed for Biarritz and then, with the Duchess, to La Croë, their Riviera home. The British, acutely embarrassed, let it be known that he would now be attached to French forces at the Italian frontier. Had that been true, his detour to Biarritz would have been highly improper; but in fact, after four weeks of his 'purely nominal job' on the Riviera, he quit. Within a fortnight, the Nazis were in Paris and the Windsors, politically unpredictable and wilful, were a source of huge potential trouble.

They fled again, this time to Spain and on to Portugal. The Duchess knew diplomats and nobles from her London days and from dinner parties at her Bryanston Court apartment. The Nazis were eager for the Windsors – at least to have them pause on Fascist territory for a while, to leave options open. Churchill was only too aware of the problem. The Windsors must be moved out of harm's way as soon as possible. Windsor tried to bargain, for visits to America, for the proper title for his wife, but there was no longer time.

On 9 July 1940 the decision was made and the Windsors were, in effect, ordered to Nassau. Churchill wanted Roosevelt to know the news immediately, and cabled the British Embassy in Washington. The message arrived corrupt and unreadable and had to be repeated, after rumours had started and the BBC in London had carried the news. Churchill told the President: 'The position of the Duke of Windsor on the Continent in recent months has been causing His Majesty and His Majesty's Government some embarrassment as, though his loyalties are unimpeachable, there is always a backlash of Nazi intrigue which seeks now that the greater part of the Continent is in enemy hands to make trouble about him.' He added, understating the point: 'There are personal and family difficulties about his return to this country. In all the circumstances, it was felt that an appointment abroad might appeal to him. . . .'

The moment Windsor knew he had to go to Nassau, the squabbles started. The British applied diplomatic pressure in Washington to have the Export Line's *Excalibur* diverted to Bermuda, so that the Windsors would not pass through New York. There was too much life – and too many British isolationists – in the city for diplomatic comfort. The Export Line was unhappy, since their passenger list was already distinguished – ambassadors from Italy, Belgium and Holland, the last two returning from newly occupied territories from which they had been withdrawn. The line was worried about insurance since, as Commissioner Truitt of the Department of Internal Communication said, the Duke and Duchess would be a 'sweet morsel' for any marauding submarines, German or Italian. Even when all the details had been arranged, there was still doubt whether Windsor would actually go when the day of sailing came – and in what frame of mind. Walter Monckton, one of his closest advisors during the abdication period, was sent to make sure that the Windsors followed orders.

He found the SS, under Walter Schellenberg, closing a net around the royal couple. Agents had already arrested known members of the British Secret Service in Lisbon, planned anonymous messages of warning to the Windsors, considered shattering the glass in Windsor villas with rifle bullets to cause alarm. They tried to build panic and paranoia in two people peculiarly liable to both, to persuade them that the British were after their lives. Monckton also listened to the stories and found them hard to discredit totally. The Marques de Estella, son of the Spanish Primo de Rivera, came from Madrid to warn the Duke that British intelligence would have him killed in the Bahamas. The story struck Monckton as fantastic, but the Duke was impressed, and so was the Duchess. It was enough to cause delay – de Estella asked for ten days to convince Monckton; the Windsors, denied official transport, were booked to leave on the *Excalibur* the next day. Monckton made a deal with the Duke; he would stay in Lisbon, listen to what de Estella had to say and stop the Windsors in Bermuda if the story had the slightest foundation. As a last throw, the German minister in Lisbon, von Hoyningen Heune, submitted to Monckton a list of 'Jews and emigrants leaving with the same boat and thus people who posed a threat to the Duke. . . .'

The situation was now wholly bizarre. A royal Duke had spent an astonishing amount of time in close contact with Nazi agents and enemy sympathizers, on barely neutral territory, while under orders to leave for a new posting. His talks, coldly viewed, were close to treason. The prospect of the Windsors deciding to sit out the war in Falangist Spain, in Franco's territory, was itself a propaganda coup for Axis sympathizers. And when Windsor and his Duchess did leave Lisbon, grudgingly and fearfully, they went under the shadow of a supposed plot to kill them by the very Government that was sending them to the Bahamas. All the certainties had shaken loose, all at once; old loyalties fell away. Windsor was produced for the last time in Europe at an official press conference in Lisbon, a bizarre occasion where journalists were specifically forbidden to ask questions. He would say little, except that work in Nassau would be his first opportunity in the government of a British colony. 'It will,' he said, 'be a novel experience for me.'

They had not meant to miss New York. Fourteen pieces of their luggage, bearing the crest of the Prince of Wales, turned up in Manhattan on the SS *Britannic*. On the journey to Bermuda the Duchess, now to be so close to America with little chance of paying a visit, gorged herself on all the typically American food she could find and said she was so glad to see it again. On a sad morning, Duke and Duchess hung at the rail of the *Excalibur* as a free-flying Pan Am clipper dipped to a few hundred feet above them and radioed messages of goodwill; it was a proof they were remembered in America, would have been greeted with affection, and the sight of a plane New York-bound was a painful reminder that they were not headed there.

In Hamilton, Bermuda, the Duke paced the living-room of Government House and talked about his beloved America. 'The Duchess hasn't been there for eight years,' he said, 'and I haven't been there for sixteen years. The last time I was there, the Woolworth building was the biggest in New York – that rather dates me.' He was curiously subdued on questions of politics; he claimed a long absence from 'the political arena and the arena of public affairs.' He remembered having a Christmas card in 1936 from Bede Clifford, then Governor in Nassau, with a photograph of a new swimming pool at Government House which had ER VIII set in tiles in the floor. 'It's funny,' he said, 'that I should be about to use that pool now.' He thought that Nassau would be very nice, really.

Monckton found nothing in Lisbon to suggest that British marksmen were waiting in Nassau, and the journey continued – the hot, long journey south. Dogs and equerries and the Buick car (Canadian-made when he was King, but American-made now that he had the choice) travelled with them, along with two truckloads of baggage. 'We have so much baggage,' the Duchess complained, 'but it doesn't contain the right things.' She regretted the clothes and silver left in France as they fled. And they had a trailer with them. To the Duchess, it was a mark. 'Every refugee,' she said, 'has a trailer.'

Over the hill in Nassau, south of the ridge on which Government House stood, the healing trade winds do not reach. Shacks crept up the hill from the bottom. Electric wires did not pass the ridge. Houses were gaudy in primer colours of blue and green and red and pink, clustered where landlords happened to have space. White outsiders saw these streets only when they were in search of some night-time excitement – a 'glimpse of Africa in the Bahamas', as the advertisements for Willy's Bar put it. This was black Nassau, full of roadside stands that sold ice, of avocado trees and silk cotton trees; all walled off, with a literal, concrete wall, from the light-brown mulatto quarters to the east.

In black Nassau, the Duke of Windsor came as the descendant of Queen Victoria – Aunti Wikki, who freed the slaves. To his family, black Bahamians ascribed emancipation, the interception of ships still plying the slave trade to other countries, the landing of the new-freed cargo at villages like Adelaide on New Providence. Windsor was a hero, by descent.

In the first days that he was in Nassau, wild rumours flew about his plans. Wharves and markets and back streets said he planned to paint the statue of Columbus, discoverer of the Bahamas, black in honour of the people. They said he had driven past the pound for stray dogs and been so moved by the whimperings that he ordered all the dogs freed. They said he had ordered freedom for the prisoners who worked in the gardens of Government House and that he had doubled their wages. They even said that Windsor had stormed into a meeting with the Bay Street Boys, and confronted Kenneth Solomon – the lawyer who led the government in the House of Assembly, served on Executive Council and stood for the certainties of white rule. He has asked who spoke for the white people, and Kenneth Solomon stood forward. He had stared the man down. 'From this time on,' the Duke had said, 'I speak for the black people of the island.'

Windsor was an implausible hero. He disliked black people. He mistrusted them and thought they required to be handled with the special expertise found in the American South. He had had little contact with blacks beyond a sight of flags and smiling faces and a gaudy welcome during his Imperial tours. Now, he was ruler of islands where only one person in ten was white. He would be helped, for a while, by the curious quiet of the Bahamian black population; 'there was,' says H. M. Taylor, later a founder of the Bahamian Progressive Liberal Party, 'no public opinion whatsoever.' Blacks, seeing no alternative to the pin-prick humiliations of white rule, seemed calm and passive by contrast with the agitation of Jamaica. For cultural reasons, they had the habit of avoiding confrontation at all costs.

In Windsor's time they would smash the plate-glass face of Bay Street, and put a torch to the police station in Grants Town, over the hill. The calm would turn to riot and fury, soon.

'We are a middle-aged couple,' the Duchess told a serious-minded American visitor. 'We do not go to night-clubs. On the contrary, we are living a very simple life and enjoying things with each other.' Simplicity cost money. Government House was to be redecorated at a cost of £2000 ($8000) – given new paint and a fresh, needed wing. The Windsors demanded changes which cost an extra £5000 ($20,000), claimed to have paid the bills themselves, but actually tried first to persuade the unwilling House of Assembly to foot the bill and then asked London if Crown funds could be used. Government House was, admittedly, a scruffy and unimpressive building. For months, the Duke and Duchess lived in other people's houses, while their official residence was brought to life.

Their first official decision was to ask permission to spend two months in Canada at the Duke's ranch near Calgary until Government House was ready for them. Lord Lloyd of the Colonial Office told them 'it would not only inevitably create a sense of disappointment but also possibly some misgiving and anxiety among the public as well.' He did make one concession, which he must have known the Duke would refuse. 'There is of course no reason why, if the Duchess feels the heat, she should not go away for a few weeks.' When their escape was blocked, they settled to work – the Duke beginning his painful exploration of the politics of Nassau, the Duchess taking on her first duties as head of the local Red Cross and working in a smell of wet paint and plaster, in a tiny bare office with cracked white walls, within the shell of Government House.

She made a proper mansion from unpromising beginnings – at the cost of rows with the House of Assembly, which thought it could not afford her style, and the Board of Public Works, which was more used to providing adequate homes for middle-range civil servants. The bare-boards austerity of the house vanished under marbled papers and pastel drapes. The worst paintings, the many which offended the Duke's educated eye, were banished. 'Don't you see I must make a home for him?' the Duchess said. 'That's why I'm doing this place over, so that we can live in it with comfort as a home.' She was certain that her fine redecorations had emotional significance. 'All his life he has travelled and a palace to come back to is not always a home. The only one he ever had, he made for himself at Fort Belvedere, he had to leave it. You don't know what that meant to him.'

For the Duke she designed (with the costly help of Mrs Winthrop Bradley of New York) a bed-sitting room, all rattan and floral prints, with a narrow desk and quadrants of sofa. Maps of the Bahamas made the walls official; New

Providence hung over the Duke's bed, in a wall recess. He had his treasures around him, like a schoolboy, as he always did: there was a rack of fifty pipes, a box made of wood from Nelson's ship the *Victory*, a midshipman's dirk, a Field Marshal's baton. Even the match-boxes had been considered; all were stamped 'Government House'. The details were royal – a capital 'E' and the insignia of the Order of the Garter set in the heavy glass of the front door; Prince of Wales feathers on the pelmets; an ashtray from 1936 marked *Edwardus Rex* – Edward the King. She even provided style in his private space where he worked and retreated. She liked to keep that space in order, to clear away the heaps of papers that represented his sort of organization. She said his disorder was 'like Churchill,' and she did not mean the comparison kindly.

For the bad paintings, the Duke substituted royal miniatures. In the drawing-room, to focus the house, he put an unflattering portrait of the Duchess by Gerald Brockhurst, stood for emphasis on a false mantel. The picture made the house into their territory, made Wallis Windsor its centre and heart in place of the official images – Queen Victoria on the cabinets, Queen Mary on the secretaire. The grand space of the ballroom was left in wartime quiet, despite its fine terrace that looked away from the town of Nassau, over the hill to gardens of flaring poinciana and hibiscus.

Money for the house was a constant battle. The cost of the curtains outraged Godfrey Higgs, a young lawyer who was then leader of the Opposition in the House of Assembly and who would later change sides and join the Government. He protested that such extravagance was unthinkable in wartime. Wallis Windsor made a point of taking Higgs aside when he next visited Government House. 'And the draperies, Mr Higgs?' she asked. 'How do you like the draperies?' Higgs wilted in face of the direct charm.

Change in Government House always meant battles. The Board of Works was capable of refusing a £10 grant for painting, or demanding that a royal palm ('for use at Government House') be bought only on their express, written authority. The bills for making the official mansion habitable

41

were thought scandalous. And all the while that the Windsors were arranging the titivation of their home, they had a separate plan: to leave as soon as possible, to lobby for a diplomatic job in America.

They sold their story to Hearst newspapers, and Adela Rogers St John came to Nassau to listen to them. The Duchess campaigned, ruthlessly, using a histrionic range she usually concealed. 'We are determined to do our duty,' she said, 'like good soldiers and he – he bears it like a saint – but it is the world that suffers his loss.'

The Windsors came to the Bahamas in ignorance of what they would find. Governors did not brief their successors, in British tradition. Sir Charles Dundas, displaced by the Duke and cornered by reporters at New York, confirmed that it was quite usual that he should have left before talking with the Windsors. 'The idea is that a new Governor can assume office without prejudice or preconceived ideas. It would be rather wrong for his predecessor to pump him with his ideas.' Windsor, unlike most new governors, had a major disadvantage: he was not an old Colonial Office hand, able to shift from post to post with little thought, nor had he experience of administration. He had to learn his job from scratch. The first thing he had to learn was that his job was more or less impossible.

The Bahamas was run by a Governor, his deputy the Colonial Secretary, a Receiver General who handled money, an Attorney General who handled the courts. Together with local leaders, these senior officials formed the Executive Council, conventionally called ExCo. They were the Governor-in-Council, the central power; they disposed of crown money, from the sale of land for example, and of money from London; they set policy on matters like immigration and took initiatives on policy. They could not, however, raise money. That power had been ceded two centuries back to an elected House of Assembly, whose members were almost all men with shops on Bay Street or legal business there, and almost all white. They alone could start and approve laws on tax; since policy depends on budget, they had extraordinary blocking power. They were financial conservatives who disapproved the spending of an unnecessary penny on health or schools or housing. They were elected, once every seven years, in elections full of rum and dollar bills; Out Islands voted by public declaration, and New Providence had its first, experimental secret ballot in the late 1930s. Members rarely visited their constituencies – once a year was considered more than enough – and they did not vote along lines the constituency might need; policy was made by and for the merchants of New Providence. Sir Arthur Burns at the Colonial Office in London called it 'their ideals of misgovernment . . . government of the people by Bay Street for Bay Street.' Monson, a senior Colonial Office civil servant, wrote in a 1940 memo that the House was a scandal:

In brief, this body represents nobody but the 'merchant princes' of Nassau, is selected in a manner reminiscent of the worst excesses of the unreformed Parliamentary system of this country in the 18th century and in performance shows itself to be irresponsible, crass or malignant. As things stand, however, the constitution of the Bahamas is more or less in the form in which it was originally created and we would only have an opportunity to alter it in the event of the House taking some step which was a danger to the external security of the Empire, or in the event of the Colony becoming bankrupt. Neither of these eventualities seem likely at the moment. . . .

Since the Colony's spending was kept very low, and import duties paid most of the bills, Nassau did not need to ask for London money, and London leverage was strictly limited. London might want social legislation, economic change, and offer substantial amounts of development money in return; but the House of Assembly refused such money as a threat to its independence. Once London money was part of the colony's budget, the threat of withholding cash could be used by London to force change. The House bellowed about its rights, and by avoiding all public spending when possible, it kept them.

The Governor was left on Government Hill to ponder this absurd situation. Dundas told London, three months before

Windsor arrived: ' . . . a fundamental fact which it is necessary to recognise is that there is no Government in the Bahamas competent to decide upon and carry out a policy of development and improvement.' He could not approach the House until he knew London's views, and he could not ask London for help until he knew the House of Assembly was at least inclined to consider a scheme kindly.

Observers might try to invest Windsor's appointment with great significance – would Britain federate her Caribbean colonies with the Duke as Governor? – but the fact was that the Bahamas was a colony which had got out of London's control by sheer neglect. It was a small, quiet enough straggle of islands in a perfect, emerald sea. It was remote and hard to police. Its history, accordingly, had veered from larceny to expediency over the centuries of British rule.

From the seventeenth century, pirates used New Providence as a base, lying up in the sheltered channels before making forays out into the Windward Passage; Blackbeard was there, watching out over the difficult channels that led into the little harbour from the east. Respectable settlers had come to Eleuthera in the seventeenth century from Bermuda. When the American colonies revolted in 1776, loyalists were rewarded with grants of land in the islands. It was a troublesome gift. In place of rich Southern land, the loyalists had to contend with soil hidden in pockets in coral and limestone rock. Cotton and sugar withered; there was no room for a plantation economy. Within twenty years the dreams of the loyalists had tarnished. Man and master had to work together to an extent unthinkable on Caribbean plantations to the south, in Jamaica or Trinidad or Guyana; the owners of plantations were not rich and distant in London, working through brutal overseers, but immediate, and hungry, like their slaves. Fishing kept people alive; there were sponges, and migrant Greek dealers who handled them, and a fleet which had by 1901 some 265 schooners and some 322 sloops and some 2577 open boats, carrying more than 5500 men and boys out to work on the sea; and during the American Civil War, the high balconies of the Royal Victoria hotel were tramped by gun-runners and blockade-busters. The shadow of Rhett Butler passed by.

Hotels became important, and not only those in the islands. Around 1900 Flagler, the developer and impresario of the swamps of Florida, finally ran out of mainland to develop. He had left a trail of grand resorts and stylish hotels on white beaches. His progress was determined by geography – he followed the railroads as they snaked south – and it naturally led from Florida to the Bahamas. In Nassau he bought the Royal Victoria and built the great pink icing-sugar mass of the British Colonial hotel, across the site of an old barracks at the westerly end of the town. More important, Flagler needed labour in Florida, at Florida rates. One in five Bahamians left home for Flagler's territory in the early years of this century.

Guns for America and beds for the tourists and jobs on the mainland were all enticing alternatives to the less rewarding business of working the sparse land. Yet the islands did grow fruit – pineapples, guavas, coconuts, oranges, grapefruit, bananas – and sent millions of them overseas. Canada had new ships that could take tomatoes north. Sisal grew and salt could be evaporated on Inagua on great, glittering saltpans tinged with the same ghostly pink crustaceans that gave colour to the flocks of flamingoes.

It all fell apart. The saltworkers took jobs as stevedores. Blue-grey fly killed the grapefruit; bad packing and careless cultivation did for the pineapples. The sisal was bush-beaten as it was dragged to the packing places, weakened by washing in salt water and often soaked again to make up the weight. Tomatoes arrived bruised and bleeding at New York, and there were chronic problems with debt and commission agents. Long before the great, wide fields of Florida and Hawaii gave cheap and lethal competition to the difficult Bahamian agriculture, the islanders themselves had almost abandoned the business. All that was left was what Dundas called 'flower-pot cultivation' – corn and peas, tomato and mango, grown promiscuously side by side in the tiny pockets of rich, red earth. 'The Bahamas,' Dundas reported in 1930 during his first tour of duty in the Bahamas as Colonial

Secretary, 'stand almost alone among the British colonies as a territory that has gone back rather than forward in productivity and contribution to British trade.'

There was a real problem of hunger, and an equally real problem that Bahamians were turning against work on the land. 'There are not a few,' Dundas wrote, 'who now regard the life of a cultivator as beneath their dignity.' Curiously, the same people were prepared to take menial jobs in the new grand hotels in Nassau; the main staff, from waiters to bands, were white, and imported from New York for the season. Dundas supposed the influence of the tourist traffic 'does rather engender a touting, opportunistic spirit. . . .'

The combination of failed farms, absent labour and growing tourism was not especially healthy, even with the commercial success of the sponge beds. But there might have been change – the House of Assembly might even have climbed down from the dizzy prominence of its rights – but for one factor. Just as American war made Nassau rich in the 1860s, followed soon by the long-term visitors who claimed to be wintering in the south for reasons of health, so now in 1920 American civic morality made the Bahamas extraordinarily successful. America wrote her wartime ban on alcoholic drink into the Constitution, and Nassau had a wild new industry.

Bay Street in 1920 was nicknamed 'Booze Avenue', a long row of shabby and unpainted liquor stores. Anyone with a boat had access to sudden wealth. Drink came legitimately from London or Glasgow to the docks, and merchants sold it legitimately, although in most British colonies orders for 5000 cases of Scotch would raise an eyebrow. Once sold, it was taken either to Rum Row, the line of boats that stood just outside territorial waters off New York; or to Bimini, where bootleggers would take it to the Florida coast; or for some brave Bahamians, it was a cargo to Florida itself, a risky business of running into the cays at night and landing fast before the Coast Guard were alert. Fortunes, later sanctified by time, were started in those years. Harold Christie, the real estate operator who became one of Windsor's political advisors, ran rum alongside the likes of Meyer Lansky. The first Prime Minister of the Bahamas, the distinguished Sir Roland Symonette, made his first money from a schooner called the *Halcyon*, which carried liquor to the Florida beaches.

The fish-town boomed. Crates were piled crazily on the dockside, stacked between the spongeboat masts which were laid on the quays. At one point, the liquor stocks of Bay Street were worth more than $10 million. 'Before the liquor homed on the Bahamas,' one bootlegger said, 'the Government had no dough at all. They was owing salaries and "gone away" was pinned up on the safe.' When the Prohibition boom came, 'the House of Assembly keeps sittin' ter consider what they'll do with all the money.' The treasury swelled so fat that villains found it worthwhile in 1926 to blow off the top of the colony's bullion vaults and steal the gold reserves. After the First World War, the colony had a £17,000 deficit and £81,000 in annual customs revenue; in 1922–23, the colony had £265,314 in the bank and £626,000 in customs dues pouring in.

The drink business softened the edges of hard morality in Nassau. Bootleggers held their wilder parties at the Lucerne, where the Chief Justice also lodged. According to the bootlegger Bill McCoy (the real McCoy), there were 'slit-eyed, hunch-shouldered strangers. . . . Nothing like these hard guys had ever crossed the trail of the gorgeously uniformed, pompous coons of the Bahamas police force.' Gun-gangs were available to discourage those who asked improper questions, and piracy of one rum boat by another was not unknown. Americans with Mob connections did their drink business in Nassau until increases in duty drove them north to St Pierre and the Canadian end of the trade. The British authorities argued, righteously, that the trade did not offend their laws, but the Governor's position did become awkward. Sir Bede Clifford, while Governor, found himself expected to protest when US Coast Guard vessels seized a Bahamian ship in US waters without giving the usual period of grace for its cargo to be unloaded. He considered – but finally, in the interests of British dignity, refused – an invitation to write the foreword to a bootlegger's autobiography. Rather complaisantly, he noted in his own memoirs that 'the Bahamians were not the only contrabanders but when it came to skilful seamanship, daring and enterprising smuggling they were in a class by themselves.'

Behind the drink trade there was a persistent shadow. Some Nassau boats took heroin and cocaine with the simple alcohol. Most captains forbade the cargo because it put them outside British law and British protection, but it still moved. The vice-consul in Nassau of one European power was arrested with a package still in its wrappers from the English manufacturers and with the stamp of a pharmacy in Nassau. Nobody talked about drugs or gossiped in the clubs, nor was it common for a man to be thought to have a taste for – say – cocaine. But the drugs traffic passed through Nassau – as it did also in the 1940s and does today – and some of the dealers bore distinguished Bahamian names.

In the rum days, the rich and stylish began to drift to Nassau in the winter. They came for the sun and the remoteness and the charm. Lady Diana Cooper, in 1925, found Nassau 'the prettiest village one could see in an old colonial aquarelle'. She remembered food that teemed with ants, chairs that tottered on the balconies; sucking oranges, breaking ice with a boot, pouring water over stung feet because scratching seemed too much bother. The women wore white boots and organdie and, on their heads, spotted kerchiefs, and were quaint; and the likes of Lady Diana found it cross-making that rum money changed the place. Within a few years, she reckoned Nassau had suffered a 'horrible earth change of brick and concrete. Gone was the primitive atmosphere. Where it once consoled, it now irritated.'

The profits from rum that reached public coffers were spent largely on developing the huge, expensive hotels. The Bahamas was determined to be a resort, a fashionable place. But as the bootleggers drifted north, harassed by rising island taxes on alcohol, the farsighted began to have a queasy feeling. If the rum money dried up, Nassau was not yet ready to make the same fortunes out of tourists. Drink made things happen; the Depression made it unlikely that tourists could be a substitute.

Roosevelt gave the Governor, Sir Bede Clifford, decent advance warning that booze was coming back to America. Easy money drifted away; and so did the more splendid rum-runners like Arizona Ted, the piano player, and the magnificent Grace Lythgoe, known as Cleopatra or Queen of the Bootleggers, who dealt in American and Scotch whiskies on Market Street, and hailed from Bowling Green, Ohio. Wages slumped. In the 1920s, a labourer could make 5s to 6s a day; now the going rate was a shilling, if a man was lucky. The tourist business brought its own labour – white and sassy, often annoyed if anyone mistook them for British. Agriculture was in disarray.

The priests and ministers and preachers saw the change most painfully, in islands whose Sunday devotions were loud and strong, even when their weekday lives were less confined by thoughts of judgement. Father Quentin Arnold Dittberner, a Benedictine, wrote:

In 1933 people were poor and undernourished because the tourist business lasted only two months of the year. Otherwise, the people lived off whatever they could gather on their little farms outside of the city. This included sweet potatoes, cassava, bananas, sugarcane (just 'cane' to them). Besides this, there were coconuts, sapodilla, oranges, grapefruit. With the poverty of the people, there existed a simplicity. They had tumble-down shacks for homes, but most managed to have a Sunday dress or Sunday suit. The squalor was not as great as would first meet the eye. They were not filthy. You could eat off the floor. . . . Their houses were neat, though very simply furnished. One day a man came to Father Arnold to ask him if he could have a box. 'What do you want it for?' The man said: 'To sit on. I have no chair in the house.'

That was the other reality of the pretty colonial town: the harsh, hungry life over the hill. At Prohibition's end the islands were again without all those activities which gave incidental employment – the making of new fortunes which gave new men a taste for households of servants, the Bay

49

Street boom which paid the wages of sweepers and cleaners and assistants in the shops, the translation of cash and profit into social aspirations. And although the great melodramas of Prohibition would fade quickly, there would be a residue: greedy colonial boys with friends in the Mob, links to organized crime that were social and friendly and, sometimes, devastating.

The prettiness of Nassau – Winston Churchill called it 'the Ganymead [sic] of the New World' in the Government House visiting book – began to need salesmen. The big hotels were ready. The Royal Victoria stood among great trees that were caught in broad-leaved philodendra, its front façade hidden from the town by a tall and wide silk-cotton tree into which was built both bandstand and dance floor, one above the other, open to the evening air. The British Colonial, coloured pink like coconut candy, lowered at the end of Bay Street, and, far out east, just before the shoreline where the rum-runners built their finest mansions, the Fort Montagu Beach stood, square and solid, between a phosphorescent lake and a gentle sea. And there were the miles of coastline, of sand and palms, where winter homes and new estates could be prepared. There were hotels; there was land; someone had to shill for them.

Harold Christie took the burden on himself – for a commission. He was old Scots stock in Nassau, from a family who were early members of the all-important St Andrew's Society that had united settlers of a certain class since before Queen Victoria's time. His father had been a wandering man, with a streak of religious fervour, who rarely concentrated on places or jobs. Offered control of all General Electric's advertising in New York State, he simply vanished after six months. He would disappear to Europe, with a handful of dollar bills, and stay away for months. He wrote verse and left business to his long-suffering wife. She sold straw-work to Georgia and played profitably with her earnings in the Florida land boom. While father went preaching the gospel of the Plymouth Brethren sect, mother built a little fortune – substantial enough to leave her badly hurt by the crash of 1929.

Harold Christie took the words and the charm from his father, the persistence of his mother, and added a total inability to manage a business. He was a salesman, an enthusiast, not a manager; that role went to his younger brother Frank. But Harold Christie was determined. Outside Nassau, nobody seems to remember a single conversation which did not somehow turn on real estate in the Bahamas – its value, its potential, its price. He had been a writer for the Knickerbocker Press in Albany, New York; he spent a year in the Royal Canadian Air Force; and by his mid-twenties he wanted to be back in the islands. He took a job as a steward on a cruise liner and at Nassau he jumped ship. His brother Percy, a proper Bay Street merchant, lent him a respectable pair of trousers to go job-hunting.

Outside Nassau, to the west, was an old sisal plantation by the sea which had become an estate called The Grove. A British millionaire called Guy Baxter was dividing it into parcels of land; Christie volunteered as salesman, was wildly successful and took either land or commission as recompense. As a bootlegger, Harold Christie made the money that kept him in cars, women, drink; but as a commission man, he started a business. He lived as high as Nassau could provide, and lived higher in Palm Beach or Bar Harbor in Maine, or anywhere among the rich where he could get invitations. He was shambling and short and dishevelled, dependent on a fugitive charm. He was good at finding the worries of rich men, full of the kind of plans and plots that would reassure them. He was lyrical on the waters and charms of the Bahamas, although with a tendency to describe most of his islands, at one time or another, as 'Eden'. But his real talent lay in selling the colony as a haven where income tax was unknown and violently opposed, where the state would take only 2 per cent of a man's personal estate on his death and nothing at all of his real estate. With that bait, Harold Christie went out among the cocktail gentry of Palm Beach, the Upper East Siders at Bar Harbor, and he sold.

Canadians had been interested from the mid-1930s in the possibility of setting up trusts in Nassau which would save them from tax. Holt of Montreal Light, Beaverbrook of the newspapers had shares in the Bahamas General Trust. Big American companies had offshore subsidiaries which acted as little more than plumbing for their flow of money; money arrived and departed from the colony's one bank to an exact timetable, staying only hours, but changing its nature by its brief time in the Bahamas. It followed that anyone with hefty business interests and a strong distaste for the progressive income tax might be persuaded quite easily to Nassau. Harold Christie went out to find such men, and he found Harry Oakes.

Oakes had gold – the Lake Shore mines in Canada – and no great taste for his civic duties. He quit medical school for the Klondike gold rush, prospected in Australia, returned to Canada when the threat of conscription for war had died away. He found his fortune either by chance (some said he had been thrown off a train for having neither ticket nor money, just at the point of his mother lode; he later gave the train conductor who expelled him a pension) or skill (he spotted what others did not: that the lodes of gold led like spokes of a wheel to a rich centre by the shores of a lake). He was a man of spectacular riches, a broad-backed, brash prospector with no social graces and a taste for riding boots and squashed felt hats; he married an Australian woman, Eunice, who drifted gracefully through the empty life of a colonial matron, arranging lilies in their various homes. They were an incongruous couple. In London, plain Harry Oakes became ambitious for a title, something to set him apart. He took advice and discovered that massive acts of charity often brought knighthoods; he financed the rebuilding of St George's Hospital at Hyde Park Corner in the centre of London. In due time, the Palace spoke; Harry Oakes, proudly, became Sir Harry.

All this was a logical progress, with one flaw: the taxman. Oakes simply could not deal with taxation. It appalled him, just as the American draft had once appalled him. Harold Christie had the right brusque approach, the ability to spin dreams of tropical living, and he persuaded Oakes to move himself, his money and his family south to Nassau. Oakes built a high house by open caves, with a swimming pool of salt water pumped from the clear sea down below; the place was huge and eccentric, out to the west of the island where sandflies still bit and the path of the trade winds was less comfortable in the heavy summers. With Christie's help – and paying Christie hefty commissions – he began to buy land. He would buy the scratched fields of a poor farmer who needed cash and could make no profit from his crops; it was like an act of charity. He bought blank scrubland, ridges by lakes and brackish salt-brown water traps. He bought the Bahamas Country Club by Cable Beach, where minor civil servants swam on Sundays. And he made himself known – blunt, awkward, over-talkative, always talking of how much he loved to live rough as a prospector while Lady Eunice busied herself with the home beautiful.

The Oakes estates had two specific values. They made work. In the rum days, anyone with a fishing smack could make money by providing transport for the cargoes of liquor. Even a small boat could be a rich investment. Women worked as packers, breaking up cases of drink, tying the bottles in triangular bundles and sewing them into canvas strips. Rum made jobs for peasants as well as merchants. When the rum trade drifted north and finally died, prospects were bleak. Only the philanthropy of men like Oakes kept men in work.

The other value was this: even without taxation, the Bahamians still contrived schemes to divert the fortune of Sir Harry Oakes into the kind of investments that Government needed and could not afford.

Bede Clifford, the Governor for most of the 1930s, was just as doubtful about income tax as Sir Harry. But he also saw that some drastic action would be needed when the Depression and the end of the rum trade hit. He took Crown money – the cash the colony raised from sales of land and so forth, which the House of Assembly could not block – and paid £37,000 for Prospect Ridge to the west of the island, above Cable Beach and its golf course, and the Bahamas Country Club. His Legislative Council – the seven men who sat in judgement on the laws passed by the House of Assembly, and on the Governor's whims at times – said the deal was too expensive and made him sell the ridge itself to estate agents like Harold Christie. Still, Clifford had the land between ridge and sea. George Murphy, a bootlegger from America who could no longer go home, built a racetrack.

Clifford, a stiff-backed, angular man, was usually obsessed with his dignity; he was the last Governor to hold a durbar, a ceremony at which the people must offer worship to him as the King's representative. But he was also an amateur surveyor and he went out with line and theodolite to lay out new holes for the Cable Beach golf course. As he worked, a stocky man in leggings and breeches appeared, discussed surveying, said he had done most of his work while staking out mining claims. Clifford said he needed a stronger dragline to handle limestone; the newcomer said he might be able to help and then, as though inspired, he said: 'Are you the Governor?'

Clifford said he had sized up the newcomer at his first appearance. It was Harry Oakes, and Clifford asked him if he would care to buy the British Colonial hotel. It was the colony's problem and it consumed money – it attracted tourists, it sheltered them, it made possible the jobs and sales that depended on tourism, but the hotel itself did not turn a profit. Governor and millionaire, out on the links, discussed what to do.

The colony put its money into subsidizing ships and planes to bring the visitors, and subsidizing such hotels as Oakes's philanthropy did not yet support. Oakes himself went from the pushy prospector who had bought much of the west of the island to an indispensable part of the island economy. As such, he bought a seat in the House of Assembly – he defeated Milo Butler, the merchant who later became a vital black leader – and within two years was translated to Legislative Council, the islands' equivalent of a House of Lords. He was established, and he was resented; and the resentment turned, bit by bit, into hatred. His money and his style – too rough for Nassau, which clung to propriety because it had so little real grace – were considered improper. His control in the west of the island was strong. He had influence, even over Windsor.

At first, in the small-town fevers of Nassau, resentment was the general tone of people discussing Oakes on Bay Street. Outsiders always said that when any two Bahamians gathered together, their main topic was how to backstab a third. In time, when resentment turned to hatred, the talk became more bitter and pointed. It became a parlour game for bored reporters covering Windsor's arrival: counting the people with motives to murder Harry Oakes.

August and September are the dog days of the Bahamas, when clothes stay wringing wet, when the high sun and the endless damps produce lethargy and short temper, all at once. Once London had forbidden them a quick escape to Canada, the Windsors had to settle – to learn their new trade in the unfriendly heat.

They borrowed houses while Government House was re-fined to their tastes. The Sigrists – Frederick Sigrist, with Tommy Sopwith, was the architect of the Spitfire fighter, and Britain's aircraft maker in California during the war – had a fine house out west which the Windsors could have: good, fake Chippendale and proper paintings and, on the patio, an eccentric screen which had been fashioned from jade and semi-precious stones. Official receptions fitted well there; official business was kept to Government House. The Duchess had only her little plastered cell, and the ADCs – more numerous for Windsor than for any previous Governor – inhabited the ballroom, like migrant, flustered birds.

The Duke listened, in those first months. He made a serious, honourable attempt to understand what might be the problems of the Bahamas. At Executive Council, with his closest advisors, he turned out to be a neat, open-minded chairman, able to keep discussion disciplined but willing to efface himself during the talk. He was good at it. He proposed no radical reforms. He played his ceremonial role carefully. There were barn dances to attend, yachting trophies to present, token appearances at any event for war charities; 'I really think,' says one Nassau lady, 'if someone had given a dance for Hitler's birthday, they would have made thousands of dollars. Nobody seemed to care what it was for. You just went ahead and you gave.' The Windsors were officially welcomed – the Duke, from the start, made it clear that all welcomes and titles and speeches must also include the Duchess, his equal partner – and there was a spectacular period of honeymoon. Local leaders, at the annual meeting of the St Andrew's Society, called him 'one of the most beloved men on earth' and hoped he would never have to leave the colony. Duke and Duchess would waltz, the fine romantic couple, and the Duke would make his constant reverses on the floor and Wallis would complain: 'But twirling makes me dizzy.' And Windsor would correct her: 'Not dizzy, darling. Giddy.' And everybody would laugh.

Windsor went to polo matches, bicycled each day to Cable Beach to swim, played golf most afternoons with his aides or with colonial officials. It was a life of a man retired, desperately full of minor diversions, and it was shot through with melancholy. Windsor, on the golf course, would often start sentences: 'When I was King. . . .' A minor official cornered the Duke at a garden party and announced that his job was frustrating. 'A job is what you make of it,' Windsor said. 'I was once King of England.' He seemed to reflect on the past years, and with no great satisfaction. He drank, as he had always done, but the effects became more noticeable. What had been binges on his great Imperial tours, kept carefully separate from his official appearances, were now sessions that happened all too publicly. He looked and acted drunk. He became loud and indiscreet. The Duchess was patient until a fund-raising evening at the Collins mansion on Shirley Street, where the Duke was too obviously full of whisky to fulfill his duties. She forbade him cocktail parties, cut entertaining except for their American visitors and a handful of politically necessary guests, took control. The Duke responded with his lifetime's pattern: like a true alcoholic, he set a fixed time for his first, necessary drink of the day – seven in the evening – and waited for clocks to sound the hour with a terrible impatience.

But although the melancholy and the reflectiveness were obvious, the Duke worked. He read the official papers. At the weekly meetings of Executive Council, he gave clemency to killers 'because the circumstances of the crime did not justify the supreme penalty'; he discussed the radio stations and the telecommunications on the island, since Beaverbrook was talking of a West Indian radio station based in Nassau, and the local officials were scared by the reorganization involved; he agreed that residents might draw dollars to spend the summers outside the sterling area, for health reasons, over the opposition of his Colonial Secretary, Heape, a man with stiff principles, a passion for the Bible and a literally stiff leg which kept him in constant, nerve-grating pain; and he overruled Heape also on petrol ration-ing, arguing that it was not needed and 'the balance of advantage from dollar exchange point of view lay with the maintenance of tourist traffic from the United States.'

As the Duke settled, the Duchess took on the duties of a Governor's wife. She was taken to Red Cross headquarters to see her workers. She was nervous and awkward at first, begging her escort not to leave her. She knew she could not easily adjust to the dowdy matrons around her, to their small-town ways. She was used to people who were either 'dear' or 'impossible', and here she would be constrained to find everybody possible. She was good at the political din-ners, small as they were; she liked to think that cigars and brandy and good food would sink political differences. Ken-neth Solomon, leader of the Government in the House of Assembly but the logical leader of the Bay Street Boys as well, came to dinner like a lamb to be fed and charmed; his wife, Lady Solomon, would chatter with the Duchess. The men would talk, seeming to agree. The Duchess proved good at good works and administration. She said she never wanted to be a committee woman; she wanted action. On the whole, she got it. Only her style still piqued the ladies of the town. They found they could easily disapprove of a woman twice divorced, especially when her elegance and wit set her apart and gave them justified feelings of inadequacy. Their little revenges included in time a new name for Government

House, which was to be topped with warning lights for low-flying aircraft. In honour of Wallis Windsor's past, they called it 'the red-light district'.

When the Duke first opened a House of Assembly session – the Duchess, being clearly more royal than previous Governors' wives, was given her own raised dais for the ceremony – he could not yet propose much that was new. There would be money to keep the Fort Montagu Beach hotel open through the winter season; he talked of Daylight Saving Time; he announced a sixpenny surcharge on telegrams, which turned out to be a breach of British Government rules about standard cable rates throughout the Empire. The single most important thing he had to say was not even a local decision. In return for the destroyers she desperately needed, Britain was granting land for military bases to America. One of them, at least, would be in the Bahamas. Roosevelt had done the deal as a way to help Britain out of an appalling financial mess – an utter lack of hard currency for buying arms and raw materials. Churchill had approved, since the base agreement tied the two countries firmly together. And Windsor told the House of Assembly, asked to approve the Bahamian details: 'I am confident the legislature will be prepared to approve. . . .'

They did approve, and their vote turned out to be much more than a patriotic gesture. It saved the life of the islands when the war came closer.

Parcels of money came regularly to the Royal Bank of Canada on Bay Street, the only bank in Nassau. They were sterling notes, sent from New York for exchange to dollars. Despite the harsh realities of wartime, the Bank of England, ladylike, still insisted that pounds would always be honoured whenever they were presented for payment. The pound must not be doubted, even when Britain was sinking toward bankruptcy.

The Bank thought itself decent, honourable, strict. It actually made an opening for a persistent and nagging scheme of Nazi economic sabotage. By sending sterling notes, captured in occupied Europe, through Lisbon to South America, from South America to banks in the USA, and from those banks to Nassau or Bermuda, the Nazis gained two advantages. They turned sterling into hard currency for their own purchases, and they deprived Britain of essential hard currency. It was an elegant device.

John Gaffney at the bank would oversee the bundles as they arrived. The notes were filthy, and often stamped with the names of banks in France or Holland or Belgium. British and American banks rarely marked their currency, but it was a common European custom. Gaffney read the stamps and noticed that almost all of them were from the great banks, the smaller *banques de dépôts*, the various houses of the areas of Europe which were now under Nazi control. As the Germans moved into Europe, they took banks; from the vaults, they took currency. Dollars could be exchanged simply. Both sides needed the currency of occupied territory – for use if their airmen or soldiers were marooned behind enemy lines. Sterling was useful for Nazi flyers over Britain; the British needed marks when over Nazi targets. Exchanges were arranged at pavement cafés in Lisbon and effected, more discreetly, in nearby hotel rooms. But most of the sterling seized in Europe was not needed for operations. It could be used as an operation in itself, of economic warfare.

All it took was the ability to take the money physically out of Europe and into America – preferably by way of South America so that its origins were masked. Couriers and U-boats did the job. Notes eventually reached New York, the staging point for major American banks with sterling to exchange. Rather than send the notes across the increasingly treacherous Atlantic, they were sent to the closest British colonies.

Gaffney sat at the receipt of the parcels, as the bank's accountant and as secretary to the exchange control commission in the Bahamas. His job was to help keep as much of the Empire's cash and liquid resources at the disposal of the Imperial Government as possible. He watched as the volume of notes grew, and the message from those bank markings became more clear. He tried to tell the Bank of England what was happening. He suggested that there would soon be a flood – a few months after the fall of Europe – and that the Bank should impose a limit of £20 in sterling notes which it was prepared to cash at any one time. The Bank, which saw sterling at the right hand of God, was appalled.

Gaffney, a Canadian working for a Canadian bank, had business in Ottawa. Before he left, he wrote himself (as accountant of the bank) a stiff note (coming from himself as secretary of the exchange control board). In it, he told himself to stop handling the sterling parcels. He did his business in Ottawa and returned by way of New York, where his bank colleagues on William Street were furious. They had, they said, between £300,000 and £400,000 in sterling notes in bags, waiting in Nassau for Gaffney to lift his high-handed ban. They wanted their money – as much as $1,600,000 – and they wanted it fast.

But Gaffney did not agree. Instead, he commandeered the services of four clerks to call every major bank in New York. They were to ask, respecting bank confidences, how much in sterling notes the New York banking community held. The amount was appalling. Gaffney cabled London to demand action. He told the Bank of England the unspeakable truth: he had, in effect, stopped payment on sterling.

London was horrified by Gaffney's action, but more horrified by what the hoard of sterling in New York would mean to Britain's dwindling reserves. If it was presented for payment, Britain would be bust. The Bank of England cabled Gaffney at the bank in Nassau; when he returned, it was to discover orders that parcels in the vaults or on their way would be exchanged for dollars without question. After that, there would be strict limits, as Gaffney had suggested.

Afterwards, it seemed ironic that one part of the Nazi money machine had been stopped in Nassau. So much else had been run from there, or through there – so much the Windsors would, in time, stake their lives on.

Wallis Windsor remembered how to be imperious. She wanted her very careful, very crafted life back – the one she had made in Paris. She might have to make compromises of all sorts, but one she refused. She wanted her maid, Marguerite Moulichon. She refused to go through official British channels. She tried to get Washington to bring her maid home.

With the Duke's help, she badgered an increasingly resentful State Department. She first wanted Maynard Barnes, at the American Embassy in Paris, to say if Moulichon was still at Boulevard Suchet, the Windsors' town house. Barnes cabled back that 'your maid left Paris fifteen days ago under safe escort for San Sebastian from which point the Spanish authorities were to convey her to Lisbon . . . it is believed by your maître d'hôtel that she has probably already sailed from Lisbon or is about to.' That was late September, and the Duchess was impatient. She wanted Washington to contact their Madrid Embassy. The State Department's patience began to fray. They called the British Embassy in Washington to try to sort out whose diplomatic activity all this really should be. It was not clear why American diplomats should act to help the maid of the wife of a British colonial official, or why the British should especially care about the progress of a French national who was in singularly little need or danger. The Embassy wrote to the Colonial Secretary in Nassau, suggesting delicately that 'strictly speaking, it would be for His Royal Highness to pursue the matter of expediting the maid's journey to Lisbon through official channels in London, always assuming that His Majesty's Government felt able to intervene in behalf of a French national.' And the State Department, reminding the Embassy that the maid was now out of the Nazi-occupied territory where America represented Britain, insisted that the fate of Mlle Moulichon was now a matter for London.

Lesser men, lesser women might have taken the very many hints. The Duchess would not, and the Duke knew the value of royal pique. He took the Embassy letter which told him of the State Department's position to an October conference on naval and air bases and actually raised the issue of Mlle Moulichon in the debate. Cordell Hull, Secretary of State, had to send a personal cable to calm the Duke who, by now, had convinced himself that the issue was vital and that the State Department was simply passing the buck.

Mlle Moulichon reached Nassau in early November, furious that the British had done nothing for her in a month in Spain and that London had failed to recover her lost luggage. She settled petulantly into the new household.

The Windsors always assumed they had special privilege in Washington. Some did come from the rights accorded diplomatic personnel; the Duke could have his six cases of wine from Sichel duty-free. Others involved furious swarms of memoranda between the heads of departments of state which turned on issues like the Duchess's washing, sent to Miami and in want of free entry to the States. 'The Bureau of Customs,' said an official letter in November 1940, 'is aware of no provision of law or practice under which articles sent to the United States by the Governor of the Bahamas or his wife for cleaning, repairing can be accorded an exemption from duty unconditionally.' The Duke persisted. In October 1941, a year later, the advisor on Political Relations with Foreign States was consulted on the issue of the washing, cleaning and the shoes and spectacles for repair which the Windsors sent to the United States.

Wallis Windsor liked to maintain her standards. A hairdresser from Antoine of Paris – the New York branch – was dispatched to Nassau to look after her needs for a while, and assorted would-be decorators and beauticians fluttered in the British Colonial hotel. She also wanted to be sure about her worldly goods – and her old home – at La Croë on the Riviera. She worried about the terms of the lease – that the Duke had first refusal on the house should it be sold, but that 'one doesn't know what sort of laws hold in France today.' The US consul in Nice reported the house still unoccupied, but the report was the last straw for the State Department. The Division of European Affairs, with larger problems to handle, scrawled on the file: 'Nassau might also be instructed to have the Windsors send their own wires direct hereafter.'

They had left La Croë at two hours' notice when France fell, and it held their world. There was furniture and silver, but also what the Duchess called the 'historical effects of His Royal Highness'. The loss haunted the Duchess as she tried to make a substitute home in Nassau. She wrote to a friend that 'Plus the worry of La Croë, we also have a house in Paris, so that you can imagine our thoughts are in France most of the time.' The Windsors still paid rent, into the London bank account of the owner, Sir Pomeroy Burton, at Coutts; but Sir Pomeroy was stranded in enemy-occupied France and it seemed unlikely the money would ever reach him. Wallis Windsor sometimes thought the estate was in safe hands – Antoine and Anna had been butler and house-keeper there since the Windsors first signed the lease, and Antoine had taken eight cases of silver into hiding in his own home. But another twenty, full of glass and china, were still in La Croë; he could find no hiding place for them. She thought the concierge 'a most trustworthy man'; she found the gardeners 'safe and loyal hands'. But she had anxieties, all the same. 'Should it become impossible to get the wages to the servants,' she wrote to a friend in St Louis, 'I worry, as a great deal of loyalty is bought.'

The Windsors had very special help in paying their servants and maintaining their life in France. Churchill and the American Ambassador in Paris personally made the arrangements in April 1941 for Windsor to pay off the 55,000 francs rent he owed, the 10,000 francs insurance, the back-pay still owing to their Paris *maitre d'hôtel* Fernand Lelovrain and the 15,000 francs rent due and embarrassingly unpaid since November 1940, for the strong room space they rented at the Banque de France. Even with all this help, ruthlessly solicited and used, the Windsors could still not feel comfortable that they had a home in France. In 1942, when America could no longer represent anyone's interests in the South of France, the money did run out. Antoine at La Croë was left penniless on 15 September.

Refugees came to Nassau to be away from the bombs in a place where they could still spend pounds sterling. They came, almost all of them, from the British upper middle class. The boys of Belmont School arrived en masse, covered in purple medicines to cure their impetigo. Women whose hus-bands were on the front lines came into the Bahamas, often with means that seemed barely adequate for expensive island life. Out of the sanctuaries in France and Monaco came the older people whose lives had been utterly disrupted by the spread of war.

Others came to the islands from more sinister places. French-speaking roughnecks arrived in open boats, after a lengthy voyage from south to north of the Caribbean Sea. They had been prisoners on Devil's Island off the coast of French Guyana, turned loose to fend for themselves when the French could no longer feed or garrison their distant colony. Some found open boats. Knowing that a landing in the bush of French Guyana would leave them no hope at all, they set out for Trinidad and then tacked north, island by island, hoping to reach America. In the Bahamas, they were singularly unwelcome. On arrival they were dumped in a mental hospital to wait for Executive Council's decision. Windsor ruled that if they were not Free French, they should simply be 'provided with a boat, adequately provisioned and put to sea'. Weeks later, he decided that if they still refused to sail, they should be sent to Haiti; four actually made the journey to Port au Prince. The rest simply stayed until, after three months, official patience was exhausted. Then, they were finally cast off, with blankets and clothing and food, refugees looking for some hope in America, without visas or charts or course.

Other would-be immigrants came from a larger tragedy. Leslie Heape, Windsor's deputy as Colonial Secretary, reported in August 1940 'a very widespread feeling in the Colony against the admission of Jews'. Even before war was declared, some German Jews had made pathetic pleas to enter the Bahamas. With one exception, they were all refused. Doctors were desperately needed for the Out Islands, and the public service, but that did not swell the list of immigrants. Jews entering the colony were forbidden to start a business or enter private practice. ExCo asked, gratuitously, that 'those of known communistic sympathies' should be excluded. The deal offered to doctors was that they pay their own passage out, work one-year contracts and then be responsible for paying their own passage back; but back, as the Colonial Office noted on the proposal sent by Dundas, 'where to?' The Bahamas was offered, and refused, the talents of men like the chief medical officer of Frankfurt, who wrote long and terrible letters to beg for any work, even non-medical work, and to promise that he had American money available for his support. He even tried to play on Nassau prejudices, to play the gentile game. 'By the way,' he wrote, 'children and father have blue eyes and blond hair, as the photos enclosed shall demonstrate.'

When Windsor became Governor he would have needed great force to wipe away that Bahamian prejudice. He did nothing to help Jews at risk in Europe, despite a stream of pleas. He even refused to do more than vaguely dissociate himself from the policy of some hotels – notably those owned by Roland Symonette – of excluding Jews on the grounds that Americans might object to their presence. The Colonial Office sent Windsor letters which had reached Churchill, in which New Jersey businessmen protested at the off-hand racism of the Nassau hoteliers, but Windsor merely replied that 'the complaint is outside the province within which the Government can dictate to private enterprises.' Leslie Heape, the Colonial Secretary, said that 'incidentally, some of these hotels do take a number of cultivated Hebrews'; Roland Symonette, annoyed by the New Jersey protesters, told them that their exclusion from hotels would be 'quite customary in the United States, where we take it Nazism does not exist.' In its polite version, real estate agents expressed the general Bahamian anti-Semitism much as Frank Christie, brother to Harold, did in 1940 in a letter to a Toronto Jew: 'I regret to say that I do not cater to Jewish clientele as house owners are reluctant to rent to them and they are not accepted at the larger hotels. It has been my practice to discourage Jewish patrons from coming to Nassau as they are very unhappy there due to social restrictions. . . .' There was a less polite version. Even after the war, when knowledge of the Nazi atrocities had at least given most in the West a decent shame about their attitudes, the manager of the Royal Victoria hotel, V. Lorraine Oiderdont, told a travel firm in Florida: 'We were very much annoyed today when your party arrived in Nassau and I found that they were Jewish . . . it is up to the agents to see that they keep at least one place a Christian resort.'

At least such ugly attitudes threatened only vacations, not lives. The Bahamas under Windsor, fearing competition from Jewish professionals and businessmen, steadfastly refused admission to Jews who wanted to live in the islands. It was suggested refugees might be found room in Nassau to wait for US visas under the quota system; Windsor and Council decided to 'reject any proposal to settle large numbers of evacuees in the Colony.' Even if they were solvent and unlikely to enter business, the refugees faced a race barrier.

Windsor stuck to his guns until 1944, when the rum merchant Eustace Myers wanted to escape colonial taxation in the Bahamas. Myers posed special problems, because the name of Myers Rum was enough to make Nassau merchants nervous. They objected, as they always did, to the very idea of someone going into competition with them. But when Myers's application to reside came before ExCo, it was evaded because it involved 'a matter of principle'. Myers was a Jew. First, it was deferred while the Attorney General was set to work out if Myers could enter as a visitor, stay his eight months, leave for a day or so and immediately return. On being told that he could do exactly that, ExCo announced that he could enter as a visitor – that he would be 'welcomed', although on reading the minutes of the meeting Windsor took that word out. Later in the minutes Council said that 'with regard to principles of admission of would-be permanent residents, Council was not prepared to make any ruling on racial grounds.'

Myers was not prepared to accept that answer. He indulged in rather public correspondence with his American lawyers, to Windsor's acute embarrassment. The Duke found himself forced to climb down. On 31 January 1945, he agreed that Myers might reside in the Bahamas; a month later, with Harold Christie and Windsor's other merchant friend, Sidney Farrington, the Nassau representative of Pan Am, still in opposition, Myers was allowed to go into business, although with due care promised for the trouble-making potential of the Jamaican workforce he planned to import. Nassau being a small town, where rules of conduct are elastic, it is not surprising that a member of ExCo at the time – Godfrey Higgs – was one of the first directors of Myers's new company.

Windsor could never quite believe that he would be kept in the Bahamas for all the war. He tried again and again to find some other job or at least to spend long periods away from the islands. He dreamed of some grand appointment in America, perhaps as a roving goodwill ambassador. As he waited, he kept a fine informality. He would walk down Bay Street for his tobacco and the Pipe of Peace. After the first weeks, people did not bother him nor did they casually engage him in conversation. He could walk as he wanted.

The way to Bay Street took him down the hill, past the old wood porches of houses on George Street, and the white cathedral and into the street itself. Bay Street had already become an abstract noun, a description of a ruling class and a government, in 1940. It was notorious. Its reality was a long street of shops, low and wide and muddled. On the seaward side, warehouses stood over sea water where the land had not been filled. In the floors there were carvings – pineapples, hammerhead sharks, the stylized curves of palm trees – from the old furniture that had been used to make them. At one end of the street was the British Colonial; at the other was Rawson Square, the official buildings before the town began to peter out to the east. Everybody congregated on Bay Street at some time, white or black, for gossip and intrigue and the time of day. There was the Jaeger shop with goods from Britain, grand pharmacies that dealt in perfumes with famous names, smaller and muddled dry-goods stores that were heaped with cartons and boxes and racks and rolls of cloth and children's clothes. Down the street, on the seaward side, stood J. P. Sands, the grocery store. One counter served whites, the other blacks. Goods and prices were the same, but if the black queue was long and the white counter empty, the douce white girls would retreat to the back of the shop rather than serve black customers. They had black trade – even from black shopkeepers – because they had goods like Fleischman's Yeast that no other store could carry.

When the mails came, white men and women with the morning to spare drank coffee at the Grand Central restaurant; blacks were asked to leave. The Grand Central was a social centre, a gossip place and somewhere to read the morning paper. The *Nassau Guardian* was the voice of Bay Street, loud and clear; the *Nassau Tribune* was a quirky paper, run by a coloured family who knew how to report the local scene. Either one was acceptable in the Grand Central. The only mixed bar on Bay Street was the Chinese place at the corner of Market Street, where blacks and whites could drink together easily; they often had common business. At Dirty Dick's bar, a black man would pay 5s for a glass of rum that would cost him eighteen pence at the Chinese. The price was the barrier. Among the lawyers and merchants there was a cinema, the Savoy, which was for whites only; there was a club, called the Club plain and simple, where the Bay Street men could talk politics and while away the afternoons with long games of poker; there was the hotel, the Prince George, where younger people went to eat dinner and to dance, looking out over the harbour waters.

Drays worked the streets, two-wheel carts that sloped low at the back. There were bicycles flashing back and forth, and sometimes grandiose limousines. Surreys with old, tired horses rattled along.

On this street men met casually to talk or plan or plot. The Duke walked among them, but he was never part of the local schemes and fantasies. He was always very separate on Government Hill.

Of all the equivocal figures in the islands, the ones who knew Meyer Lansky, the ones who wanted Jews kept out, the ones who ran rum or guns or drugs, there was one that everybody suspected and nobody would openly denounce. He was Axel Wenner-Gren, the Swedish financier. In the evening of 17 October his great yacht, the *Southern Cross*, bought from Howard Hughes, slipped into Nassau harbour after a long absence. Wenner-Gren already had, by mail from Rio, his introduction to the Windsors – 'a new and interesting family ... sympathetic understanding for totalitarian ideals.' He would be their greatest temptation, and their near ruin. They had come through those twenty-eight days in Lisbon with a loss of dignity, but no more. Now, Axel Wenner-Gren would ask them to do much more, and he would play on every anxiety in the Duke's mind – anxieties about safety, money, Windsor's position in the world and the swelling tide of Bolshevism.

For that, Nassau was the perfect place. Love for London was thin. Many white Bahamians reckoned they would be involved in war when the first German warships steamed into the New Providence Channel and not before. Island isolation bred an instinctive distance from big, dangerous political wars happening elsewhere. Certain of the Bay Street Boys had no love for Britain, which constantly tried to interfere with their privileges, and their talk sometimes sounded as though they might have a taste for some of the brute certainties of Hitler's Germany. At least one Allied consul was presumed to sympathize with the Nazis.

Even in this amoral world, Wenner-Gren was suspect. His great yacht, radio masts high, steamed in and out of the harbour regularly. Rumour said it carried oil for submarines; or that it scouted for U-boats, guiding them to their prey. Rumour said Wenner-Gren's new hurricane harbour, set in the centre of Hog Island, would be used to provision German vessels. On this trip, he could report the rescue of the crew of a training plane which had 'dropped 150 yards from the *Southern Cross*'. In the first days of war, the *Southern Cross* had picked up 376 survivors of the torpedoed liner SS *Athenia*. Wenner-Gren reported the rescue direct to Roosevelt – the two had met briefly – and assured the President that 'it is hard to imagine in view of probable consequences that Germany intentionally would have sunk the steamer.' Such rescues, such coincidences became rather common on the voyages of the *Southern Cross*, and some began to ask how Wenner-Gren could have so fine an instinct for disaster. Did he, perhaps, know where the Germans were to strike next?

For Wenner-Gren certainly had a curious concept of the world. He tried to use the sinking of the *Athenia* to persuade Roosevelt that new peace efforts were needed in Europe. 'Seeing at first hand the misery, suffering, tragedy and horror of this one incident, I recall your own expressed views and I believe that the disaster, if properly utilised [*sic*], might form the basis for new peace efforts with prospects of success.' This was an eccentric interpretation of an act of brigandage. Yet Wenner-Gren was confident enough to ask Roosevelt to send a destroyer instantly to Nassau – the *Southern Cross*, he complained, made only fourteen knots – so that they could discuss the matter. 'You surely agree,' he said, 'that no efforts . . . should be spared if there is the slightest chance of preventing the looming holocaust.'

Wenner-Gren was always ready to intervene, to believe that his own pragmatism could save the world from the awful consequences of its ideologies. He had an ambitious wife; he had generally right-wing views, with a special emphasis on the bond between Nordic peoples. He worked against war, but for a greater 'fairness' to Germany. He wanted to believe his views counted for something.

He felt excluded from political affairs and convinced that he, and other great captains of industry, were the natural powers. He wanted to be a diplomat. In 1939, he even went on a curious mission to talk peace with Goering, taking as presents a Field Marshal's baton, a can of China tea and a signed portrait of himself.

His diplomacy looked foolish, and his wartime actions on the *Southern Cross* had nothing to do with the provisioning of U-boats. The way the Nazis used Wenner-Gren was more subtle and arguably much more dangerous. He was Krupp's front man, an architect of Sweden's neutrality, Goering's financial helper, a man who could be relied upon to act out huge schemes of subversion where money gave the Axis an opportunity that local politics and sentiment might have blocked. Wenner-Gren was to be the middle man between Nazi ambition and the rich and powerful of Western Europe; and he was to help take German power into South America. For all this, his chosen base was Nassau.

He had come to the Bahamas in 1938, a notoriously rich man who controlled Electrolux in America and Sweden, and had a controlling interest in Aktion Bofors, the gun-makers. He had a public passion for anthropology, for expeditions to remote places; those expeditions, to digs that Wenner-Gren was financing, often coincided with Nazi interest. Wenner-Gren trailed through Peru with more high-powered radios than shovels on what he called an archaeological expedition; it was at a time when the Germans wanted to consolidate their influence there. He sponsored expeditions up the Amazon at the one time when such explorations might have had strategic significance. The *Southern Cross* carried samples of Bofors wares on all her voyages.

His explanation for the move to Nassau sounded familiar. He wanted to avoid penal Swedish taxation, he told the Governor, Dundas; he was also moving 'in view of the imminence of war in Europe'. He bought land on Hog Island – he wanted the name changed to Paradise Island – and worked on the making of a great estate, with fine trees and exquisite flowers and captive tropical birds. He called it Shangri-la and said: 'We are happy to be home.'

Wenner-Gren was a benefactor, a creator of jobs. But his move to Nassau was not simply that of a rich man in search of a haven. He admitted as much in a 1943 brief to the American Secretary of State which was designed to free him from the Allied blacklist. He talked of visits to Mexico in the 1930s and said: 'My visit became a revelation and I tried to visualise what Latin America, if rationally developed, might mean to the economy and progress of the entire world. The unlimited scope of creative activities naturally appealed to me. I therefore decided to invite British and American friends of mine to participate in the study and possible real-isation of a few specially interesting projects. A logical place for headquarters of such a Swedish–American–British combine would be Nassau in the Bahamas. On my way back to Europe I stopped there and acquired a home and began to prepare for the necessary organisation.'

The explanation is partly true, but it leaves out some vital details. Wenner-Gren had investors who were neither British

71

nor American nor Swedish. He had some Nazi backers. His Mexican schemes, just like his archaeological schemes, happened to concern a country of peculiar interest to the Axis powers. If Roosevelt took America into war, then the strategic importance of Mexico – oil, frontiers, mineral potential – would be huge. And Mexico was wobbling. Money might win the day.

In the early years of the war, Mexico seemed to dislike the totalitarian states and lack confidence in the democracies. She had cut diplomatic ties with Britain in 1938, after expropriating all foreign oil companies and taking control of her own mineral assets. The British, rudely, suggested that Mexico could not pay for the oil assets. The Mexicans immediately sent a cheque and withdrew their Ambassador. Mexicans had long, painful reasons to mistrust the power of America. Even though the centrist Avilo Camacho succeeded the reformist Cardenas as President in 1940, and seemed to like America more than his predecessor, intelligence services still had worries. 'The danger is,' British intelligence files said, 'that a hostile or distracted Mexico might be used for the purposes of sabotage and lend itself to Axis infiltration.' Camacho was turning his policies away from the popular basis of the continuing Mexican revolution. His brother Maximinio, governor and self-appointed chieftain of the Puebla province, had a taste for money and the contacts with men like Wenner-Gren to procure it. The Camacho brothers were close; pressure on one would sooner or later change the mind and attitudes of the other.

Eight days after the *Southern Cross* docked in Nassau, Wenner-Gren was at Government House, dining officially. British intelligence had a fat file on him. American intelligence, and especially Adolf Berle, the Under Secretary of State responsible for intelligence, had grave suspicions. They seemed out of kilter with Wenner-Gren himself. He was a tall, broad, blond man, charming and rather impressive; he talked a lot of 'brotherly love'. He said he had seen pitiful hunger demonstrations in Nassau and created a thousand jobs. He said the islands could be the most beautiful spot in the world, if developed, and his own house would stand in

Paradise Town. He would have parrots and toucans flashing between his great trees and he might even have stateless artists, intellectual refugees to live there, 'a completely neutral, unpolitical and humane activity of assistance'. If anyone brought up darker suspicions, he had ready answers. He had indeed intervened in the war between Russia and Finland, but not as a German front man. He had simply wanted negotiated peace. He had known Goering, certainly, but only as he had known British politicians, in the cause of peace. The Americans suspected him because of a terrible misunderstanding, that he had once called his agent Bigge to meet him in Rome and their intelligence operatives had thought that Bigge must mean the big man, and the big man must be Goering.

Wenner-Gren was plausible and seemed more visionary than cold-eyed schemer. His wife, more obviously ambitious, drank heavily; he watched her always. It gave an uneasy edge to dinner parties or to cocktails. All Wenner-Gren wanted was a compromise and peace, he said. In that, he agreed with Charles Bédaux, the Windsors' friend who always thought France and England would plunge into very advanced socialism after the war, just as Windsor feared; and that war was an unnecessary, bloody adventure, just as Windsor thought. Together, Windsor and Wenner-Gren were friends of the kind of American businessman who thought war was bad for trade, that America had no business in an old-fashioned European squabble, that businessmen should be above politics and operate where they wished, that Communism was a greater menace than Nazism, that war would only be for the preservation of the resented British Empire. Their associates often had Irish or German ancestry which helped explain their unwillingness to see any moral dimension to Britain's struggle. They wanted what Wenner-Gren wanted – 'a wall against Bolshevism'.

The links became a scandal very quickly. Warren at the State Department was told by a member of his staff in January 1941: 'The most recent information I have regarding Mr Wenner-Gren indicates that he is in constant and close touch with the Duke of Windsor and that both of them are

73

seeing a great deal of prominent and influential American businessmen, particularly from the mid-Western states, where a strictly commercial point of view would appear to prevail in business circles with regard to relations between the United States and Germany. There would appear to be certain indications that Wenner-Gren, as well as the Duke of Windsor, is stressing the need for a negotiated peace at this time on account of the advantages which this would present to American business interests. This angle, I think, should be closely observed. . . .'

It was a throw-away phrase, 'as well as the Duke of Windsor'. Everybody – everybody diplomatic, that is – knew that the Duke talked peace whenever he could. He suggested talks and compromise. Denver socialites would go back home from the season and tell their friends about the Duke's views. He would not keep them secret on his American trips.

He knew the dangers of association with Wenner-Gren. In November 1940, Leslie Heape was sent down to talk with the American consul, John Dye. Their talk was confidential. Heape was worried about an architect called A. J. Lothian, who said he wanted to photograph Mayaguana from the air. The island lies to the south of the Bahamas, and it was poor even among the Out Islands, but it was about to be the site of an American base. Heape said the photographs were to be for a neutral citizen, and not an American; Dye 'knew he meant Wenner-Gren, as Lothian has been doing some work for him at his palatial winter home on Hog Island.' Dye reckoned pictures of Mayaguana before dredging and building began would be of little intelligence value, but he agreed it might be wise to have a regulation banning aerial photography in the area. That evening, Dye met Windsor at a war benefit – a dance with a broadcast revue as a special attraction, where listeners could phone to promise money. The Duke wanted to know if Heape had discussed the problem, and with due discretion – they mentioned no names – the Duke and the consul discussed it again. Dye gave his opinion; Windsor said: 'Excellent. That is what I had in mind, but we wanted to first have your opinion.'

Dye discovered later that Lothian had already been to

Mayaguana – in company with Harold Christie. He reckoned Christie might be using Wenner-Gren's money to buy up potentially valuable land. The remoteness of Mayaguana made that seem unlikely, but Dye made no public comment. Wenner-Gren might be sinister, or he might not; Dye would defend him. 'I shall continue to take that attitude for the present whatever my real knowledge or opinion. It is more useful.'

Windsor, too, would hear nothing against Wenner-Gren, even when he was actively organizing regulations in case Wenner-Gren might be a spy. With protection on Government Hill, and his increasing influence with local grandees, Wenner-Gren had all the base he needed for his move on Mexico.

The story later would be that the Windsors advocated a negotiated peace only before the fall of France, that in the Bahamas they were staunchly loyal to the war effort. They were not. They had their little circle in Nassau – Oakes, Wenner-Gren, Christie and the visitors – and nobody would challenge them on their views.

All the time, the war came closer to the islands.

On 29 October 1940 there was a bleak north-west wind that set the sea rising. A woman on Eleuthera, Mrs Lewis Johnson, dreamt that night that she would go to the beach and find something astonishing, washed ashore by the high seas. She went down early and found a boat – a ship's lifeboat. In it, exhausted and burnt black, were two men, Robert Tapscott and Roy Widdicombe.

They had been sailors on the tramp steamer *Anglo-Saxon*, out of Newport in Wales, bound for South America with coal. At nine on the evening of 21 August, a ship came close. The men heard five shells, fired at point blank range. They scrambled for the deck under a steady spray of machinegun fire. The German liner SS *Weser* had attacked the *Anglo-Saxon* and she was determined to leave no trace. Even before the ship could founder, the *Weser* piled incendiaries into the steamer. She became a terrible column of fire and then, inexorably, a silence.

Seven men swung into the lifeboat, four already injured seriously. Others died of exposure later. Widdicombe and Tapscott, aged twenty-one and nineteen, kept themselves alive from rainwater that filled the tarpaulins and flying fish that leapt into the boat. They crossed some 3000 miles of ocean in an open 18-foot boat, their hair and skin burned with salt and the sun. They were taken to Nassau and a brief celebrity.

In hospital, they were visited by the Duke and Duchess. The Windsors were moved. The boys were absurdly young, and beginning to recover their morale. The Duchess brought milk pudding, laced with so much rum that the sailors said they were 'tiddly' after eating it. The lifeboat was auctioned to raise money for the Red Cross and in December, on stiff gilt chairs at the Royal Victoria, Widdicombe and Tapscott were stars in a special edition of Ripley's 'Believe It Or Not', the radio version of the newspaper cartoon strip which brought little wonders (record parsnips, freak materials) to the attention of America. Afterwards, in the strip itself, the Duke had a supporting role, as an exiled king in a little corner: 'The Duke in the Bahamas, Believe It Or Not.'

The Duchess suffered terribly from an infected tooth in December 1940, and it seemed she would have to go to Miami for treatment. No white person entered the Bahamas General Hospital; it was unthinkable. Unfortunately, she refused to fly. She had claustrophobia and she had almost cured the Duke of his old passion for the air; it had been the Prince of Wales who inaugurated the King's Flight of the Royal Air Force. At first they planned to take the regular sailing of the SS *Munargo* to Miami, but when the ship was delayed they needed an alternative. Nothing could be more natural than to accept the invitation of their new friends, the Wenner-Grens.

And nothing could be more embarrassing. In Miami, Wenner-Gren was confined to port as a suspected subversive. The ship's crew were assumed by American authorities to be virulently pro-Nazi. The ship itself carried Bofors guns which Wenner-Gren would indiscreetly try to sell; his sales methods led, soon, to a ban on the *Southern Cross* passing through the Panama Canal. But the yacht had enormous style, and the Windsors appreciated that; and as they came into Miami, their smiles were almost painful with relief and joy. They had left the islands at last and reached America.

The tooth infection proved more serious than anyone had thought. The Duke stayed at the bedside in St Francis Hospital. He was comforted by an older nursing sister who idolized him. 'Every time I turned round,' he said later, 'she put a whisky and soda in my hand. Dear old girl.' By the weekend, the Windsors had moved to the Miami Biltmore. The Duke was visibly nervous. He would come down to the lobby, walk a little, toy with the leaf of some ornamental palm and then, quite suddenly, retreat to his room. When he left the hotel to play golf, he was noticeably solemn. He was worried about the Duchess, of course, but something else was on his mind.

Lord Lothian, British Ambassador to Washington, had just died. Windsor wondered if Churchill would possibly give him the job.

He wanted Washington. He wanted the sense of being in a real position. Wallis was from Baltimore and she had known the Washington diplomatic round. He knew how to handle receptions and appearances; his performances had been extraordinary. More, there was the question of money. As Governor in the Bahamas he had a salary of £3000, and unlike most men with comparable wealth and some sort of title, he drew his pay. In Washington, the allowance (*frais de representation*) was £17,500 as a kind of expense account free of tax and an extra £800 for clothes. It would be wonderful to come back so comfortably to the real world.

Talk started fast. More than fifty telegrams and two thousand letters were sent to the British Embassy in Washington and to the White House in a concerted campaign. Some Americans evidently believed that Roosevelt could choose the next British Ambassador, a diplomatic nonsense. Senator A. B. Chandler told the world: 'The British couldn't pick a better man.' An anxious Washington correspondent cabled Roosevelt to shout down the Windsor lobby, to say that 'no more unfortunate appointment from the viewpoint of Anglo-American relationships could be made.' Across the cable, Roosevelt scrawled: 'There isn't a chance.'

Windsor, on the steps of the *Southern Cross*, volunteered to the press: 'I have not been offered the Ambassadorship, but I would most certainly accept it if I thought it to the interest of our two countries.' The royal campaign was singularly inept. Roosevelt cared deeply who came to Washington; he needed a substantial figure who would help convince Americans of the seriousness of the European war. But Roosevelt did not make the appointment, nor could he easily be seen to favour one or other of competing candidates. He knew that Churchill wanted 'a public figure' of substance, which was not the reality of Windsor. Windsor's name came often into conversations about those who harmed Britain's image in the United States.

The Windsor legend turned heavily, in America, on the charm of Wallis Windsor, the question of what she had that other women had not, how she won the King. Even in Nassau, American tourists would stand and finger the dust on her car and go home happy; they simply wanted to say, 'We touched Wally's car.' Admission to her old family home, $1 at the time of the abdication and 25¢ in the bleak years after the planned Bédaux trip, now recovered to 40¢. Wallis Windsor's stock was rising.

The Duke, by contrast, seemed more lightweight than he should. The very clumsiness of his campaigns suggested that he was no diplomat. And the Nassau connections of the Windsors were worse than embarrassing. Roosevelt himself, early in 1941, wanted agents put on the *Southern Cross* because 'it was easily possible that the Wennergren [*sic*] yacht might have evidences of suspicious activities on board.' He wanted 'greater energy . . . in covering the activities and connections of Mr Axel Wennergren.' Windsor launched his job hunt from the wrong gangplank.

Roosevelt's private files held letters from Bingham, American Ambassador to London at the time of the abdication, which painted Windsor as pro-Nazi. 'The Duke of Windsor was surrounded by a pro-German cabal,' Bingham wrote, with the startling rider that 'many people here suspected that Mrs Simpson was actually in German pay. I think this is unlikely, and that her strong pro-German attitude was the result of flattering propaganda.' Bingham had reported specific instances where Windsor had behaved in an embarrassing fashion; in December 1935, for example, he wrote that 'the Prince of Wales had become the German protagonist. . . . Quite recently, at a large public dinner he made another pro-German statement which was not well received by the audience and which was hushed up in the newspapers.'

At Hyde Park, the Roosevelt's land joined the estates of Herman Rogers, an old friend of Wallis Windsor who never quite fell out of love with her. Such little points started a chain of neighbourly duty and the Roosevelts were often kind. When the Bédaux tour of America was planned, Eleanor Roosevelt tried to smooth out the awful difficulties of protocol involved – helping to calm the strong embarrassment felt by the British Ambassador and his wife. 'They are having a dinner for them,' she wrote in one of her stiff memos to her husband, 'but it was with the greatest difficulty that they obtained permission and they will not like to be asked to meet them here at the White House.' When the trip had to be cancelled, Roosevelt was kind again. He wrote to sympathize with Windsor about the 'misunderstandings', to remember a speech Windsor once made at Annapolis.

All this had no great significance, beyond Roosevelt's rather splendid courtesy. Windsor thought it did. Roosevelt came to the Bahamas aboard a US warship to inspect the base site at Mayaguana in December 1940. He had already explained his journey to King George: 'Early in December,' he wrote from Hyde Park, 'I hope to get a bit of a holiday by going over to the Bahamas and several other prospective bases. That destroyer arrangement seems to have worked out perfectly.' Windsor was eager for the President's arrival; he flew to Mayaguana full of hopes. The talks were good – Roosevelt, as usual, allowed no notes to be taken of the substance. But it was not the friendly reunion Windsor had hoped. He was on the list of State Department Christmas cards signed by the President, but the letters exchanged were cool and polite. Roosevelt acknowledged Windsor's card not with a promise or an offer but simply by writing: 'It was indeed good to see you again after all these years, and when an airbase is finally decided on, you and I will have to make an "inspection trip" to see it.' He mentioned a 'nice letter' from Herman Rogers, and hoped that Cannes would survive the war. And that was the extent of Roosevelt's interest. He had more pressing concerns than Windsor's arbitrary ambitions.

One thing is clear from the little, failed campaign. In December 1940, Windsor genuinely believed he had done nothing treasonous, that there had been nothing in the days in Spain and Portugal which would specifically exclude him from the chance of a post like the Washington Embassy. He must have known how carefully the British Government had watched his actions. If he had signed any pact, done any deal, beyond considering the prospect of a war spent out of battle, out of duty in some Spanish villa, he would have known himself disqualified from the American job. He had a terrible ability to fool himself, to go from motive to motive, action to action without perceiving links or consequences. He lacked political sense. But if he had come to some agreement with the Nazis already, he could hardly have been put into Washington as a pro-German agent. He was never subtle; he was notorious for being at once wilful and blunt. He would have been no great Ambassador in the British interest, but there was no possibility at all that he could help the Germans as an undercover man. The idea is absurd. And since it is absurd, it makes unlikely any stories of actual compacts with the Nazis. Windsor's links would be dangerous and disreputable, on the verge of treason, but they would not be as simple as that.

Wallis Windsor was high-pitched and emotional when the *Southern Cross* left Miami. She had been home, after almost a decade. 'I've been very happy here,' she said. 'I'm very, very proud of my country and very grateful for the reception and kindness of everyone. Everything here is so vital and alive.' The contrast with the Nassau Christmas that awaited her was unspoken, but unmistakeable.

80

The Duke promised that 'Now that we've found the way, we shall come again' and with the crew singing and the crowds cheering at the dockside, the Windsors sailed home. Home now to the Duchess, when her temper frayed, was 'that lousy hole'.

The Miami trip offended many. Already, journalists in Toronto and New York were preparing the stories which would make it publicly awkward for Windsor to pretend he knew nothing of Wenner-Gren's activities. The stories would make it seem that by knowing the man, taking his hospitality, the Windsors endorsed him. The Duke seemed wonderfully innocent of the trouble ahead.

At 9.45 on a bright morning, the *Southern Cross* came into Nassau. Sergeant Holder, the Scotland Yard bodyguard, led the Windsors' beloved cairn terriers solemnly ashore. Wood, one of the ADCs, greeted the Duke and Duchess.

'Where are we going?' asked the Duchess.

'To Government House,' said Wood.

It was finally ready for them. They had stayed in the Sigrists' house until the Sigrists returned, and then they had taken from Harry Oakes a sprawling house by the Bahamas Country Club called Westbourne. To answer the unspoken question, Wood told the Duchess: 'Everything has been moved from Westbourne.' They had a home.

And they had an official Christmas. There were Christmas trees for children of the Bahamas, and for the evacuee boys from Belmont School. The Duchess told the assembled mothers that she thought they were all very brave, and the Duke was down on his hands and knees, playing with toy motorcars before an enraptured audience of small boys. There was the paupers' treat, given by Marion Carstairs, a tough lady who had used her fortune from Standard Oil to compete with men for racing trophies and shooting prowess. Carstairs had her own island, Whale Cay, and she guarded it with a shotgun against unwanted visitors; she roared from her house on motorbike, shorts rolled up and hunting knife at her waist, and she organized a fine private kingdom. She built roads and a church, made jobs for dozens of men and women and usually kept her distance from Nassau; she thought disease lurked behind every flower. Her lunch for the poor was an annual event, hard to organize and expensive, and she oversaw it as she supervised the affairs of her island. Her boy scouts served the chowder; her Whale Cay band played. To the Windsors, as to all her social equals, she was 'Jo'.

After Christmas ceremony, the Duke addressed the islands on the radio. His speech was equivocal and odd. Alongside the simpler words of Churchill – 'Peace? When we have beaten them!' – it seemed limp. The Duke of Windsor refused to take his propaganda duties seriously. He would say, very nearly, what he thought.

He talked of the 'strife and quarrels of the old world' in which Britain had again become entangled; he said that 'leaders of great peoples have stirred up in the peaceful masses feelings of hatred which fundamentally they neither feel nor understand.' He reminded the islanders that the American continent had long contained 'two virile peoples . . . peacefully, side by side.' He talked of the new world after peace, of colossal readjustment and a solution for the future. Such talk, six months after the fall of France, was not timely. Britain still thought she was fighting to keep her prewar power, against huge odds. Sudden peace could all too easily mean sudden defeat. The Windsor abstracts – 'justice, sanity and good will' – were codes that were easily broken to show his private concern for a negotiated peace, at almost all costs. None of his speeches in Nassau was casual; he worked on them with painful concentration.

In the swirl of parties and dances, the words were mercifully lost, and none too carefully interpreted. The unwanted Christmas present arrived a few days late. Wenner-Gren gave £5000 to Nassau charities, of which £1000 was for charities in which the Duchess took a special interest. The same day, Canadian papers denounced him as a friend of Goering who had funded university research in order to have access to areas where top secret military work was being prepared.

Wenner-Gren defended himself; all his defences, and they were many, were voluble and windy. He talked of difficult times 'in which men live with suspicion constantly perched on their doorsteps'. He said he had retired from active business life, that he lived quietly at Shangri-la, 'uplifting less fortunate peoples'. He cared only about 'social and scientific progress that rises above the din of war and human suspicion'. He complained bitterly that the German press had called his wife 'an American Jewess' – 'she has not a drop of Jewish blood in her veins'. The defence contained one simple lie. Far from retiring, Wenner-Gren was engineering a bank, a $100,000,000 investment and the discreet and illegal transmission of money to Mexico for a list of friends that included the Duke of Windsor.

With the new year, the season started in earnest. The Duchess imposed style on the parties, the rather eager and sweaty and hard-drinking social life of Nassau. She emerged in stark white and gold, necklace and earrings of heavy gold, with even her gloves gold-trimmed. She sailed into society, witty and bright and startlingly attractive. A new hotel opened, named for the Windsors; at the Fort Montagu Beach, the imported New York band launched a new waltz, named for the Windsors. Tourists stopped at the grandest houses in the town and asked if they were 'the Duke's palace'. Big houses came to life and big hotels were full.

They were invited to Cat Cay, a tiny island to the north which was the joy, and investment, of the New York advertising man Louis Wasey. He had a small casino, a little resort and spectacular fishing and a nine-hole golf course which he asked the Duke to declare open. In the harbour at Nassau, Alfred P. Sloan, head of General Motors, had his yacht *Rene*. It had the right degree of style for the Windsors, and Sloan was congenial company; he had been a staunch investor in Nazi Germany, and he always argued that great corporations should not be trammelled by political morality. Sloan wanted peace and prosperity now, even if the world had to accept an expanded and powerful Nazi Germany. The Duke, on the whole, agreed.

There was another man waiting at Cat Cay. He was an associate of the Duke's, another mid-Westerner who believed that America should steer clear of war and a peace should be settled at the earliest possible moment. James D. Mooney was one of Sloan's right-hand men, the head of the defence effort for General Motors. He harried the State Department for help in his quixotic schemes to settle the war in 1940. State refused, since senior diplomats believed Mooney also saw himself as the American Quisling, when the Nazis took over.

Mooney was an Irishman who, according to a senior diplomat who knew him, 'is so against England that he would be prepared to see the whole world go down in order to satisfy his feelings with respect to England.' He also had the same certainties that other businessmen shared – that his own brand of corporate commonsense could somehow override mere political arguments. 'Mr Mooney,' said a State Department report, 'considers there is no sense whatever in the present war and that both parties should be compelled to make peace so that business could go on as usual.' He shared with Windsor horrific memories of fighting in the First World War, and he saw European war as the working out of old and bloody imperial feuds which had nothing to do with real American interests. In 1940 he told alumni of the Case School of Applied Science in Cleveland, in a speech curiously passionate for such a gathering, that ten-fold horrors were now imminent. He feared 'general hysteria will be increased in our country by the war news and propaganda, war psychosis will have been generated and eventually some dramatic incident will be seized upon to precipitate us into the war.' He ridiculed the rhetoric of British statesmen. 'Germany and Italy re-armed to eliminate this fear that their food supplies and commerce would be cut off. England and France are fighting for their lives. Germany and Italy are fighting and striving to keep from being starved to death. These aims of the belligerents have nothing to do with making the world safe for democracy.'

Mooney's arguments were not pure emotion. They were also $100,000,000 worth of calculation. That was the amount General Motors had poured into Germany since Hitler came to power. Sloan argued that General Motors, as 'an international business operating throughout the world should conduct its operations in strictly business terms, without regard to the political beliefs of its management or the political beliefs of the country in which it is operating.' Mooney's successor as head of General Motors export division, Graeme K. Howard, had a more detailed strategy. He followed the GM line which was, essentially, that Japan should be assigned the Far East, Germany should take Europe, and the British Empire should be 'adjusted'. There was nothing innocent about GM's decision to invest in Germany, nor in the consequences.

For Mooney was considerably more pro-German than his talk of American interests would suggest. He had been wooed by the Nazis. He went to Berlin in 1937 as General Motors' spokesman and he spoke of the cripplingly high cost of licence fees for cars. It was a usual GM line, with a highly unexpected result. The moment his speech was finished, a German government official rose to announce that the licence fee would be cut to $10 immediately – 'as Herr Mooney has suggested'. In 1938, while still an officer in the Naval Reserves, he accepted the Order of Merit of the German Eagle, which also went to Henry Ford and the aviator and isolationist Charles Lindbergh. He served on the board of the German-American Board of Trade and used its bulletin as a platform for his views. He thought America should stop criticizing Germany and Italy and 'join France and England in offering trade and financial help to the dictator countries in exchange for guarantees of non-aggression and arms limitation.' He expressed some general sympathy for the British, as one might for an exhausted prizefighter whose final destruction is an ugly sight, but his usual line in private was: 'I know Hitler has all the cards.' He believed Germany needed more room to live. He reinforced, loudly and from a position of great corporate influence, every element of the Nazi position that was publicly touted.

He did more. The $100,000,000 GM poured into building the Nazi industrial machine was inevitably diverted into the Nazi war machine. GM arranged to build an Opel plant, under Mooney's general supervision. The plant was built more cheaply than seemed possible. Mooney asked no questions. He did not ask about the armed guards in the factory. He claimed he did not realize that the plant was built by soldiers; when, very soon after its completion, the plant was seized by the Nazis and converted to tank production, he did not protest. GM had contributed a vital element to Hitler's war machine, and their best explanation was extraordinary naiveté.

For Windsor to associate with Mooney was highly eccentric. For all their common views, Mooney had already been identified as a potential danger; George S. Messersmith, then in the Havana Embassy, had told the US State Department that 'During the past few years, something has happened to him. I am personally convinced that he has become mentally unbalanced.' Every time the Duke sounded off, he encouraged the isolationists to believe that they had British allies – influential, significant allies. British isolationists certainly existed, as did sympathizers with the general Nazi line, but they lacked the royal charisma. It was not obvious to Americans just how far from the centre of things Windsor had always been. He could be made to seem the voice of the Establishment – talking freely, talking openly with a man who had already tried to negotiate a peace between Germany and Britain, and who was suspected by diplomats of fancying himself as America's Quisling.

After Cat Cay, Sloan's yacht came into Nassau harbour at night, a feast of lights. Etienne Dupuch of the *Nassau Tribune* was at the dockside. He had five hungry news services to feed with copy, and he hoped for at least some quote from his prime news story.

The yacht tied up. Dupuch waited, patiently. Quite suddenly, all the lights on the *Rene* were doused. Dupuch heard the noise of a motorboat, setting out across the harbour, toward Hog Island. The Duke and Duchess had urgent business at Shangri-la, so urgent that they would go there even before Government House.

The business was, in part, financial. On Windsor's behalf, Wenner-Gren was holding $2,500,000 in the Bahamas. Some of this was for Windsor's own benefit; all of it was available at his request. It represented Windsor's strategy for keeping his personal money safe from the fortunes of war in Europe. It also represented a floating fund which would allow the Windsors mobility, not least in their investments. The Duke would spend more and more time in America on 'private business' when he got the chance, even though London exchange control monitored the money he could have. Thanks to Wenner-Gren, he could evade exchange control when he wanted. The same trick had already been organized for Harry Oakes.

But Wenner-Gren was playing on more than the Duke's greed. He could use the Duke's fears. He was the first to warn the Duke that the Germans might try to land in Nassau to capture him. The Duke had a terror of submarines, of sudden attacks, and Wenner-Gren fuelled it. 'There were no defence facilities to speak of in Nassau, and as I happened to have a number of automatic rifles since our cruise in the pirate-infested China Seas,' Wenner-Gren explained later, 'I offered these rifles, including ammunition, to the British or Bahamas Government for the defence of the Bahamas.' It was a less than perfect gift, since Windsor had to point out the guns were not of standard bore, and ammunition would be hard to come by once Wenner-Gren's supply was exhausted. Still, he accepted the gift, and he agreed to Wenner-Gren's request – curious, given the publicity that usually surrounded his acts of charity – that the gift be kept secret.

Fear of capture, of assassination were common terrors of the Duke. He was trapped between images of himself: the man who defied the seductive Nazis, the man who tricked the stuffy British. He began to embroider on his fears. He let it be known, in 1942, to J. Edgar Hoover, that he most feared being taken from Nassau by U-boat and being exchanged for Rudolf Hess. In Britain, the prospect of a royal kidnap – Lord Hailsham was particularly concerned about the fate of the 'Little Princesses' – was taken seriously. It would be an excellent engine of blackmail. Churchill knew that Windsor's loyalties were questionable, and that the submarines were prowling the New Providence Channel, leaving sometimes smoke and oil on the water, and sometimes the sea-wrecked victims of a sinking. He took the matter in hand in August 1942.

> Am I not right in thinking that the only attack against the Bahamas possible is by a party landed from a U-boat? If so, Government House seems to be the obvious quarry. A U-boat would not have the facilities for finding out where the Duke of Windsor was if he were not there or were moving about. The right rule is, one may always take a chance but not offer a 'sitter'. I am therefore in favour of putting an electrified fence around Government House and the other places mentioned, but not interfering with H.R.H.'s liberty for movement otherwise than by informing him of the dangers. It is essential that the seat of Government should be protected against a U-boat raiding force, and for this purpose additional platoons should be sent.

Windsor could still remember the Lisbon days, when Monckton had been left to check whether or not British intelligence planned to murder their ex-King. Early in 1942, men from the Highland Regiments came to Nassau in part to act as his bodyguard. Island defences were rudimentary – machine-gun nests on awkward corners which held no machine guns, and pillboxes made of palm thatch, vulnerable to a few blasts from a .303. The Bahamas Defence Force rallied manfully, but could not always persuade its members to come to parades wearing uniform. Exercises in storming Government House were consistently and depressingly successful. One night, despite the barbed wire and the sentries, Duke and Duchess watched from the verandah as their attackers slipped into the grounds, broke the lines, and entered Government House. The Camerons commander had a special taste for bursting into the bedroom of Gray Phillips, the Windsors' amiable and angular and long-suffering comptroller, and declaring him a captive as he woke.

The lack of defence and the constant repetition of second- and third-hand threats – what the Germans would do, what the British might do – added to the strain of the Bahamas. The American friends, and the Bahamian uncertainties, were a cruel and effective process of preparing the

Windsors, already isolated, already malcontent, for other adventures. They would not present themselves to Hitler; that, they could have done in Lisbon. Instead, they would be available for schemes and propaganda much subtler than a spell as trainee Quislings. What Schellenberg had tried through little terrors and harassments in Lisbon, the British helped complete in the Bahamas. They reinforced the amorality, the self-preserving force in Windsor. And while, as a private person, he might have posed little problem – simply required surveillance or punishment or both – as the ex-King of England, as the romantic Duke, as the exile wandering far from his home and calling for peace, he was ripe for exploitation. Worse, he wanted more than anything to be taken seriously, and anyone who did so would have his attention; he had become so accustomed to listening to advisors that anyone who had his attention might change his mind. He was distant from local politicians, and from his colonial civil servants. The men who had his mind were the likes of James Mooney, Alfred Sloan and Axel Wenner-Gren. The risks were higher than in Lisbon, and the stakes as spectacular.

At the start of 1941, and throughout that year, the Windsors played out the formal comedy of the Nassau season, and they worked hard at their appointed tasks. But they wanted escape, and they knew now that the British would not offer it through the Washington Embassy.

The Nassau season filled their time. It opened by tradition at New Year and lasted a scant three months full of fierce indulgence. Along the beach at the Fort Montagu stood the cars, the cabriolets, the high-hooded convertibles, while sun-bathers perfected their tans for nights of dancing at the Jungle Club. They would come by the Orange Blossom Special – 'first and only air-conditioned train to Florida' – out of New York at 12.30 p.m., a 'one-night-out all-Pullman' train to Miami. From there, there were still boats or else the $35 round trip with Pan Am's seaplanes. The liners came to the bar of the harbour, and the diving boys were waiting for them. Veterans moved out at dawn to the side of the big ships, a flotilla of little boats each with a boy who dived for

89

nickels and quarters thrown from the liners – pennies, tourists noted rather crossly, were no longer enough – and surfaced with the money in his mouth.

Once off the boats, the welcome was enveloping, sensual; black girls became part of the marketing of the place for their supposed litheness and sinuousness and easy ways. Drink was cheap – gin 4s 6d (90¢) a bottle, Bacardi rum 5s 9d ($1.15), an appropriate tip was 3d (5¢) and the Moët et Chandon Dry Imperial was 'guaranteed to be identical with the wine sold in England'. A small island would cost only $2500. A cook expected no more than 14s a week ($2.80) and would also do housework. Life was easy to organize.

Nassau had not yet won its post-war reputation as 'that sunny place for shady people'. Only those on the fringes of society were likely to spend an entire winter season in the islands. That left Drexels from the Mainline of Philadelphia, and serious money from New York scattered along the shoreline; the Duke of Sutherland would spend the winter at Old Fort and the Dukes of Leeds and Manchester, less prepossessing specimens, were often present. Hog Island itself was a sort of 'luxurious quarantine', reached from Nassau only by boat. In wartime, some of the familiar names from the 1930s dropped away, but they were replaced. Captains of industry came for the sun, and sometimes left captive corporations in the islands for tax purposes. The rich tourists came, and were flattered by the social hostess who would check at their rooms when they first came and tell their local papers of their fine vacation. From the day the season opened, Nassau was fashionable, with pretensions; Altman's windows on Fifth Avenue were devoted that season to Fashions for Nassau, and the pages of *Vogue* and *Harper's Bazaar* took up the theme. Nassau was sold by its Development Board on a degree of style that the Windsors reinforced: 'Your gown,' said the advertisement, 'by Worth or Molyneux . . . your suntan to complete the winter ensemble – by Nassau. Perfect bathing days assure an even coat.'

Time had to be filled, carefully. There was fishing – 200-pound blue marlin close to Cat Cay, and tarpon off Andros, bonefish or kingfish or wahoo and the great northerly run of tuna in the spring. Etiquette prescribed which sex pursued which fish, since kingfish were thought to lead to blistered hands – almost as distressing for women as the need to ask a man to boat the fish when it had been hooked.

There was tennis, and boating and remote cays. (Noel Coward especially liked remote cays.) There was sailing – social at the Royal Nassau Sailing Club, sporting at the Nassau Yacht Club where a younger crowd were thought to lead a wilder life under the leadership of Roland Symonette. He was already a local politician, and a man who had consolidated his riches from rum-running in property and shipyards and other businesses; but he was still thought not quite white, with his Out Island birth and his Indian features and his shuffling walk. At formal occasions only one other man walked like that – 'not like a man does', according to one observer – and that was the Duke of Windsor.

Eccentric sailors also appeared, although not by the pool of the snobbish RNSC or among the wicker chairs and hard drinking of the Yacht Club. Group Captain L. W. B. Rees came with a boat that looked like a huge, lost egg. It was hung with tarpaulins, supposed to resemble the covers of grain-holds, and with port lights and verandahs which were like rowers' galleries, and the Group Captain said he was the Goddess Isis, trading from Rome to the Levant.

The great social events were fish-hauls – a ritual of decent cocktails, frosted glass and fine absurdity, with frocks pinned up to the waist, and trouser legs rolled high as the gentry took a net out and blocked a creek. Upstream, beaters howled and flailed the water with long sticks and drove the fish down so that the net could encircle them. By the net, the cocktail boat sculled, its attendant dressed in perfect white; there was beer, and baskets of limes and cans of sugar and ice. Guests weighted the bottom of the main net with their toes, and often tumbled forward into the frenetic fish. Yelling and beating and awkward balance, along with the strong drinks and the sun, made a wild day. In the haul there would often be barracuda, young shark, groupers and snapper and weakfish and parrotfish, which the revellers said had 'the type of nose which would put Hitler off fish for a week'. As

91

the net closed, the black servants waded out among the fury of fishes beating to escape, and used a two-prong gaff to dispose of the unwanted ones.

The formal retainers would approach and put on a fire whatever from the catch seemed good to eat; and a little sea of expensive flesh would organize itself on the sand with fish and drink, and congratulate itself on fending off another day.

Social geography was dominated by the clubs. Far to the west, past Cable Beach, stood the Emerald Beach Club where the Duke and Duchess had first been welcomed to the islands. Its moving spirit was Sir Frederick Williams Taylor, a Canadian banker whose claims to distinction were his wife and his granddaughter, Brenda Frazier. His wife, at seventy-five, was presented by her current lover with the largest and most grand of the old rum-runners' houses, as a token of esteem and love and, presumably, appreciation.

East from the Emerald Beach was the Bahamas Country Club. If Emerald Beach clung to a certain exclusiveness, a slight Canadian atmosphere as well, the Country Club was positively democratic; on Sundays it teemed with junior civil servants and their children. It had been founded by Chicago money; it was maintained on Harry Oakes's money.

On the ridge just before Nassau itself stood the Bahamian Club, an unlovely square building which was almost the most desirable of the clubs. Inside, there was a place for playing blackjack. It was of dubious legality, although since 1939 it had a licence engineered by the one-eyed commercial lawyer Stafford Sands. It was regarded by white Bahamians with a degree of awe – the truly exclusive establishment to which a very few of them might yet aspire. Their main social centre was the Club on Bay Street – poker, drinks, and talk. And they would never enter, except in very exceptional circumstances like war, the finest of all the clubs – the Porcupine.

That establishment stood on Hog Island in a sweet garden of high trees. Its members were the very rich, who for years had drifted south to the islands on their massive yachts. J. P.

Morgan, on the *Corsair*, trailed through the emerald waters before his financial empire took him back to New York, and Vincent Astor would come on one of his several yachts, called *Nourmahal,* sometimes with Franklin Roosevelt as guest. Some of the rich wanted a club in Nassau – a place for yachtsmen of a certain class and standing. In November 1927, Nelson Doubleday of the publishing house signed the first Articles of Association. The charter members included a Mellon, Frank Munson of shipping, the inevitable Lady Williams Taylor, Seward Prosser, president of Bankers Trust, and Dwight D. Morrow, a partner in Morgans, who gave his profession as Ambassador and was chiefly noted for recurring nightmares that one day he would be rich.

Doubleday was followed by Arthur Vining Davis, founder of the Aluminum Company of America, who was already turning his mind to property in Florida and the Bahamas. Davis was the animator of the club, the guardian of its fierce standards. At business meetings of the club, he would listen impatiently to accounts of some candidate for membership – his fortune, business, style and reputation – and cut short the eulogy by barking: 'Yes, but who *is* he?' He liked his company as dry and as predictable as his martinis (he used an atomizer for the vermouth). He conserved the Porcupine, against all those who might mar or dilute its great richness.

For it was a good place – a beach of white sand with awnings and striped deckchairs, and gardens with casuarinas feathery against the sky, and palms and the vanilla scent of poor man's orchid in the spring. It had absolute certainties of solid money in every stone and path.

For the less grand, the less rich, Nassau offered the places over the hill – assorted 'native bars' like Weary Willie's. And if a man's tastes were more basic, and if the girls on Rawson Square seemed all too brash, he could drive out east beyond Eastern Parade, where the major brothel stood, a barrack building full of love – for everyone, with money, who was white.

Everyone wanted the company of the Windsors. Would the Duke go to the air carnival in Cuba, to the Hialeah Races or the President's Birthday Ball in Miami? The State of Michigan brashly offered summers more temperate than Nassau's; advertising men in Baltimore thought the Duke would find their company congenial; Houston charities wrote fiercely, as though it was part of the Windsors' duties to visit Texas for a country fair. Such invitations went through cumbrous channels, since it was custom that royalty must enter the United States only on the direct invitation of the President. If the Windsors could not come to America, though, America was hell-bent on visiting the Windsors – often with great lobbying beforehand. Even the Speaker of the House of Representatives, Sam Rayburn, tried to stir the Nassau consul into fixing a royal audience for thirty-one girls from the Hockaday School in Dallas – 'mighty fine girls', the Speaker assured the State Department

As tourist attractions, the Windsors were a huge success.

There were eccentrics for their amusement. Each day, a notorious trio of man, wife and mistress would walk to a beauty parlour, each to have his or her identical grey pompadour perfected. A couple out at Cable Beach adored their dogs so unquestioningly that they had their dining-room tiled and drained, so as not to miss one moment of the animals' company, even for calls of nature. There was also one royal pretender, one other exile: high on Prospect Ridge lived the claimant of the Austro-Hungarian throne, with her prosaic American stockbroker husband. They lived among flags, with a household that even in high summer appeared at all times in impeccable white gloves.

The Windsors went to the races at Montagu Park, down by the sea at Cable Beach. They arrived after the first race, left after the fourth; presented a cup, assessed the bloodstock – which was ponies, at best threequarter breeds; graced the wooden stands and betting booths for a while. (There were, of course, separate betting booths for the ladies.) They would briefly see the big bluff figure of Harry Oakes, in riding breeches, felt hat and boots, ambling across the lawns with his hands stuck deep in his pockets, whistling a little nervously. Oakes never enjoyed such occasions, nor would he pretend. Coat, tie and shirt were to him social conventions he could not take seriously. But he waved at the crowd as they barked at him, looked neither to left nor to right and dived back into the bush whence he had come.

The Windsor name went on trophies for every sport – cups for the Miami–Nassau ocean race, for golf at the Bahamas Country Club, for polo at Clifford Park. The Windsors went to parties given by the Leader of the Government, to dances at the Jungle Club with parties that starred the Wenner-Grens and Alfred Sloan and assorted relics of the Argentine diplomatic corps. When the Royal Victoria hotel opened a patio of shops, the Duchess was there, and made her token buys; when salesmen from Electrolux passed through, visiting their owner, Wenner-Gren, the Duke went out to present them with golfing trophies. Together, they went to dances at the Emerald Beach and the Duke would say wistfully, 'I sincerely hope I shall have the opportunity of getting away for a spell this summer, and showing the Duchess my ranching property in the foothills of the Rocky Mountains which,' he added rather superfluously, 'I have the good fortune to own.' Bessie Merryman, aunt to the Duchess, came to stay, and repaid the hospitality by reporting that she had it on good authority that the Duchess was flying weekly to secret assignations in Puerto Rico. Aunt Bessie would not reveal her sources, but she told the rumours even to the American Government.

The season's known names began to congregate. The Messmores from New York – the Knoedler Galleries – starred at the Windsors' Christmas party and stayed on, with Mr Messmore indulging his unpleasant habit of telling jokes in fake Scots and Cockney accents, and yodelling after dinner. The Goldsmiths came in from Monte Carlo, no longer a refuge or a proper place for hotel owners, with the six-year-old James Goldsmith in tow, and the Duchess of Leeds, who bitterly complained that the Rolls-Royce she had been forced to abandon in Paris was now gracing the streets of Berlin.

The season involved great effort – a slightly sweaty air of too much alcohol and too little air-conditioning. The wartime etiquette of being rich and stylish was complicated –

some Anglophile Americans like Leonore Messmore would buy no clothes until the war was over, and most felt a new outfit every evening was not acceptable. And the usual social equilibrium was upset by the first of the refugee women – from England, often, and with husbands overseas, and with too little money and blank evenings to fill. The women were a new, disruptive factor. They complained of the dullness of Nassau evenings, and they needed male company. Little games blew up into little storms.

At grand events, there was an earnest air of determined enjoyment. The gap was huge between the Windsor style – costly, exact – and this enthusiastic partying. Grand events were like the Head-Dress Ball, where everybody, for charity, arrived in bizarre hats. First prize went to a spinster from New York who wore the head of a swordfish stuck with flowers. McAndrews, the prissy American vice-consul who lived with his sister, arrived under a huge sponge which was draped with sea ferns and a real crawfish. Among the model aircraft, the turbans, the woman who came with half her head still in curlers and face mask, the Duchess maintained her standards: a tiara, but of rice-shells.

Her season was a very moderate consolation. The Duke, at least, had his daily bicycle ride to Cable Beach, bodyguard at his side, and his swim, his round of golf with acquaintances; he had the work of being Governor, which involved apparent power, if limited by political reality, and he had his beloved, worshipped Duchess. She, who needed style and wit, had only the season – and her solid committee work for the Red Cross.

The great events were the rugby matches against Yale and Princeton. Yale played Nassau and lost. Princeton arrived weeks later in better shape. Wisely, they played their first game fresh off the ship, to avoid the excessive strain of Nassau partying. They also, thanks to a certain vagueness about the differences between armour-clad American football and the more vulnerable British rugby, put several key Nassau players out of commission for the series. Before the third game, the Windsors entertained at Government House. The Duchess asked politely which members of the team

96

might be from Baltimore, and the Duke joked – 'The British Navy likes rum,' he said, 'but the German Navy sticks to port!' The guffaws were deferential. The Americans found the Duke charming, but downright natty – he wore startling blue canvas deck shoes, as no American sophomore would have dared.

And there was the Bahamas Fair, a curious mixture of educational event and demonstration of civic pride, with booths for the islands and their products. It was as though the islands brought tribute to Nassau, and put it on stands that were thatched with palm fronds. For Whale Cay, Marion Carstairs built a fine pavilion with a picket fence and flagpoles for the American and British flags; with a scout troop that gave the Duchess a guard of honour into the fairground; and, in the pavilion, models of the church and houses on Whale Cay that lit up from inside while a recorded church bell rang. The Duchess went with the Duke from stall to stall, carefully, even regally charming and informed. It was a parody of royal duties – showing interest in sugar cane and straw baskets, coconut hats and shell tiaras. The Duke bought jam and stood on a low wall to watch the old, blind grace of turtles in a pen; and on the last day, showed their terrier Pookie at the dog show, trotting him before the crowd with fierce concentration and winning a diplomatic second prize. Pookie, the papers said, was 'the most popular dog in the show'. The Duchess showed flowers – yellow, green and white with pink-tipped tuberoses – and peered at the crafts (a wood Madonna) and the curiosities (skin and bones of a five-year-old mackerel shark with the embryo of an egg that was found in the body; the skeleton of a whale that had washed up on the island of Andros; the mola-mola fish, killed by a ship's anchor). It was like an older sort of carnival, with bizarre things to see, and it had a great Ferris wheel imported for the occasion. It was the perfect provincial event and Duke and Duchess walked through it with commendable liveliness of feature and eye. They were good at this – professional and kind.

And Sally Rand, the fan-dancer, came to Nassau and danced for the Duke and Duchess at a Red Cross benefit.

Her arrival scandalized the black politicians, and it evidently upset Government House, since there was an official ban on reporting that the Windsors had actually seen Miss Rand's Famous Fan and Bubble Dance. Miss Rand, unperturbed, went her pretty way, all blue eyes and golden hair, with manager and hairdresser (other dressers being superfluous) and posed behind curtains of special balloons, made by her own company to her own specification to be perfectly round. Her other customer, she said, was the US Government, who bought her balloons for target practice.

And movies came. In Paris, the Windsors had attended the world première of *Pygmalion*, the movie teased by the Hungarian producer Gabriel Pascal from the play by George Bernard Shaw. Pascal, who liked to be consistent, wanted the Windsors now for the première of his version of Shaw's *Major Barbara* (which Shaw, said Pascal, 'frankly admits is the greatest picture drawn from his works'). And since the Windsors could not leave the Bahamas, the movie was brought to them, for a world première at the all-white Savoy Theatre on Bay Street.

The Windsors made Pascal delay the showing for a day. They expected a guest so important that such trivial matters had to be put aside.

Maximinio Avila Camacho, governor of the province of Puebla, brother of the President of Mexico, a kind of chieftain in his own region, was installed in the penthouse of the British Colonial hotel as guest of Harry Oakes and Harold Christie. On 20 March 1941 he spent two hours with Windsor at Government House – 'I was,' he said, 'impressed by His Royal Highness's knowledge of European and American politics.' The conversation was wholly improper. Windsor was the representative of the British Government; those he entertained were presumed to have some official existence in British eyes. Camacho was closely associated with his brother and the Mexican Government. Britain and Mexico had broken off diplomatic relations in 1938, and would not restore them until October 1941. Windsor should never have entertained Camacho, let alone discussed politics with him, let alone announced the fact.

Their meeting was worse than a breach of diplomatic conventions. It was the outward sign of Windsor's increasing involvement with Oakes and Christie and Wenner-Gren and Mexico. Windsor saw Camacho because Camacho required wooing. Royal hospitality was an excellently seductive start.

The prospect of making money in the Bahamas must, by 1941, have seemed rather remote. Outsiders were forbidden any activity except the buying of land, and those prices rose explosively only when postwar migrants came to the islands to escape what they feared would be a confiscatory socialism in Britain. Only after 1945 was Bahamas land a safe investment. Harry Oakes was essentially a philanthropist now, providing work for the unemployed as they cleared his bush and made his roads and filled his swamps – all preparation for some future boom in land prices which nobody could yet predict. Oakes's investments in hotels were not paying off; none of the islands' big hotels made money. Worse, Lake Shore Mines – the very centre of Oakes's fortune – was under some pressure, its earnings and value both declining. Oakes saw the need for some more active investment, and he could not see it in Nassau. He confided in his future son-in-law Alfred de Marigny his doubts about his advisors, and de Marigny wrote of the Oakeses to his friend Georges de Visdelou, 'They are surrounded by sharks whom they distrust, and for this reason they make hardly any use of their capital in Nassau.'

Harold Christie sensed Oakes's restlessness. He also knew how much the firm of H. G. Christie rested on the commissions from buying and selling for the Oakes Estates. He set about using his contacts – from Palm Beach and Bar Harbor and the rest of the watering places of the rich – for an unusual purpose. Instead of seducing buyers to the Bahamas, he was trying to find Harry Oakes a new home for his money. Together, Oakes and Christie visited Mexico City on 18 July 1940. Oakes was talking very publicly of investing in highways or oil. The next day, the Harolds went to visit Maximinio Camacho, since they firmly believed he held great influence over his brother; and Harold Christie introduced Oakes to State Senator John Hastings from New York, a financial front man with extensive contacts, a kind of upstate Harold Christie. Hastings was in Mexico at the time and the three kept in constant touch. Hastings later claimed that it was either Oakes or Christie – he could not remember which – who introduced him to Axel Wenner-Gren, and the Swede, late in 1940, arrived in New York armed with a letter of introduction and started talks with Hastings.

On purely financial grounds, Mexico glittered. There was a dream of huge oil fields – always an enticement to the Duke, who nursed his own fantasies about oil being found on his Calgary ranch. There was a pressing need for homes and highways and railways to keep pace with what looked likely to be vast industrial development. Mexico was not on the front line of war, her banking system was developed, and anyone with political contacts could establish a sophisticated financial empire, ready for use. The Mexican Revolution, true to its ideals in the 1930s, had been turned to the Right by Camacho. Money was welcome, and Maximinio Camacho was the welcoming committee.

In all of this, there was only one problem. Neither Harry Oakes nor the Duke of Windsor could legally send one penny outside the sterling area without exchange control permission – London for the Duke, Nassau for Sir Harry. The Oakes dividends from Lake Shore Mines arrived each quarter at the Royal Bank of Canada, where they were handled with the respect proper to their vast size. Once the money had left Canada – legitimately, since Oakes was a resident of the Bahamas, and both countries were within the sterling area and the same general framework of exchange control – it was trapped. It could go to England, but Oakes did not pretend to have even residual patriotism, and he could hardly justify investments in a country which was on the verge of a wartime economic collapse. No other part of the sterling area offered him the opportunities he wanted. Canada would tax him too highly; he had been through Australia before. What Oakes wanted was no tax and a hope of profit – which Mexico offered. But to get his money to Mexico would mean passing through exchange control in Nassau. Oakes never did apply for permission, but in 1941 he emerged as a sizeable stockholder in the newly formed Banco Continental, alongside Hastings from New York. The deal was illegal. In wartime, it was outrageous.

The Duke also was badgered by exchange control and would have reason to see the money rules as a device to keep him in his place. It was literally used that way; when he wanted to be in America in 1941 at the same time as his brother, the Duke of Kent, he was denied permission and, in case that did not work, denied dollars. In Paris after the war, he bought his francs on the black market in such quantity that his bankers found it embarrassing to explain the flow of used notes to the Windsor accounts. In the Bahamas, he needed a more tricky device.

Axel Wenner-Gren was stakeholder for Windsor – and, it is possible, the man who was responsible for physically shipping bullion for Oakes from the Bahamas and Canada to Mexico. Since Oakes owned gold mines, and currency transactions would have been extremely difficult; since Wenner-Gren had the *Southern Cross*, jaunting in the Caribbean; and since the records prove that Oakes did manage the magician's trick of holding all of his money in Nassau in a legal trap, yet using enough of it in Mexico to become a substantial backer of a respectable bank, the idea of Wenner-Gren running an illegal cargo of gold into Mexico is actually the easiest explanation of the mechanics of the deal. Wenner-Gren's advantage from all this was simple. He was a rich man, but his riches were not liquid. He could not simply sell his stake in Bofors in wartime and pocket the cash; and he would find it hard to dispose of a huge asset like control of Electrolux. More, those were the foundations of his fortune. Wenner-Gren wanted to make splashy announcements in Mexico, to talk of a $100,000,000 investment, when State Department officials estimated he could not put his hands on more than $250,000 in cash. Other people's money was Wenner-Gren's liquidity.

His money machine was spectacular. He had legitimate bank arrangements anywhere guns or vacuum cleaners were

101

sold. He was a neutral in the war, able to organize his empire as he wanted. He certainly had money in London, in Nassau, in America, Mexico, Norway and Sweden. Through commercial investments – or substantial expeditions financed by his foundations – he could negotiate in Peru or in the Amazon basin. He might be an 'international hoax' to the Americans monitoring his affairs, but they were naive in assuming that only his own money passed through his companies. Through Mobilia SA alone in 1941 passed some $300,000 – money which, once handled in Nassau by Mobilia subsidiaries, could legitimately be sent to a private resting place in Panama where Mobilia was registered. Washington saw this as self-protection: 'It appears quite possible that he has been distributing his assets in such a way as to get them under cover or out of reach. It is interesting to note how early he began. . . .' Actually, Wenner-Gren played banker to a set who wanted their money out of the reach of war.

The catch with Wenner-Gren was the Americans' continuing interest in him. Maximinio Camacho's links were embarrassing the President of Mexico, since Maximinio was 'more "out in front" than the President would like him to be, particularly with respect to his connections with our friend Axel Wenner-Gren whose very blatant display of his wealth and proposals to invest his capital in Mexico may yet prove embarrassing to the President,' according to diplomatic sources in the Mexico City Embassy of the United States. Some other name was needed on the Mexican investments.

Harry Oakes was the front man. Oakes, Christie and Wenner-Gren used the Duke to give some style to the proceedings. The talks in Nassau were an important part of that. The Duke and Camacho talked for two hours – the Duke conveniently spoke fluent Spanish. At the very least he was breaking every diplomatic rule and giving help to a scheme that he had every reason to believe defied exchange control. Actually, he knew more. John Hastings, the New York fixer who by now had been introduced to all the major partners in the scheme outside Mexico, was also in Nassau. He confirmed later that he had discussed investments in Mexico with Christie, Oakes and Wenner-Gren. Indeed, by July 1941

Oakes had committed himself to Banco Continental, a new Mexican venture, and the American Embassy feared 'it now seems to include Wenner-Gren. We understand that Wenner-Gren's influence in such an institution may not be for the best interests of the United States.' On 1 August 1941 the Bank first opened for business with authorized capital of 5,000,000 pesos – 50,000 shares of 100 pesos each – 'Don John A. Hastings' on the board and, by its first balance sheet on 31 December, $7,000,000 in deposits. It seems likely that Wenner-Gren was already involved, and the State Department would be told the next year – through good sources in Mexico City – just how much Windsor had entrusted to Wenner-Gren's money machine.

Blacks were invisible men to Windsor. They simply did not figure in his scheme of things, except as servants – in Nassau, he acquired the houseman Sydney who later went with the Windsors to Paris. He let it be known that he disliked and distrusted them in general. He wanted social reforms but, as he told doctors who came to report on the state of public health in the colony, 'such proposals would not change the social relationships between the races'. The Duchess was more direct. 'We Southerners,' she told an island dinner party, 'always flatter ourselves we know best how to deal with coloured people.'

Etienne Dupuch, editor of the daily *Nassau Tribune*, was infuriated by Windsor's attitudes. Dupuch was a fairly usual Nassau mixture of races – black, French, with a passion for all things British – and a Member of the House of Assembly. He knew he was outside the inner circles of power, but he was still effective; he had organized, since war began, a war materials committee which sent scrap and canned food to Britain, on the calculation that money was useless if there was nothing to spend it on. Bay Street made one spirited attempt to remove Dupuch from his prominence by creating a rival committee – the grounds were that a coloured man should not have a position of such importance, let alone steal the patriotic bluster which secured the position of whites. When that failed, Dupuch remained a significant figure in

103

Nassau. The Duke let it be known that he had great respect for Dupuch, when he was talking to whites. To Dupuch himself, the picture looked very different.

When the Duke was furious with Dupuch's reporting for Associated Press, he summoned the Miami bureau head for AP and set an *aide de camp* to wander through the gardens with him promising more cooperation if only AP would employ a man 'not of that type'. Since AP was more interested in stories than Government hand-outs, the bureau chief went back to Dupuch and laughed about the clumsiness of English diplomats. When Dupuch found a Scots engineer with plans for badly needed reservoirs in Nassau, he proposed the man to the Duke. Windsor first assumed the man was black, and said a coloured man could not do the job. He then thought Dupuch must have found a white Bahamian, and said there was none qualified. His attitudes exasperated Dupuch so much that the introduction never took place.

Such irritating bias produced private fury, but little public action. 'There was,' says H. M. Taylor, later co-founder of the Progressive Liberal Party which now rules the Bahamas, 'no public opinion at all, no political consciousness.' Black businessmen were rare, and under terrible pressure because their credit was limited. Black politicians – only five Members of the House of Assembly – were conservative by nature, and some, like the lawyer A. F. Adderley who served on Legislative Council, were positively aristocratic. The loudest of them all, and the most effective, was Milo Butler.

He had a small store selling ice and groceries to the east of town. 'It was very difficult to make a living,' his widow, Lady Caroline Butler, remembers, 'because if you didn't have finance to pay them on the spot for their goods, then don't mind how long you'd been trading with them, they'd bluntly turn their backs and refuse you. The bank didn't lend money because if he gets money he is going to climb over their heads, and the bank was easily advised – the same clique was lawyers for the bank and on the bank committees. And if my husband did catch the bankers with too many whiskies in him and get him to say yes, and if he got the loan of £50 or £60, he'd split it with a friend. I always said, "Milo, this is only enough to get you confused and get you into trouble. . . .'' And that was true. You didn't have time to turn over what little you got before you had to pay it back.'

In his store, Butler was a big presence – booming, passionate, talking constantly of 'My people, the black people'. To some blacks in the 1940s, that sounded like racism, although it is hard to see how black Bahamians could have advanced without radical change in the power and privilege of the whites. In military intelligence reports, he appears as 'labour leader and trouble maker'. He took some of his prestige from his mother, a gentle woman who had founded the Mothers' Club in Nassau and had worked quietly for some reforms; and he was kind, almost indulgent, to his customers, as the white merchants rarely were. 'People were so poor, so destitute that everybody wanted to get a start . . . they were going out to rub and scrub for the higher ups.'

Butler was no radical in a modern sense. In the House, he was a great supporter of measures which allowed merchants a few cents more profit. But he did articulate a feeling over the hill that was usually a great sadness, and in his hands became a great anger. Anger, at least, could start change. Bert Cambridge, one of his black colleagues in the House, insists, 'He was damn well racial. Everything where he was concerned was my people, my people, the black people. We're being mistreated. In a sense he was right, but his policy was to influence the hatred of the races.'

Butler had sailed into the House of Assembly at a by-election when Harry Oakes was appointed to the Legislative Council – the first secret ballot in the Bahamas. He had been roundly defeated before when the ballot was open and votes were exchanged for rum and cash. He bought himself an English dinner jacket – the sure sign a man wanted to be in the House, since it was obligatory for all Members. He was the awkward black voice, which the whites answered by bullying. If Butler would not withdraw his opposition to a measure, the whites would simply lock him in the men's room until the vote was over.

Those whites had no considered philosophy of racial superiority. They were simply more insular than they knew.

Political currents in the Caribbean as such never brushed past the Bahamas, and the white lawyers, even though they might travel as widely as a Stafford Sands who went from Brazil (after a Pepsi Cola franchise) to America (after great client corporations), lived in a separate, limited, rarified world. Their closest regular contact with America was shopping trips to Miami, itself a city with separate drinking fountains for blacks and whites. Their ignorance, however, left them with certainties. They disliked spending money. Most of all, they disliked spending it on blacks – which was spending with no hope of a return.

In late 1940, they tried one of their most astonishing coups. They tried to abolish secondary education for blacks. Only one school took black pupils beyond the age of fourteen, Government High School; the other secondary schools were fee-paying, and black children were excluded by the simple device of the known cruelty of white children to outsiders in their midst. Windsor admitted to London that the move must have 'a bad psychological effect on the coloured population'. The only argument for shutting GHS was that its very existence took the pressure off the Government-subsidized Methodist school, Queen's College, to integrate its classrooms. London saw that 'Here is a colony with a large measure of self-government so exercised by its House of Assembly, in which one racial section is predominant, as to exclude the coloured section of the community from receiving efficient secondary education.' The proposal was quashed, although GHS did not get adequate funds for such 'frills' as science teaching for many years. It was the kind of move which would have seemed dubious in the 1900s, and by the 1940s was a scandal.

Windsor wholly missed the beginnings of black consciousness. He did not try to understand the anger of black politicians telling him that something must be done. In his own mind, his paternalistic mind, he knew that already. He wanted to end hunger and deprivation. He worked hard. 'It may be that he and the Duchess were sent out here to get rid of them, so to speak,' the US consul told Washington, 'but he is taking his job seriously.' He asked for better housing when he had seen what the islands already had, and for lower import duties on the basic foodstuffs which kept most islanders alive. He planned new agricultural development, modelled on Roosevelt's Civilian Conservation Corps (launched in 1933 as a way to find work for men between seventeen and twenty-five, and to create forests, build dams, eliminate malaria by mosquito control, stock fisheries and fight forest fires). The value of CCC that attracted Windsor was, in Roosevelt's words, 'the value to the men themselves and to the nation in morale, in occupational training, in health and in adaptability to later competitive life.' It meant small pay and big hopes, but it also meant the kind of spending the House of Assembly resented most.

All Windsor's caring was tempered by his suspicion of blacks, a feeling that they required special handling. When he wanted a labour officer for the islands, he asked for one 'familiar with Negro idiosyncracies and understanding of the traditional handling of Negroes in the Southern States'. When pressed to make the House pass bills on workmen's compensation and trade union rights, bills that would have made some deep social difference, he merely said: 'regret no prospect of getting workmen's compensation legislation enacted here in the immediate future.' The London officials noted coldly on the file: 'A useful contribution!'

In the event, what made change happen, and what saved the economy of the Bahamas when America went to war, had nothing to do with Windsor. It was the building of bases – first American, then British – in the islands. Roosevelt anticipated the problems – the 'colour line' issues, and the question of whether to pay top local rates or better; Churchill produced the grand rhetoric. On 27 March 1941 he announced to colonial Governors the final agreement. 'I have today signed the document implementing the agreement of September last for the leasing to the United States of bases in the Bahamas and elsewhere and I wish to express to you my strong conviction that these bases are important pillars to the bridge connecting two great English-speaking democracies. You have cause to be proud that it has fallen to your lot to make this important contribution to a better world.'

Churchill had finally paid for the warships Roosevelt had provided for Britain over howls of protest and threats of impeachment for breaching America's neutrality. Now Roosevelt would come to inherit the very old and sour problems of the British West Indies.

War in Europe baffled Bahamians because the British seemed not to want their help. At the fall of France, some brave boys borrowed dollars illegally and made their own way, in defiance of exit permits and exchange control, to Canada and to Britain as volunteers. Godfrey Higgs took himself to his army contacts and expected to be drafted any day, but although a healthy professional in his early thirties he was never called. London wanted only white airmen and they had to be young.

There were awkward questions when a liner full of black Jamaican recruits passed through Nassau on its way to Britain. The Colonial Secretary suggested they had been taken because they were skilled technicians. He was probably right. Recruitment of blacks, even recruitment from the colonies, was a touchy issue. The British military never did come to terms with its own racism. But there were still curious elements to the Duke's behaviour.

He suppressed a Colonial Office telegram, asking for recruits for the Royal Air Force. When he finally announced its contents, in April 1941, he declared: 'I received a telegram to this effect from the Colonial Office some time ago but I have purposely delayed imparting its contents because in recruiting response to impulse is infinitely preferable and more genuine than response to an appeal.' The argument was curious: having failed to volunteer because they thought Britain did not want their help, Bahamians were now told that they should have guessed the change of mind in London; if they had not guessed, then their volunteering was somehow second rate.

Recruitment for the Navy was equally odd. Bahamians knew the sea and ships; yet when in February 1942 there was an appeal for volunteers for the British Navy, it was not published. Instead, the Colonial Secretary was told to ask three leading white men – Herbert McKinney, a Nassau merchant, Rev. Brown of Spanish Wells, Rev. William C. Dyer of Abaco – 'if any substantial number of suitable applicants were likely to respond to such an appeal.' The next month, ExCo decided against any public appeal on the grounds that they had already, privately, found a handful of suitable white candidates.

Such equivocal ardour from Government Hill left Bay Street's cool approach to war seeming less sinister than it might otherwise. Britain and her problems were very far away from the record 1941 tourist season. And Britain seemed determined to keep her distance, to make no demands on the men and women of the islands. There was little challenge to the kind of sentiments that an anonymous merchant, signing himself 'Bahamian', expressed in the *Tribune*: 'I did not bring [my son] up to be a soldier, I did not spend hundreds of pounds on his education just to have him go out to fight Hitler and probably get killed, furthermore the shock would kill his mother. We in the Bahamas have nothing to worry about, the United States will always protect us if Britain can't, time enough for Bahamians to think about fighting when the Bahamas are attacked. . . .'

Sometimes, London could seem appallingly insensitive. Widdicombe and Tapscott, the sailors who had beached on Eleuthera after weeks of bleak exposure in the wild Atlantic, had become a problem. One month after they landed, the Ministry of Shipping in London tried to order Widdicombe back to work, since all hands were needed for the Atlantic run. The Colonial Office was appalled. Lord Lloyd wrote of 'the lack of imagination and of the sympathy and understanding to which Widdicombe is entitled in view of his ordeal.' He accused the Ministry of 'patent inhumanity' and refused to tell Windsor to send the men home.

Widdicombe showed no signs of wanting to leave the Bahamas when money for his keep ran out. Tapscott, Windsor said, was 'psychologically unfitted for further service at sea'. He might have been a hero in the Bahamas, but his family showed no interest in him and he had no wish to go home. 'He is,' Windsor reported, 'unwilling to go to Canada and desires to go to the United States where he is assured that he can earn a living by lecturing.' The Colonial Office wondered who had 'got at' Tapscott. The hero began to melt away in the sun to a man whose family deserted him, and who had no home.

Widdicombe left for Britain and work again. His ship was due in Liverpool on 17 February. His wife had come from Newport to greet him. A civic lunch, a hero's return, had been arranged.

On 16 February the ship on which Widdicombe was travelling sank – victim of a torpedo, like the *Anglo-Saxon* before her. Windsor cabled immediately, for Mrs Widdicombe, a message full of the tears he had shed before in field hospitals, for the wounded, for the dying.

'The Duchess and I,' he said, 'were deeply shocked. . . .'

Royal privilege did not protect a Governor from criticism, although Windsor used to claim it should. He instructed Etienne Dupuch that it was not customary to criticise members of the royal family, and Dupuch simply reminded him that he was a politician now. He would have to accept harsh words.

The *Tribune* said: 'At a time when the colony needs government leadership and inspiration, it is totally lacking.' Godfrey Higgs told the House of Assembly: 'I have reached the stage where I don't like to give any more power to the Governor in Council than I can help. We all feel that the Governor in Council is out of touch with the House and with the colony.' The jokes also started. Alvin Braynen, a politician who had married into property and an oil business, raised the case of a Bahamian who had an American wife and American-born children. His wife could not join him in Nassau because of immigration rules; he could not send out US dollars to help her because of exchange control. 'Nothing,' Braynen said, rather archly, 'should keep a man from the woman he loves.'

Windsor was not proving a bad Governor – not after Clifford, or Dundas, who was so unpopular that American residents petitioned for his recall. The tourist season had

110

been astonishing; the publicity – fourteen and a half pages in *Vogue*, eleven in *Harper's Bazaar*, Duke, Duchess and Nassau fashions making guest appearances on Movietone News – had been brilliant. For all the prowling submarines, the Windsors had succeeded in keeping the war at bay. There had been squabbles, but they had been mostly resolved. A public gardener had been appointed and started his duties by building a rockery and lily ponds at Government House for Windsor, whose main activities in gardens were design and hoeing. The House objected, and rules were drawn for the time the public gardener was to spend on more obviously public spaces. In Executive Council, the Duke had chaired effectively – listening to everyone, seemingly democratic, and finally quite decisive. The ancient battles – locals against the underpaid, sometimes arrogant colonial officials; Government Hill against Bay Street and the House of Assembly – were not capable of resolution without drastic reform.

It was not the actions or derelictions of the Duke which started criticism. It was a general nervousness in Nassau. The last tourists were going home. For the next season, the great ships were not yet guaranteed, and the seas were becoming more dangerous. Tight money controls meant a new dependence on American custom – Canadians could come to Nassau since it was in the sterling area, but to get there they had to pass through American ports and that meant dollars which they could not buy. Would the Americans still brave the U-boats next year? This season had been very good, but with the customary fatalism of men so dependent on chance for their survival, the Bahamians did not count on the next. Times were not certain any more.

Duke and Duchess took themselves to Miami in April, not with Wenner-Gren. They went for long money talks with Sir Edward Peacock who, besides being Governor of the Bank of England and the usual go-between in settling Anglo-American financial differences, was also unofficial financial advisor to the royal family. Peacock was too busy to come to Nassau and waste an extra day in travel, but he made himself available in Palm Beach. Despite the swirl of parties that had been planned – this was the Windsors' debut in American society – the Duke cleared twenty-four hours of every social activity for the talks. Money alarmed him; he needed reassurance. And he built his stay around the telephone. In Palm Beach, he could make uncensored private calls.

The rich on the Beach expected more diversion, more spectacle from the Windsors than they delivered. There were cocktails for 300, the sponsorship of Douglas Fairbanks Junior, golf for the Duke and a roster of old friends, including Captain Alastair Mackintosh (from days when the Prince of Wales was always with Freda Dudley Ward) and even childhood playmates of the Duchess. But their first engagement with American society after abandoning their terriers in Miami ('for,' the Duke said, 'a little spring overhaul') was warmly greeted. This was the territory and heartland of the very rich. It was the territory they would inhabit after the war, when there was nothing else to occupy them and when their wartime behaviour had cut away for ever the possibility of official position or recognition.

They dreamt of visiting the Duke's Canadian ranch. The Duke spoke so often of his land – his only land – with its breeding stock of animals and its Dartmoor ponies bought because children could not learn to ride on the huge working horses. The subject came up so often that the Duke was forced to deny publicly that he planned to retire. Both Duke and Duchess complained of the impossibility of making plans or keeping to schedules. 'For one thing,' said the Duke, 'it isn't easy to get a ship now.' It was clear that they felt their lives had been dislocated and the Nassau routine was no substitute for the sweet anarchy of their earlier life.

The Duchess changed her mind once while in Palm Beach. She took a ride in a plane – Harold Vanderbilt's plane. Before, she had always pleaded claustrophobia; that was the reason the Windsors gave to those who wanted to know why, on a previous visit, they had accepted Wenner-Gren's invitation to travel by the *Southern Cross*. Now, she found a way to come to terms with the wretched machines. 'Soon after the plane left the ground,' she explained, 'it developed a motion like that of a ship and then I felt a little more secure. . . .'

'Men get tired,' said Milo Butler, 'of being debarred from happiness.' He wanted a rise in the colony's minimum wage – 4s a day. His arguments were battled by white politicians like Godfrey Higgs – 'Much of the labour employed in this colony is hired as a form of charity,' Higgs told the House of Assembly – and by black politicians like L. Walton Young, who had labour forces of their own and spoke from the wallet. Butler was opposed by Stafford Sands, spokesman and relative of the Bay Street Boys, a one-eyed, big-bellied man who announced that even the minimum wage was a definite disadvantage to the people of the islands.

Windsor had to contend with these men. The sponges had died out, and war conditions made it impossible to bring materials from Britain and hard to buy them in America. Construction work was almost at a halt. Windsor did not believe, like the Bahamians, that something would turn up. He wanted reform. Yet even the simplest of reforms – raising the wage level fixed years before, now that the cost of living had risen a full third since war began – was blocked. Government business in the House was constantly blocked. The Duke was frustrated and baffled and angry. The Windsors' feelings were exacerbated by what others wrote of them – Janet Flanner, in *Life*, saw them in a kind of beatific limbo. 'Untouched physically, financially, socially or otherwise,' she wrote, 'life has flowed along easily – almost sweetly – while millions of people in Europe, Africa and Asia are being terrorised and our way of life is being threatened.'

Summer heat began in May and June and the Duchess could not tolerate it. Work and strain left her sickly thin. She had never been substantial; she was to have a haggard and painted look, but always smoothed and organized, as immaculate as a miniature painting. The first knife-twists of a stomach ulcer were beginning, hurts she would never lose for the rest of her life. She was working, working with survivors from torpedoed boats, playing the gracious Governor's wife, trying to use her social wiles to smooth the

Duke's path and perfecting him as much as she could. He required not so much help as direction – someone to check and rewrite speeches, someone to tell him what must be done. She concerned herself with the welfare of black children, something no white Bahamian woman would consider. She found it nearly impossible to find volunteers for her clinics, and settled for the wives of ADCs and Government House staff. Together, they weighed, checked, organized. She worked hard with the Red Cross ladies, sorting the knitting, organizing the care parcels ready for the forces overseas. She was doing a job, competently, and under great stress. At the same time, she must have seen the implications of their involvement with Wenner-Gren and Oakes and Christie.

At best it would be a wonderful escape from their cramped world in Nassau – new places and a new degree of financial security. That mattered to her. Even when, many years later, she was finally told exactly how much the Duke of Windsor had left – it was all for her – she persisted in thinking herself a poor woman. At worst, the Windsors were sailing even closer to the wind than in Lisbon. The danger of discovery was terrible. It was hard to see what punishment they would now devise for her beloved David and herself – what could be worse than this sort of house arrest in Nassau? But there would be a punishment.

Nassau closed around her as the summer came – the awful, enveloping heat that held so much moisture clothes stuck to your back as you left cover. She hated the landcrabs, cemetery-white, that scuttled along the sidewalks. Some days of public duty, she stayed, on the Duke's orders, prostrate in bed. He would apologize for her absence and say he had prescribed a day of peace and quiet. Her temper, usually perfectly controlled, became waspish at times. A child proffered a book of raffle tickets to her, called her 'Your Royal Highness'. The old hurt of the title flared again. 'I am not Your Royal Highness,' the Duchess snapped. 'I am Your Grace.' The child was left to make a careful apology; the Duchess was left in the wake of a fury that embarrassed her.

Nassau exchange control allowed people the money to

114

leave the islands for reasons of health in the sticky season. Why should not London give Windsor the same rights?

London had rather good reasons. Windsor was not the only member of the royal family who was determined to be some sort of roving goodwill ambassador. His brother, the Duke of Kent, was lobbying to go to Canada. R. A. Butler, inside the Cabinet, was supporting him, although with a passing fear that a scheme also to send Kent around American factories might just misfire as 'there is . . . the coincidence that the Duke of Windsor is visiting America about this time.'

Windsor wanted to go beyond Miami in America to see old friends and visit Wallis Windsor's territory. He also wanted to see his only property, his ranch in Canada. Kent, meanwhile, was welcome in Canada and determined to extend his trip to America. For London's taste, there were too many chances that Kent and Windsor would meet.

Kent was the favourite brother of Windsor, the younger, brighter and more thoughtful man who had been pulled from assorted disasters – women, drugs and one near-suicide – by Windsor's influence. If the influence was still strong, the consequences would be unpredictable; more, a meeting with Windsor would embarrass the Court. But the brothers could hardly be kept apart by force or diplomacy if they were in the same country. The situation required management.

For a start, Canada did not want the Duke to come. A brisk wind of Canadian morality had prevented the Windsors landing there before – as exiles and as refugees – and it had not abated. The Prime Minister of Canada let it be known that he would prefer that Windsor did not come, although, of course, he would make no objection should the Duke request the trip. If he had to accept Windsor on Canadian soil, he wanted him directed from America to his ranch with no visits to eastern Canada. He would admit it was impossible to separate the brothers' visits, but he still wanted it done. Otherwise, if Windsor and Kent met, there would be 'awkward situations' and perhaps 'undesirable speculation in the Press'.

The diplomatic activity designed to keep Windsor in his

place was conducted with an air of furtive embarrassment. Nobody wanted to give Windsor orders, or to articulate the objections to a meeting. These were matters of royal privilege – a royal duke to be free to travel, a royal court to be free to stop him. Nobody wanted to say exactly why Windsor was such a problem. They preferred discreet memoranda which spelt nothing out. Yet it was painfully clear that the aftermath of Lisbon – reinforced by his behaviour in Nassau, and intelligence reports that told of the introduction given to Wenner-Gren by friends in Rio – was utter isolation. When Churchill considered whether he needed some royal figures to tour the West Indies to 'comfort some of those unhappy islands who are so much upset about the bases', he proposed to send the Kents.

Lord Moyne clung to his hope that Windsor would spare everybody the multiple embarrassment of the American trip. But time was against him. Month by month, the heat settled on Nassau, humid, heavy, implacable. Even Wenner-Gren had slipped away for Peru, where his archaeological expedition was working its way into a country which the Nazis wanted to seduce. 'Under prevailing world conditions,' Wenner-Gren announced, 'cruises on the seven seas are not very appropriate, I certainly do admit' – he loved his words and rarely felt he had enough of them – 'but the approach of the stormy season here in Nassau, where in the case of really difficult weather there is no protection for a large ship like the *Southern Cross,* makes a voyage no more hazardous than staying at anchor.'

'If the Duke of Windsor's journey takes place,' Lord Moyne wrote to Churchill on 17 July, 'I think we had better not appear to be dictating his plans, but should invite him to send in a detailed itinerary and dates so that we might make the necessary arrangements. I would also suggest that we leave it to him to propose a visit to New York as if this is not in his mind it would be much better to avoid it.' New York was thought a particular problem because of its isolationist community of exiled Britishers and Windsor's endless chances for passing among old friends and would-be friends with his gospel of compromise and a negotiated peace. Windsor might also speak publicly, and the consequences would almost certainly be acute embarrassment for a British propaganda service already harassed by isolationists trying to have them removed as illegal foreign agents.

'It would no doubt be possible to ask the Duke of Windsor to defer his holiday,' Moyne added, 'but I expect his patience will be rather strained as the weather in the Bahamas in September is trying and it may no longer be at its best in Canada in October.' Some terrible deference still informed London's attempts to deal with the Duke. Other governors could be posted to new continents at a moment's notice, it seemed. Windsor could not be told when he might and might not take his holidays. Churchill finally had to intervene, and insist that Kent make his trip in July, returning to Britain by the end of August, and that Windsor would have to swelter in Nassau until the third week in September. 'Matters,' wrote Churchill, firmly, 'had better be arranged on this basis.'

Halifax, successor to Lothian as British Ambassador, was sent to Sumner Welles, acting Secretary of State, to ask if the President would have any objection to Windsor 'passing through the United States in September to go to his ranch.' Roosevelt magnanimously said he would have none at all, and in fact he would be glad to have the Duke to lunch.

Everybody hoped that there would be no incidents, nothing embarrassing. Adela Rogers St John conspired with the British Embassy to produce lists of advice, dos and don'ts: do not land in New York, stay at grand hotels, go about in café society or accept invitations before the President has spoken; do visit the ancestral places of the various Wallis Warfield Simpson clans – Montagues and Warfields; do not travel with an excess of luggage. It was excellent advice. The Windsors did not listen.

They found ways to survive summer. They made a silly August trip to Williamson's Photosphere – the World's First Undersea Post Office – which lay off Hog Island. Williamson had a barge with what looked like a giant cornflakes package on it. Beneath, reached through wide piping, was an observation chamber on the seabed where visitors, strapped in a padded bosun's chair, could watch divers and fish. Two

ADCs – Drury and Wood – swam down to the Photosphere and waved to the Duke and Duchess inside. 'He seems,' said the Duke of Drury, watching the air bubbles rise, 'to be breathing heavily.'

Out on the road past Cable Beach, there were terrible sounds – growlings and lowings, fierce and long – coming from the back of a car. An American tourist passed to see the Duke and Duchess convulsed with laughter in the back seat. The Duke had bagpipes and was playing loudly. The Duchess was begging him: 'No more, no more. . . .'

The Duchess confined her feelings tightly for the most part, and paid the price with her ulcer. She gave a perfectly controlled performance. Nothing was let out – not her feelings for the lizards and the huge, metallic palmetto bugs; for the terrible, wasting heat; or for the ants found nesting one morning in a $40 jar of cold cream. She had a steel façade. The times when she could relax – the rare dinner parties out of Nassau, the trips to other islands – became particularly valuable.

The Windsors' visits, announced only hours in advance, created chaos. Rosita Forbes had a newly built house on Eleuthera which they decided to visit. She found herself with a single pork chop in the refrigerator, begged a chicken and a half from neighbours who promptly volunteered to help cook. The politician Roland Symonette, who was building her house, appeared with huge steaks and cans of vegetables. A little war of cooks established itself in the kitchen. Everyone was nervous. At the worst moments, when there were sounds of a car, the maid would start babbling: 'My Lawd, My Lawd, de Lawd comes. Hallelujah tis de Lawd,' to be greeted with sharp upper-middle class scorn. 'Nonsense, Malvina,' said the neighbour. 'You can't have religion now.'

The Windsors arrived, battered from twenty-six miles over a barely existent road. Two gardeners had been swiftly disguised as butlers for the day. They charged forward to shut the door and their heads collided violently. Their revenge was the total darkness of the house, since they wanted the Windsors to appreciate their handiwork in the garden, and the way to make sure of an inspection was to run the only

118

electric cable out of the house and into the thick of the lilies and marigolds.

The Duke and the Duchess talked freely that night, of Nassau and its complications, human and political; its cabals; the odd atmospheres. War was producing its own tensions; a clergyman told an Allied consul at a smart lunch he was nothing but a Nazi; a greybeard at a polo match threatened to knock down a contemporary who said Britain had no fight at all. Everybody was on edge, and no action came to hold the attention. The Windsors talked of this, and as they talked they tried to exorcize the place.

By the end of August, even the ADCs had left. The Windsors were alone in Nassau; their sole familiar support was the kind and angular Gray Phillips. Even their official life on Government Hill had been narrowed down. London chose that moment to send word that the Bahamas were not to be allowed the dollars to buy the SS *Cobb*, a superannuated liner on the Havana run which the House had planned to bring back after ten years of retirement to guarantee some transport for the tourists of the next season. The *Cobb*'s condition had been suspect just because she was available – other and stronger ships had already been taken by the US Government – but she had been the only certain hope.

And the round continued. Jamaica restricted its imports from the Bahamas, but the regulations went astray in the mails and nobody knew what they might mean; the Government prosecuted its own Government Ice Shop for selling ice after 10 o'clock on a Sunday morning and sent the manager to jail for a day; official notices called for the conservation of scarce gasoline, and the Duke and Duchess were urged onto a tandem bicycle to dramatize the alternatives – both, within yards, fell off.

Wenner-Gren tried to buy an island, Grand Bahama. The plan became a crisis. London asked Washington for the American view, and the answer was direct: although nothing was known directly to Wenner-Gren's disgrace, the Navy would like London to turn down the plan. The Naval officer said: 'I do not believe it would be a good policy for them to grant favours to a pal of Goering at a time like this.'

119

Windsor intervened. He sent word by way of Halifax in Washington that he would like to know 'what it may be that the United States Government had against Wenner-Gren'. Windsor claimed that the Swede was 'disposed to make large investments in the Bahamas which would be very helpful to the native population and that as Governor of the Islands he desired to know officially what reason there might be for his not approving and encouraging such activities on the part of Wenner-Gren.' Sumner Welles told Halifax that the State Department lacked proof of actual wrongdoing, but that 'his links with high Germans are very intimate and suspicious'. It was not a sufficient answer. Halifax decided to tell the Duke that he would look into the matter but that, since it was a delicate subject, he doubted if he would obtain any information.

By July 1941 Windsor had been persuaded into a nominal scheme to watch Wenner-Gren's movements. Washington, through the US consul, Dye, contacted Windsor's deputy, Heape, and Heape took the issue to Windsor. They agreed on an order – more easily issued than enforced – that yachts were to enter the Bahamas only at ports, and that they were to give the names and nationalities of all crew and passengers.

The Duke knew the rumours that surrounded his dinner friend, his banker, his accomplice. He could not have known that British Intelligence had just warned the Americans of these rumours: that Wenner-Gren was helping Germany get her oil supplies, sponsoring a movement in the USA whose purpose was to overthrow the Swedish Government in favour of a Nazi regime, and masterminding a cartel whose purpose was to control the world's wool trade and cut Britain off from her traditional sources of supply.

Such stories filled the Wenner-Gren file. More embarrassing, the links with Windsor became a prime reason for suspecting Wenner-Gren. The argument became circular, as more was known of the attitudes of the Duke and Duchess. Adolf Berle, coordinator of intelligence at the State Department, reckoned Wenner-Gren was not to be trusted because of his 'continued friendship with the defeatists in Britain

. . . his appearances with the Duke of Windsor in the Bahamas', as well as his South American activities. When in November 1941 Wenner-Gren was barred from the Panama Canal, the file shows as reasons: '[he] has been in very close contact with the German authorities; he is also a close associate of the Duke of Windsor.'

For the first leg of their American journey, the Windsors took a plane. It was only the second time in the Duchess's life that she had flown and she was obviously nervous. The captain tried to comfort her. 'I'll bet you were the sort of little girl,' he said, 'who had her head in the pillows when it thundered.'

'I was,' said the Duchess, grimly, 'and I grew into a woman who never quit doing just that.'

Five thousand people crammed against the airport fences and gave them a triumphal landing; cars filled parking lots for blocks. There were cheers and 'by night fall,' the *Miami Herald* observed, 'there was a distinct impression that if this fellow ever wants to come back, establish a residence and run for the city commission, it will be just a pushover.' They travelled north by train, in a private pullman, utterly absorbed in each other except for the two hours when the Duke insisted on his royal prerogative and rode the footplate along with the diesel engine crew. The cairn terriers (three of them) travelled like attendant princes.

In Washington, they were politely welcomed. The awkward fact was that this royal governor, this romantic figure and ex-King of England, was being watched as a potential subversive. Nobody could directly refer to the fact. Nobody could forget it.

The Embassy provided morning cocktails, the party proper for guests of moderate importance. The issue of curtseying surfaced again. It seemed rather rude to deny the Duchess so simple an honour. Edwina Mountbatten curtsied, Diana Cooper curtsied, Edwina d'Erlanger refused on the grounds that Wallis was really just an American, like her. Roosevelt saw Windsor for a half-hour, but had to postpone the promised White House lunch. 'I am very much distressed,' he

121

wrote on 24 September, 'but I know that you and the Duchess will understand why we think we ought to defer the luncheon tomorrow.' Eleanor Roosevelt's brother had been on the point of death for weeks. 'My wife is constantly at the hospital and I am standing by. We count on having you both to lunch with us on your way back to Nassau. I hope in the meantime you will have a wonderful vacation in Canada. You both must need it after the very poor summer climate of the Bahamas.'

The Duke used his royal rank in Washington to gain access to anyone who might have refused to see a mere colonial governor. Since the Bahamas would need ships and planes for the next winter season, he went directly to the President of the United States Maritime Commission, the President of the Civil Aeronautics Board. He also spoke publicly, with that flat and disappointed tone which marked his wartime speeches. 'Of course,' he told the National Press Club in Washington, 'when London and other cities were bombarded and Great Britain was threatened with invasion, I could not help wishing, like every Briton in every part of the world, to share the fortunes of my countrymen at home. In wartime, however, one serves where one is told, and although it is a very different post to the one I held in the First World War, I have applied myself to the administration of the Bahamas to the best of my ability.'

They headed north, away from their moderate success in Washington, where even Halifax had been coincidentally out of town and unable to meet them, and out for a grand progress through America. The magic held. At Chicago, it took six burly policemen with night-sticks drawn to protect the Duke as he went for a stroll; at St Paul, Minnesota, two thousand people came to cheer them; by the time they arrived in Canada, the royal charisma, without the royal planning or the royal bodyguards, had become a distinct problem. Thousands hemmed them in when they tried to walk the streets of Moose Jaw; they had to abandon their sightseeing in Calgary because of the thousands who had turned out to welcome them; they had to drive immediately out to the ranch, some sixty-four miles away. Old signs standing along the way announced: 'Prince of Wales Ranch: 18 miles'. On their journey, they even had the proper touches of headline melodrama. At Woodstock, Illinois, a man snatched at the rails of the observation car where Duke and Duchess were standing just as the train began to gather speed. Anxious FBI agents pulled him on board and lectured him severely. He turned out to be a press photographer, but his only motive in the sudden leap for the Windsors' platform was a simple need to catch the train. And in Canada, at a brief stop, the precious cairns were taken out for exercise, strayed across the tracks, and were quite forgotten until the train had pulled out of the station and gone some miles. The reunion was emotional.

They remembered the weather more than anything at the ranch. 'It was quite cold while we were there,' the Duke said, 'and freezing weather had already begun to set in.' The Duke had not been there for fourteen years. The land represented his certainties, his own property, in his name, bought and paid for. It was all he owned. But more than nostalgia drew him to the E.P. – the initials stood for Edward, Prince. He thought there was oil under his land. Surveys of neighbouring land looked promising; together, the Duke and Duchess visited the productive Turner oilfield close by. The Duke made fantastic plans. Since he owned the mineral rights on most of his land – the only Canadian landowner with that privilege – he would be a great tycoon and Standard Oil would find his oil for him. The Duchess caught his fever. A year later she was still writing to friends saying that she hoped soon to be the wife of an oil magnate.

In the crisp days of early October, they went walking together among the fire-colours, among mountains cool with high snows. It was a lovely place, and a lovely time. The Duke's lack of official standing did not seem to matter, although there were awkward moments: he tried to visit a Royal Canadian Air Force base at High River, but the guards turned him back since he did not have a pass. The Windsors had the great luxury of quiet and cool, and they were together in decent privacy.

Official duty broke into it. Without rain or storm warnings, a force of wind bellied up from Turks Island and struck the Bahamas on a Sunday evening. It had the full force of a hurricane. Great trees stiffened in the wind and were torn out of the ground, taking cables with them; palms shook and the coconuts flew, lethal missiles in the storm; gardens across the islands, and farms, were churned and flattened and destroyed.

News from the Out Islands took time to filter back to Nassau, but when it came, it was appalling. The great wind had left ninety families homeless on San Salvador, 120 on Watlings Island, 300 on Cat Island. Sloops had foundered and been lost. Wharves had been weakened and torn down. Farms were washed away. Even in Nassau, which missed the main force of the wind, schooners were lifted bodily into streets. After the hurricane had passed, there was still no rain. Fruit trees had been beaten bare and crops destroyed not by the pelting rain that usually goes with hurricanes, but by the dry salt wind coming off the sea.

The Windsors could do little in Calgary except send cables. They had no intention of returning to the islands before they had visited New York and Washington; they were not at all sure when they would next get the chance. They might not be useful in Nassau even if they returned. The Duchess cabled her distress, and her certainty that the Red Cross and the Daughters of Empire would be able to care for all those who suffered. 'I only wish I was there to help you in your work,' she said. 'Let me know if there is anything I can do or that you need.'

The Windsors turned south to Baltimore – Aunt Bessie Merryman had carefully equipped herself with an extra ration of gasoline for the visit – and the city stood in line to cheer. A prima donna assoluta sang 'Home, Sweet Home!', a six-car cavalcade needed 550 policemen to keep it moving through the crowds. A cousin heard Wallis Windsor laughing aloud in the shower, and asked what was the joke. 'Oh, nothing,' she said. 'I'm just thinking of my old existence in Baltimore and now look at me!'

She was a star. As with any star, it was hard to say whether the public actually loved her, or wanted to consume her. It was certainly true that neither of the Windsors was much protected by the usual restraints on public comment about royalty. If they abandoned or betrayed their public – now baying ecstatically for them – they would be lost, mere rich individuals, no more a legend. Together, the Windsors had the power of a star to influence, to change styles. They also had the peculiar position of royal relations whose family is still on the throne; that is, they represented the family, whether they liked it or not, and through the family they represented an entire ruling class in Britain. In the mixture of those two roles lay their huge potential for disaster. As stars, every eccentricity, every extravagance, was good copy, and part of what was expected of the Windsor style. It could not be conducted in private. Yet as royalty, they represented a struggling nation which had no money, barely adequate food, a problem in paying for the arms on which its survival depended. People could easily imagine that their attitudes were common among the British Establishment and could draw the dangerous conclusion that only wartime controls stopped others in Britain speaking their minds. And the very presence of the Windsors in the luxurious asylum of America, in grand hotels and grand circles, was enough to make a statement – about defeatism, irresponsibility, mindless extravagance, and how the British could manage all three while claiming to be the hungry, suffering champions of democracy.

As propaganda, then, whether they liked it or not, they came back to Washington. They lunched with Roosevelt, had a party under the Rotunda for a dozen or so Congressmen and their wives who had to be hastily mobilized by telephone. One Texas wife presented the Duchess with forty-eight roses, one for each State of the Union. They tactlessly snubbed the local Red Cross, who had organized tea and cakes and roses for them, but repaired the damage by a later visit. The Duke went from Washington to inspect the camps of the CCC, hoping to find a model for the Bahamas, and managed to do the Maryland part of his journey as a private citizen. At the borders of Washington DC, though, on his return, the inevitable detectives and motor-cycle escort arrived to protect him.

And then, New York. The Duke threatened to talk 'straight from the horse's mouth, for publication'. The British were apprehensive. The Windsors were given a tickertape parade in lower Manhattan. They lunched at the British War Relief Society and went to play darts with the seamen. They were greeted with shouts of 'Hurrah for the King!' The Duchess took aim and scored a bull's-eye and the Duke told her not to try again: 'You'll spoil your luck.'

And a man called William Worthington Breen, a seaman who during the First World War had served alongside the Duke, asked: 'When are you coming home, sir?'

It was a harsh question, all the more so because at that moment Wenner-Gren was preparing to leave Vera Cruz in Mexico for Nassau. He expected to stay in the islands briefly, and then return on the *Southern Cross* to Mexico. He expected the Windsors to be passengers and he did not know if they would ever return to Nassau.

The Duke said only to Breen: 'One day soon. I hope.'

The royal duties and civilities went well. The Duchess pursued her interest in children – an untypical, unexpected concern which was obvious in the Bahamas. She went to visit Inwood House on West 15th Street, a home for unmarried mothers, and she talked like a social worker rather than a socialite. She discussed birth control, and its advantages, and she admitted that there were so many Catholics in the Bahamas – 'we haven't stressed it, for that reason'. The Duke saw Henry Ford in Detroit; together, Duke and Duchess visited the Brooklyn Naval Yard. The Duchess agreed to write 'Some Favourite Southern Recipes of the Duchess of Windsor'; Eleanor Roosevelt would write the foreword and British War Relief would take the profits. Duty seemed satisfied. 'I'm not nearly so interested in clothes as people think', the Duchess said. 'I'd much rather talk about Red Cross work and infant welfare.'

But they took an entire floor of the Waldorf-Astoria, their suitcases and trunks required a railroad car of their own, and packages from the designer Mainbocher and Bergdorf

Goodman's store were taken into their hotel. Mainbocher chose to talk of the clothes he had made for the Duchess and their 'tummy emphasis', which seemed to be literal – a twist of black velvet over the ducal belly which was otherwise shrouded in fine white silk crepe. The Duchess was furious. All her careful work in Nassau would be set aside if she were seen to be simply returning to type. 'I haven't been in a shop since May 1940,' she said, 'before I left Paris. I'm trying to collect money for a third clinic, but I hope you don't mind if I buy one or two dresses.' Rumour said she bought thirty-four hats; she said five. 'Since I am actually shopping for a year, I don't think anyone could consider this outrageous.' She dealt acidly with reporters who asked about the bulk and number of their baggage. 'I read about 106. I've never counted them,' she said. 'But if you wish to, I'm sure we could arrange it.'

The appearance of great virtue had evaporated. All that was left was a couple in café society – precisely what Adela Rogers St John had warned against. The Duchess had worked hard at persuading New York department stores to take Bahamian coral jewellery; the Duke was serious about a Bahamian CCC. If only they had moderated their style, and if they had not had the peculiar magic of royalty, they would have done honourably. But great lovers, however notorious, do not get tickertapes for the strength of their passions alone. They went along with the acclaim and privilege of royalty; they did not take the full measure of the responsibilities. It was a tiny reminder of the basic truth about the abdication – that kings rule for as long as they behave themselves in a way thought proper for kings, which, in a world which valued stolid bourgeois families, was none too easy for the Windsors.

Everything made news. An over-eager adolescent from the German–American Bund broke into their hotel rooms to 'check off the guests'. Back in Florida, whole floors of the Miami Biltmore, closed for summer, were reopened for them; the manager flew from New York to open the fifteenth floor for the Duke and Duchess – two bedrooms, two bathrooms, a private dining-room, a vast sitting-room – and the fourteenth for the long-suffering Gray Phillips and the rest of the entourage. Such luxurious actions dimmed their political clout, but they remained attractive symbols who could pull a crowd, symbols for Americans who feared war, for those who liked Germany and Hitler, who wanted a barrier against the great force of Communism to the East. The Windsors proved wonderfully decorative – ideal fronts.

They came back to Nassau on a dull, dark afternoon, where huge damp Union Jacks hung at the gates of the newly opened land airfield. They had wanted so much out of America; they had wanted America to continue. Back in Nassau it was clear that, try as they would, they did not have and could not aspire to the kind of role they wanted.

Something else troubled the Duchess. The Windsors had seen doctors in Baltimore who had diagnosed a duodenal ulcer, the source of the Duchess's pain. She would have to return to hospital in three months, they said, to see if an operation was needed. She would hide the pain until then. She always did.

'Are you aware of the bitter comment made in the United States papers on the ostentatious display of jewellery and finery at a period when the people of this country are strictly rationed and, if so, will you make representations to the Prime Minister to have this Governor and his wife recalled since their visit is evidently doing a certain amount of harm and no good?' Alexander Sloan, Labour MP, broke the conventions of the House of Commons by attacking royalty in quite that way. He was joined by the London *Daily Mirror*. Taboo had broken down, and the Windsors were a target in Britain, also.

They tried to defend themselves – claiming that reporters had counted individual thermos flasks as items of luggage, that the Duchess had shopped only at a Red Cross arcade, that 80 per cent of the press coverage had been favourable, that the baggage was needed because of the cold weather in Canada – but the explanations and excuses sounded absurd.

Now the Mexican visit was close, it might attract the same talk that their American progress had produced. Windsor had never been good with the press, and his impatience had often been obvious; Wallis Windsor could manage more equably, but she also found the sense of being observed and analysed offensive. It would have been natural for them to dream of escape – based on the funds Wenner-Gren held for them, their expectations of oil money from Canada which remained high, the fact that Cuernavaca already held Oakes and their other friends from Nassau. But they would again be in contact with German sympathizers, with active Nazis; the general suspicion of Mexico at this time had risen so high that J. Edgar Hoover put Cary Grant on the suspect list for a plan to buy land near Acapulco. If they went, it would be an extraordinary act of defiance. People would wonder, inevitably, if they ever planned to return.

In the middle of the hurt and confusion, Windsor had to handle a real political crisis. Kenneth Solomon, doyen of the colony's lawyers, 'a sort of political boss' in the Colonial Office's view, the leader for the Government in the House of Assembly and a member of Executive Council, sent an utterly formal note of resignation. He was quitting ExCo forthwith. In the town, he had the aura of a martyr, someone who talked darkly of rights being abridged. He would not be more specific, since he had a clear interest in such sympathy as his resignation would provide: he wanted to be the next Speaker of the House of Assembly.

Solomon had gone before Windsor could fire him, and the firing was on orders from London. In May 1941, Lord Moyne told all colonial governors to stop treating appointments to their Executive Councils as a lifetime affair. Nobody should serve more than eight years. The Council should reflect more aspects of a colony's life. In Nassau, where the Executive Council, with members like Solomon and Harold Christie, had always reflected the same political ascendancy that ran the House of Assembly, such a new ruling was revolutionary.

Windsor at first delayed telling ExCo what was afoot. He finally read out Moyne's cable on 25 November; within four days, Solomon's resignation was public scandal. Bay Street would not let it drop. Godfrey Higgs asked in the House why he had resigned and Solomon told him: 'If it has been a shock and surprise to the community, I hope it will mean that Members of the House will realise what is taking place with respect to their rights and privileges.' Solomon meant nothing of the kind. He wanted mystery and sympathy. His own letter of resignation had shown that he knew exactly what was happening, had been told that it was a question of general Imperial principle and nothing to do with either personalities or the specific, and odd, constitutional position of the Bahamas. He had announced his leaving as 'in consequence of the information which H.R.H. the Governor communicated to members of the Council . . . and as a result of my conversations with His Royal Highness. . . .'

Solomon never forgave Windsor, for he always insisted on feeling that the Governor was responsible for the terrible slight he had suffered. The Duchess and Mrs Solomon were friendly, not least from their shared civic duties, and the Duchess would trust to her oldest formula of brandy and cigars to bring two sides together; she would, for an evening, succeed, and it would mean nothing. Solomon, never a great friend, had become an enemy, and the opposition to Government Hill carried the new weight of a man who had served there for years.

One calculation was exactly right. To replace Solomon, Windsor chose a man he had come to respect: Sidney Farrington, a man of intelligence whom the Bay Street Boys found acceptable, the local representative for Pan Am among other things. It was a clever choice. It was formally announced on 8 December 1941.

But with the attack on Pearl Harbor on 7 December 1941, the Windsors' schemes, the life of the islands, fell apart. On 8 December Congress declared a state of war with Japan. On 11 December Germany and Italy declared war on the United States. War was around them, now, and all its consequences. The quiet life was over.

For the islands, the single most serious consequence was

the death of the tourist trade. The SS *Kungsholm*, used for cruises to the Bahamas, was requisitioned by the US Government because of the 'desire of the United States to be relieved from the burden of protecting vessels unnecessarily proceeding in waters of the Western Hemisphere.' By Christmas, Nassau merchants reported their trade halved. The vast, pink halls of the Fort Montagu Beach hotel would not even open for the season. The SS *Yarmouth* was switched from the islands; Pan Am reverted to seaplanes instead of the land-planes it had been using. The season became a fantasy. Even the weather turned absurdly sour. A quick and vicious cold wind struck the fishing fleet and sank seven boats, one of which carried all the Christmas goods for an island.

In face of everything, the Windsors worked on. The Duchess performed the formal opening of her infant welfare clinics – white walls and varnish, plain sinks and austerity. She formally laid the keel of a wood minesweeper at Symonette's yards. The Duke said firmly that he wanted the election of 1942 to go ahead, wartime or no wartime. And they established a convention for more serious times: that they would attend war charity functions, but always leave before the dancing started.

At sea, just out of Vera Cruz, Wenner-Gren heard the news of Pearl Harbor and turned back. The Americans soon put him on their blacklist – aliens 'banned' from doing business or having financial dealings in America. Nobody could touch his property, cash or other assets. Those parts of his empire that had engaged the Duke of Windsor and Sir Harry Oakes were now walled off for the duration of war. Soon after the American decision, with some show of reluctance, the British followed suit. Wenner-Gren announced only that he was 'watching the situation'.

The escape was blocked. It was Nassau now or nothing for the Windsors. Only there could they retrieve some of the dignity lost in the past eighteen months – lost in Lisbon, in Nassau, in the financial dealings with Mexico, in the Nazi links and the damage done to British standing in the United States. There was no chance now that they could innocently retire to Mexico, among their dubious friends, with the capital Wenner-Gren held for them, in a compatible world where war could be evaded and most people sympathized with the German cause.

They were besieged by two final ironies.

On 10 December the battleship HMS *Prince of Wales* was sunk by Japanese aircraft off the Malay Peninsula. David Windsor had loved that ship.

And the Duchess was named top of the list of the best-dressed women in the world. All her seriousness was dissolved by her style. She shared the list with Mme Felipe A. Espil, the wife of the Argentinian diplomat who had once been the love of Wallis Warfield's life.

And in Nassau, they knew the trap had sprung.

PART TWO

RIOT

'I am sure that my appointment as Governor of this colony was as great a surprise to you as it was to me.' It was New Year's Day, a proper turning point. Windsor tried to take control of his destiny by talking to the islands on radio. He would be honest. He would be personal; he wrote all his speeches, subject only to the revision of the Duchess's pencil. He had no screen of official writers. Instead, he showed his pain and even some of his uncertainty; and, more than that, he showed how he intended to make sense of his time in Nassau. It was as though he aimed for a kind of redemption.

'I had, as you know, retired altogether from public life in December 1936. . . .' It was not true. He had wanted to return after those two years of voluntary exile, but he had been excluded. There was no Prince of Wales, no second string to a king who found kingship a difficult task. He thought he could fill the role, but his brother George VI was not his friend. He must stay in the cold. '. . . but with the declaration of war I naturally offered my services to my country. After a brief but not uneventful post with the French Army. . . .' Nobody would listen to him, although his reports made excellent sense. He knew he was untrained, ill-educated, but he also knew that he had some abilities. They were refused. ' . . . A curious course of circumstances prescribed that I come to the Bahamas as the King's Representative. . . .' It was a moderate account of those days in Spain and in Lisbon, the haggling over a royal title for the Duchess which came just before the final, ignominious order to get to the Bahamas. He seemed to savour the irony in being here, at last, the King's representative. That, he had been for all his youth. It was a role denied him after he left the throne.

135

'While I had no long years of colonial administration to fit me technically for this position, I have ... travelled the world enough to give me a fairly comprehensive knowledge of the constitution and political and social aspirations of most of the colonies under the British flag. However, following the wise precept that "a little knowledge is a dangerous thing" I have until now purposely trod very warily in my approach to all things that would irrevocably affect the internal policies of this colony in the future. . . .'

It was his moment. He would come into control of his little kingdom. He would change the pain and poverty. He would make reforms. The Bahamas had long been the safe point of Britain's possessions in the Caribbean area. The black majority despaired of change, of finding any true alternative to the slights and suffering that the white minority offered. But the whole of the West Indies was beginning to change. Riot and reform, sometimes real and sometimes cosmetic, were common to many of the islands; that was the reason Windsor could not be sent there in 1940. In Barbados, diplomats reported, 'coloured politicians are making the most of the precarious situation brought about by the war. . . . There is a definite breaking down of old barriers between black and white.' In Antigua, 'the more intelligent natives are using the situation to enhance their racial position.' In Jamaica, 'the situation is being used by local agitators to stir up racial and anti-local government feeling.' In Guyana, 'among the negro population petty lawlessness is on the increase while . . . [there is] some unrest among the East Indian element. . . .' Island by island, it was seen that protest could work, strikes did bring change, revolt was effective.

'My experiences,' Windsor said, 'may perhaps have given me a wider range of ideas which sometimes prompt me to make suggestions, even be they only a little progressive, which will not radically disrupt your life and economical set-up evolved after many years, and to which you have all become accustomed. However, times change and a little give and take, here and there, will eventually save a great deal of misunderstanding and bitterness.'

It had become improper to talk of change in Nassau; there

136

was altogether too much of a crisis. Windsor wanted to discuss both change and causes. 'Now, through no fault of her own,' he continued, 'America has become a belligerent power, but we Britishers welcome her as an ally.' The phrasing was curious, a reminder that Windsor was never happy with war rhetoric. 'The normal life and business of the Bahamas has been but little interfered with until now, but with the coming of hostilities to this side of the Atlantic, the situation has changed appreciably . . . we must face facts and realise that we can no longer regard these islands solely as a tourist resort until the success of our Arms and those of our allies bring peace to the world again.'

He declared war. 'It will be a privilege to help you readjust your finances and economics to the changes of which we have but a slight indication today.' He also identified a problem which would not impress the Bay Street merchants, with their talk of labour being a commodity subject to laws of supply and demand, and no others. 'The immediate financial situation does not depress me as much as the threat that the already high number of unemployed will increase.'

Windsor's speech was brave. All that he wanted, the House was likely to oppose; either it involved spending the colony's limited revenues, or else it meant dependence on London for funds. They would accept neither. Kenneth Solomon gave the opposition new weight and by appointing Sidney Farrington to ExCo – Farrington was not a Member of the House of Assembly – Windsor had reduced his own minority representation in the House. He would have to fight the often pig-headed insularity of the lawyers and merchants of the town as best he could. Moral talk was no leverage. They simply did not accept it. If Windsor was to be successful at all, he would need every ounce of political skill he might have.

Windsor talked of income tax – since there might be problems in importing goods that carried duty and there were no more tourists to buy them; the House said 'No'. The Duke wanted to cut tariffs on essential goods and foodstuffs; the merchants agreed, but increased the price on the shelves. He wanted money for a labour camp, for Out Island development, for the development of any industry that would create jobs. The House bridled at the thought of competition, of outsiders doing business in the private garden of the Bahamas. They refused to spend more public money. They also refused to pass those basic laws – on shopworkers' hours, trade union rights, workmen's compensation – which would have released substantial funds from the British Government for development.

The first lively issue was unemployment. The first reaction of Executive Council was to ask whether home-owners in Florida might need domestic servants. They were quickly convinced that exiling some maids and gardeners would not solve the problem.

The Duke formed a committee. It hardly seems a radical move, but it was the first necessary stage; since the House alone could take the initiative on spending money, local opinion had to be convinced. A good committee might do the trick. Committees led inexorably to boards in the local hierarchy; boards might take action, especially if the Members of the House of Assembly among their number could be convinced that the best ideas had come from them.

Ideas about basic strategy were wildly varied. L. Walton Young, the black MHA, had been furiously annoyed by the war games around him – mock blackouts, mock exercises and the irritating fact that the school sirens, blasted each morning of term at 8.45 a.m. to tell the children that school was almost open, had been commandeered for general, but unexplained, military use. Young reckoned the Bahamas should send 500 fighting men forthwith to America. 'It might,' he said, 'open the way for 10,000 to be employed in American industry.'

Others had less imagination. George Murphy, a bootlegger who could not see America again, had become head of the Agriculture Board, and was naturally convinced the Bahamas would be saved by growing things. 'Every time we see another bushel of sweet potatoes or another crate of tomatoes going down to the wharf,' he said, trying rather desperately to tie good farming to brute patriotics, 'we'll know that there's another sock for Mad Dog Adolf, the Boastful Benito and Sawed-Off Hirohito. . . .'

The Development Board continued, optimistically, its siren calls to the elusive American tourist. Its emphasis, however, had changed. Nassau was said to be in a ring of powerful US bases, a 'sequestered island just off the coast of Florida' with a 'quietly expanding two-year-old war crusade and at the same time carrying on a determined crusade to preserve the quiet and picturesque charm which has delighted visiting Americans.' The campaign proved hopeless. On 13 January, the Royal Victoria hotel abandoned the season, and shut its terraces and patios, boarded up the dance floor and bandstand that both perched in the same vast silk cotton tree.

The Government needed to know how many people were unemployed. The writing of the register became a political issue – because the man who used to do it was also the islands' immigration officer, and not a Bahamian; because of the House's suspicions, articulated by Godfrey Higgs, who asked exactly what the Government had in mind once the unemployed had been listed and counted.

As yet, the answer was: very little. Politics interfered with any new business. On the southern islands, close to Cuba, the Erickson brothers had revived the salt business. They offered a hundred jobs, chartered a motorboat to take their new workers south, accepted 160 of the applicants. On the day of sailing, only fifty-six turned up. Once they reached Inagua, their new workforce rebelled. Only twelve were actually prepared to work. The Ericksons sent back word to their friend and ally, Etienne Dupuch, that 'these men have come solely for the purpose of an outing'. A few days in the heat of the distant islands seemed to produce some calm, but ten or so of the men remained obstinately troublesome. The Ericksons were outsiders; outsiders were resented; it was a curious coincidence that their workforce should prove so troublesome. It was so easy to arrange that outsiders should have trouble.

Registration of the unemployed was finally approved. The Duke in person took the chair of an Economic Investigation Committee. The first proposal from that committee bore the

139

stamp of Windsor's American researches. He wanted an agricultural training camp which would keep men busy and train them as farmers. Harold Christie was left to move the proposition in the House. His argument was crude, but effective: if men did not work they became vagrants; vagrants under the Vagrancy Act went to jail; keeping a man in jail cost more than clearing some earth and trying to train farmers. The men would draw only 4s a day, could live in houses they built for themselves, could work for their keep. They could grow peppers and sisal, sesame and spices. They would have real work.

The House was unconvinced. The merchant, Eric Solomon, thought unemployment was a problem of Out Islanders with too strong a taste for Nassau life. 'It's not training the people want. They want moving pictures to get them back to the islands.'

Windsor got his farm. Harry Oakes provided the land, far to the west, and men were selected for training – 'good work and conduct generally' being the main criteria. The authorities promised, rather bleakly, that 'arrangements will be made for those men who desire to return home from time to time.' The lime kilns were set burning, and the great pines were torn down, and the Economic Committee busied itself with other schemes – herbs for the Americans, thyme, sage, sesame, ginger, pimento, paprika, dill and the small, fierce orange goat peppers; more fishing, farms on the Out Islands, sisal and straw-work, boat building and book-binding for an English firm which had chosen Nassau for its wartime exile. The ideals were good. The practice remained problematic.

To Windsor, it seemed the only possible policy in the circumstances. He found allies among the Bay Street Boys – Christie, in particular – who shared his views. The proselytizing was well done. He could not have anticipated one problem. His policy fitted old circumstances, but the circumstances were about to change utterly.

In May he told the colony that his own labour camp would suffer 'what might be regarded as a temporary setback'. The island had been chosen for 'a certain extensive Project' which was likely to absorb all available labour for the next three or four months.

The airmen were coming to Nassau; airstrips and barracks and offices would have to be built; the town would have money again. Their presence would undermine all Windsor's bargaining position with the House. But it would also create a paradox. The more Nassau sacrificed for the war effort, the more affluent and comfortable life would be. War was coming closer, with the parties, the shows, the jollity and the drinking of the old-style season.

The law gave the House of Assembly a life of seven years. The precedent of the First World War would suggest that the House could have extended its life for the duration of hostilities. 'If the Government insists on an election,' Eric Solomon said, 'I will consider myself exempt from contributing to any war fund.' It would be so convenient if the House could simply continue, with no election expenses, no costly rum and cash bribes for the voters, no tedious trips to the other islands – which, in name, the merchants represented in the House. Nobody expected a serious change in the ruling group. An election would be purely cosmetic.

There was a catch. The House might want to extend its life, but ending its life was the Governor's prerogative. Windsor could dissolve the House at any time. Stafford Sands knew that, and tried to persuade the House to tolerate an election. But his fellow Members were not so easily appeased. The Governor had let his views be known, and that was enough to set the merchants bridling. 'The Government should be doing more important things,' Walton Young declared, 'than dabbling in politics.'

The House, capable of fury at the slightest provocation, passed two bills. One extended its life, and so delayed the election. The other took to the House the sole right to condemn any regulation made by the Governor.

The result was a real constitutional crisis, and one which Windsor could sidestep only for a while. Above the House of Assembly was the Legislative Council, which had to approve bills coming from the senior House. LegCo blocked both the House's new bills and the House showed righteous

141

indignation at the body. Young said: 'They can't even stay at home unless they can satisfy the Attorney General that it's impossible for them to be present to vote – as directed.' He said the House had been slipping for twenty years. 'In past years, the Executive used to consult the House but now the Leader just brings a Bill down and pulls strings to get it on the statute books.' He remembered when he first joined the House that the Colonial Secretary stood to attention when a Member entered his office, and a Governor was always approachable. Today, a Member had to put his case to a clerk before he could even make an appointment with the Colonial Secretary. He could not even sit as a Justice of the Peace. 'If I go to the Magistrate's Court,' he said, 'I am obliged to sit among thugs.'

Such was the beginning.

Funds for security of the islands were blocked on the grounds that security 'will probably involve the establishment of another department with a cushy job for someone.' A defence vote of £7000, most of it already spent, was thrown out altogether because one member of the House committee on the bill had not been shown a final amendment of no great significance. When the Government wanted to change harbour dues, the bill was thrown out because 'it is not competent for . . . the Government to proceed with any matter involving taxation . . . such a matter should have reached the House by petition.'

Hallinan, the Attorney General, added to the havoc. While LegCo was dealing with a bill that would have given the House of Assembly an automatic majority on all boards and committees – and brought administration from Government Hill to a complete stop – he observed: 'Members of the House on the board will be more inclined to be political than practical'. The insult, as it was perceived, was deeply resented by the House. Hallinan made it worse that weekend. He went down on a Saturday morning to the printing works at the *Guardian* newspaper, the official Government printers, to demand a copy of the amended Agriculture Board regulations. The rules were no great secret, but an elaborate protocol kept them within the grasp of the House alone until they were finally established and sent to LegCo. To see a copy, Hallinan should have made formal application to the Speaker of the House. He did not. The Chief Clerk of the House was consulted, but he would not approve the printers giving Hallinan a copy because the matter had not yet been proofread. He could take no responsibility for its accuracy. Hallinan, exasperated by the tangle of minor privileges and small-town precision in which he found himself, snatched the papers and left.

It was a mistake. Eric Solomon turned to his favourite sport of baiting Government Hill. He wondered if Nassau was too quiet for Hallinan, and if his native Ireland would not offer more of the violence to which he was accustomed. 'For the last decade or more,' he said, 'it has been impossible to teach English officials that they are not sent here to govern the colony but to assist in their small way the Government of the colony.' Such arrogance was moderated in the speech of Stafford Sands to a great and silken pomposity. 'There seems,' he said, 'to be a constant and growing misunderstanding between the representatives of the people and the Government.' He spoke of studied insults, of Government overriding the House. 'The time is not far distant,' he said, 'when the House and the Government will reach a showdown.'

Such passions were not new. The legislature of the Bahamas had been granted so bizarre an independence – like Barbados and Bermuda, the others of what the Colonial Office called either the 'three Bs' or else the 'three bastards' – that its members had come to believe their own rhetoric. They did not represent the people. The people voted according to who gave most, since election days were a party and they had no reason to see that voting might ever change anything. The Members, interrelated by blood and business, were a tiny elite, a part and only a part of the white Bahamian ascendancy. Once elected, they were almost impossible to displace provided there was sufficient Bay Street money behind them. By taking to themselves all the semblance of political activity, and most of the language of politics, they left no room for other forms of political consciousness. They

143

were at once the ruling class, and the opposition to Government. Their success, such as it was, depended on being the only people present to exploit opportunities. They opposed foreign investment, new companies coming to the Bahamas, even Jewish immigration on the same grounds: they needed a monopoly of economic life in order to remain effective.

Given the vulnerability of the merchants, their passions are understandable. When they defended the House, they defended the curious economic system which kept them powerful and rich and clearly dominant in the Bahamas. When they attacked Government, they attacked all the forces which could, all too easily, destroy their hegemony if they once dropped their guard. It followed that, whatever the issue, the Government were of necessity the radicals. They were the only group with the slightest interest in change.

Windsor showed no personal enthusiasm for changing the trade union law, or the law on compensating injured workmen. He regretted to London that such laws were not possible, but in the mildest tones, and London's annotations show how sceptical they were of his sincerity. But he did want to engage with the social problems of the islands – to save them from collapse and then to provide something better than the shacks and hunger and pellagra which all too commonly were the lot of the black majority. Unlike other Governors, he wanted to know what was happening. He would urge priests on the Out Islands to see him in Nassau when they passed through, so that he could hear what was happening in the homes of islanders. He went out to visit the shacks of the poor in a way that earlier Governors would not have considered.

His reactions were emotional, often naive; variants on his South Wales cry that 'something must be done'. They were also brave and honourable, and in their defence he would wage a long and eager battle.

'My heart sinks,' the Duchess said, 'when I see the doctor write out the prescription for an undernourished case – milk, cod-liver oil and fruit juice – because we can't cope with it. But one day we will.' The socialite Wallis Windsor was perfectly sincere. In Nassau she, too, did battle. She redeemed her glossy, carefree reputation. A report on the Bahamas by Rockefeller Foundation doctors in 1944 said: 'The Duchess of Windsor, American-born, is the only person known who has practised philanthropy, at least in the interests of health for the poor Negroes.'

She saw problems that other white ladies preferred not to consider. She worked with black children in her infant welfare clinics, and only wives from Government Hill would join her. She broke an important white taboo – having physical contact with black children to measure and weigh and tend them. She also knew the syphilis rate, which was unspeakable to the whites. The best serious estimate was that one in three of the population of the Bahamas suffered from syphilis – either contracted venereally, or inherited. Public health could not deal with a disease that was endemic, and public health did not try. Its main task was removing nuisances on the white side of the ridge. The Duchess not only saw the horrific effect on infant mortality. She proposed a clinic – funded, like the others, from the Duke's pocketbook – for the children of mothers with syphilis. Nassau did not talk of such things.

Other Governors' wives had attended to more genteel pursuits – the training of domestic servants, for example, which required only the most remote supervision. Wallis Windsor, with virtually no support and with the Duke's money and her own, tried to tackle less comfortable issues. She would prove herself even further when the airmen and soldiers came. She took the usual duties of a Governor's lady – being head of the Red Cross – and performed them very well, despite a natural and surprising timidity in face of committees and ranks and infinitely proper ladies.

Some problems could not be alleviated by private endeavour – the syphilis rate itself, for example, or the finding of sufficient nourishment for the children with pellagra. Tuberculosis was endemic. Public service doctors were scarce, and the five sanitary inspectors, according to their own chief medical officer, were 'untrained, poorly paid and add to their income by buying and selling land'. Off the island of New

Providence, there were two doctors – one a Burmese lady of uncertain training – and a shoal of 'graduate nurses', many of whom had never gone further than primary school. For the whole population over the hill, there were exactly five communal privies; the protection of water in white areas depended largely on the provision of little silver fish that ate mosquito larvae in the water-butts by each house. A major task of sanitary inspectors in the town of Nassau was to check fish in the barrels.

The Nassau hospital – the Bahamas General – was primitive and full of an air of malign squalor. Visitors often found the lavatories blocked. The administrator left the building at 3.30 sharp each afternoon for the Club on Bay Street and a game of poker; any medical or social problems that arose had to be handled the next day. No white went to Bahamas General, even for the setting of a broken limb; private doctors did that. Worse cases were taken immediately by plane to Miami. Since it was only for blacks, and since blacks were not truly represented, it followed that there was little pressure to reform the place. Lepers were left some eight miles from Nassau in what was called the lazarium. A menu on the wall promised fish. Fish was served only if the lepers succeeded in catching any.

The Windsors had seen for themselves the tragic neatness of the collapsing, shattered shacks that some people over the hill called home. Given what the Duchess did, and what the Duke felt, the emotional burden must have been far greater than they would show. They wanted the sort of political action they could not possibly deliver, not now that the House was on its high dignity and Government Hill again isolated. They began to feel a great frustration.

Without a season, Nassau still kept its social life. There was again a Head-Dress Ball, but this year the crayfish and sponges had been replaced by bizarre military themes – shells and flags and gunboats, a woman wearing twenty toy soldiers on her head, and an American woman who carried a huge and patriotic model of the Capitol, illuminated. Flags and V-signs began to replace the garlands of earlier years. Oc-

146

casional murmurs reached Nassau from London – stories that the rich were sitting out hostilities in luxury, stories of privilege. They were true, but only so far as the rich could buy themselves out of the sidewalk suffering of Britain. The rich in Nassau were the older rich, ruled out by age or illness from active service; alongside them were the war wives and their children. It was certainly a great advantage, mostly bought and paid for, although many of the women had arrived with barely adequate means. It was less than a scandal.

Except that the more staid Bahamians detected an influx of 'perverts and undesirables'. They may have remembered the legendary swarm of interior decorators and hairdressers which descended after the Windsors arrived, to serve the needs of those who hoped to invite or be invited to dinner, and who startled the daylights out of the British Colonial hotel. In reality, the solvent in the fabric of society was the bright, lonely war wives – and the first of the soldiers.

For the Canadians had come, and the Cameron Highlanders, reconstituted after the agonies of Dunkirk and now perched in the pink pile of the Montagu Beach, guarding the person of the Governor and doing escort duty for prisoners of war. There were still no more than platoons on the island, but the Duchess began her first canteen for the forces. And everybody noticed that the big-hipped ladies who once patrolled Rawson Square had now moved their place of business to Montagu Beach. They embarrassed the local residents, and they disturbed the tranquillity of the Montagu Beach itself, half public, half private, where wartime had brought down what had been a sharp social boundary between the two halves; and Nassau worried for its daughters, swimming so dangerously close to soldiers.

Once Wenner-Gren was on the blacklist, the great estates on Hog Island had to be closed up. The horses were sold, the fast motorboats dismantled and put in store, the larders and cellars cleared and the staff reduced from thirty to seven. The cost of running Shangri-la had been £12,000 a year; for the war years, that was cut to £3000. The rarest of the rare birds were taken to Paradise Beach, and the rest that had flown crying and screeching among the great trees of the estate were sold or given away.

Five Swedes and a Finn, previously in Wenner-Gren's employ, were abandoned in the Bahamas. Of them all, the saddest was Georg af Trolle, a baron. He had been secretary to the great man, a director of real companies, an aide; he had been married in the upper-middle-class style of Nassau, in the cathedral; now, he was an irrelevancy. His sole support was irregular contributions from an official committee set up to administer Wenner-Gren's assets; his wife could neither touch nor control her own assets in Canada. Neither could get a United States visa, because of their late employer, nor transport back to Europe. They were poor and trapped, and constantly worried that their income might one day cease altogether. Af Trolle took to importuning Swedish bank directors for help in sad letters which offered his services in bringing Wenner-Gren's money, 'a Swedish credit, back to Sweden'. A little late, he told the same bankers: 'Big finance I more and more condemn as being too unpatriotic.'

The great schemes of Wenner-Gren on Grand Bahama had produced one concrete result: the Grand Bahama Packing Company. Windsor had set great store by its business of packing crawfish; Marion Carstairs had sent produce to be canned there and shipped to Britain for war relief. Now, it was in dire trouble. It had been entrusted to a man called Lawrence I. Becker, who simply failed to account for the proceeds of the entire 1940–41 season. Next year, he sold nothing, and packed the unsold fish in crates marked 'East Coast Fisheries, Miami', which made it impossible to sell to any of the local rivals of East Coast. The men left to run the Wenner-Gren empire took Becker, successfully, to court.

The blacklisting of Wenner-Gren made it possible to examine some of the files of his companies – Bank of Bahamas, Mobilia SA and so forth – and trace the full extent of the cash that had passed through his hands and out to shadow companies or other hands. It also made possible a search of the grounds at Shangri-la, where rumour had put a pen for submarines and Walter Winchell in his newspaper column had astonishingly claimed there were landing strips, and a harbour able to take destroyers. 'As a result of continuous rumours to the effect that there are various forms of secret facilities, appliances and stores available to the enemy on the Wenner-Gren estate on Hog Island, the public is officially informed' – the announcement came from the Colonial Secretary, Windsor's second-in-command, in February 1942 – 'that a most thorough search which has been made of the property has failed to reveal the existence of anything of a suspicious nature. It is hoped that this announcement will allay entirely any anxiety the community may have felt as a result of the rumours.'

As for Wenner-Gren himself, he sat out his war in Cuernavaca, making furious petitions to Roosevelt and to Cordell Hull for release from the blacklist on which he assured them – 'as a gentleman' – he had been wrongly placed. When he needed money he borrowed – as Adrian Alvarez – from the Banco Continental in whose founding he had been so instrumental. With that money, and cash and securities that reached him from Nassau, he bought interests in a ritzy silver shop, a Cuernavaca hotel and a bus line. His wife still wrote to the Bahamas asking above all for Bob Martin's conditioning powder for dogs – the large size.

The money conduits between Nassau and Wenner-Gren were never quite stopped. In December 1941, Wenner-Gren was expecting $750,000 from Nassau. In February 1942 J. H. Anderson was rumoured to have taken the money out to him. Anderson was an accountant who ran the Bahamas General Trust, a corporation whose main business was the provision of trusts which would allow rich Canadians to avoid tax. Its founders had included Lord Beaverbrook and the likes of Holt of the Royal Bank of Canada; in the early 1940s, before Mexico had gripped him like a fever, Harry Oakes planned to increase his share of the company; Arthur Vining Davis emerged as owner in 1943, with men like Harold Christie still holding small parcels of shares. During the war, the trust was largely dormant. Anderson, however, was not. He was constantly rumoured to be on the point of taking employment with some great financier, and the only

149

one likely – the one to whom he was closest – was Axel Wenner-Gren. In February 1943 the British found him in Mexico City and warned him that if he made contact with the Swede, it would be at his own risk. He was also, it seems, Wenner-Gren's bagman for a while, until both local and American authorities took a closer interest in his journeys.

Out in the New Providence channel, the submarines worked their way. Half-drowned seamen were brought to Red Cross centres where the Duchess and her workers cared for them. 'Enemy submarines attacked shipping in Florida Straits,' the Duke cabled London in February 1942, 'about 130 miles North West of Grand Bahama. Am informed that the United States Naval Air Base at Exuma will not be in operation until May and am taking up with Commander-in-Chief, America and West Indies, possibility that enemy submarines are sheltering among unoccupied cays and that air patrol is necessary. . . .'

London told Windsor to take his problems to the Americans, on the grounds that the Bahamas fell within the American defence zone. He lost no time. He cabled back: 'As the matter most urgent, I consider it more expedient to make immediate personal contact with Commandant 5th Naval District, Miami. If you agree, please inform Washington and I will fly to Miami immediately upon receipt of your approval.'

At that point, London began to worry. The Duke seemed hell-bent on a return to America. He had the perfect excuse. Halifax in Washington seemed to consider he had had his share of dealing with errant ex-kings, and after talks with Sumner Welles he told London: 'I hope the Duke's visit may be confined to his naval business.' Churchill himself had been involved in the approach to Washington for help. Now the Colonial Office, in a margin note, promised to do their best to help Halifax confine the Duke, to 'try to insert in their instructions to the P.M. a tactful hint . . . but doubt whether it will be easy.'

American naval authorities were told none of this. They only knew the Duke was delayed in Nassau. London cleared his visit, but with only enough time for him to do precisely what he was officially setting out to do. He made contact with the Americans and told a startling story. The Bahamas, he said, were 'totally undefended against any scale of attack, except perhaps of a minor landing force from a single plane in the vicinity of Nassau . . . the general state of the Bahamas at present is that there are no guns in the island larger than machine guns and only two of these.' Communications to the mainland depended on Pan Am lines. Surveillance of the scattered cays and rocks depended on what Pan Am's pilots could see from their cockpits. The Duke, still nervous about a submarine kidnap, also warned the Americans that there were numerous shelters where submarines could be serviced without being observed, and where, even if they were spotted, it would take days for news to reach Nassau.

In Nassau, the Duke and his advisors met again with the Americans. They sorted out improvements in communications between Nassau and the naval base at Key West, a field office of the Seventh District Intelligence Organization and an inshore patrol squadron at Oakes Field. Weather reports were to go from their present insecure cipher to something more certainly safe.

The Americans were impressed by Windsor's eagerness to help. Given his record – as isolationist, as seeker after negotiated peace, as a man tainted by economic treason – his new-minted enthusiasms may seem ironic. But they are not. He knew, now, that there was no alternative except to work within the British system. He would lobby and bully to make his way out of Nassau, but he could not expect to organize his life anywhere else for the moment. He had a certain sentimental patriotism, and once America was committed to the war he could no longer cling to a neutral, sympathetic power as his model. He only had one job and one chance, and he would make the best of it.

'All of the discussions,' noted Captain Cranshaw for the Americans, 'were conducted on the basis that "We are all on the same team, trying to win the same game." '

Harold Christie had been busy in Washington, bothering his

contacts in the State Department. On 26 May 1942, he arrived to explain his links with Wenner-Gren, and to claim that it was he who had made the introduction to Maximinio Avila Camacho. He told Winters of the State Department that the blacklisting had been 'a source of considerable embarrassment to him and to Maximinio.' Rather grandly, he announced that he was prepared to accept the blacklisting – he really had very little choice – but that he was still sure Wenner-Gren was 'completely above board'.

And then he announced he was going to Mexico, but was 'evasive as to the reason'. The State Department was now puzzled. Christie made very little sense on the subject. He clearly had some high contacts in the Camacho family, but he was talking of placing US capital in Mexico, since British money was not available, and it was hard to see whom Christie might represent. On Bahamas real estate, he was the only expert; on Mexican oil, he was a hustler no better or worse than a dozen others, but rather less credible just because of his long association with selling islands. More, for a man who was supposed to be taking an interest in Mexico, he was asking very curious questions. He repeatedly presumed, for example, that the US Government would discourage all non-US investment in Mexico. State assured him that Washington was opposed only to investment by 'interests inimical' to the Allied cause. Yet Christie persisted.

His behaviour struck the State Department as odd only because they did not consider the simplest explanation. Christie actually wanted them to say the words he kept putting in their mouths. He wanted to be told that investment from outside America was not acceptable in Mexico. That way, he could return to Nassau and tell Harry Oakes that his Mexican dreams could not yet come true. He could keep his richest client, his richest source, in the Bahamas, and with him would remain all the prominence and wealth to which Christie had become accustomed.

The State Department made notes on the conversation and filed them. There seemed little point in the conversation, but a record might be useful, some day.

Edward

GOVERNOR.

Edward, Governor.
The Duke's signature
on official
documents

The arrival. On
a fiercely humid
August day, the Duke
and Duchess of
Windsor first set
foot on the islands
which were to be
their place of
wartime exile

Above Lisbon, 1940. A fearful Duke embarks for Bermuda, convinced that British intelligence plans his assassination. Behind him is long-time advisor Walter Monckton

Left Bermuda, 1940. The Duchess faces life as 'a refugee'

Opposite above Bahamas, August 1940. Exhausted and dazed by the heat, the Duke and Duchess were already planning an escape from their islands

Opposite below Bay Street, Nassau

'Our home for the duration.' The local *Nassau Magazine*
shows Government House and the Duke's newly decorated
study – dominated by photographs of Wallis Windsor

'I have never worked so hard, I never felt better used.'
Wallis Windsor's war involved work for soldiers,
children and the Red Cross

Below 'A job is what you make of it.'
The Duke pins a medal on a policeman

Backgammon at the Prince George
hotel. The more raffish side of
Nassau life revolved around men
like Alfred de Marigny (left)
and J. H. Anderson, who was
later the bagman for financier
Axel Wenner-Gren

Invisible men. Black Bahamians treated the Duke with a mixture of awe
and suspicion. He mistrusted all of them

Milo Butler. He fought for 'my people,
the black people'

Bert Cambridge, musician turned
politician

Reminders of war. Among
the shipwrecked were
sailors Widdicombe and
Tapscott who survived an
Atlantic crossing in an
open boat

Meeting the troops. Duke
and Duchess animate a
Broadway ball for British
servicemen

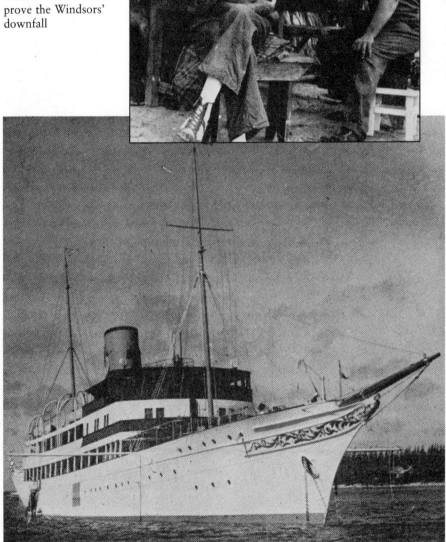

Hunter: Axel Wenner-Gren (centre) on a duckshooting expedition with lawyer Stafford Sands (right) and white Bahamian Charles Bethell. Wenner-Gren was to prove the Windsors' downfall

Southern Cross, Wenner-Gren's yacht, once the personal ship of Howard Hughes, lies in Nassau Harbour. Roosevelt wanted agents placed aboard to check on Wenner-Gren's money games and arms dealing

The money-go-round. Maximino Camacho (centre) was wooed by
Harold Christie (left) and Sir Harry Oakes in a major, illegal investment
that Windsor helped

The money-go-round. The Duke and Duchess, always anxious about
money, talk with the royal family's advisor Sir Edward Peacock

The greatest scandal. Sir Harry Oakes's murder finally discredited his friend the Duke

The Miami connection. Duke and Duchess accept passports from the Miami policeman who wrecked the Oakes investigation – Captain Edward Melchen

Victim Sir Harry Oakes, richest baronet in the British Empire, stands
bluff and awkward with his wife Eunice

Survivors: café society welcomed the Duke and Duchess, even after the scandal of Nassau. His boyish charm now seemed a little thin; her style remained a practised, perfect performance

The marriage was announced, but rather late and in rather subdued tones, between Nancy Oakes, eldest daughter of Sir Harry, and Alfred de Marigny, sometimes known as Count, a Mauritian gentleman with a lively history that had once titillated proper Nassau and now appalled them. Pretty Nancy, the rich girl, the girl who liked the Bahamas, had been a social star – a pure, wealthy social virgin, worshipped and cossetted by her father, protected by her mother as she drifted through life in a haze of good intentions. It was bad enough she had married, and ended her role in fantasy. To have married de Marigny, only days after her eighteenth birthday without asking her parents' permission, was scandal.

De Marigny was much-married, a charming man, tall and slim and athletic, who had a particular elegance of manner that allowed him to carry off his taste for bright, tropic colour. He had come from Mauritius with little more than his French accent, and sufficient funds to keep alive, and a wife, and a friend called Georges de Visdelou, who had a title as questionable as de Marigny's, but rather less charm. De Marigny's most visible means of support was his wife Ruth, of a New York stockbroking clan. Together, they bought houses and property on Eleuthera and lived an idyllic life. In March 1940 Ruth divorced de Marigny and in December that year she persuaded him to move out of her house. He had plans now for a chicken farm. He sailed his yacht brilliantly and called it, to the fury of the tight-curled ladies, the *Concubine*. De Visdelou had no apparent occupation except for a pretty black girl called Betty Roberts, who tore tickets at the Savoy Theatre for a living.

The pair upset Nassau profoundly. Not even the indictment of a Member of the House of Assembly on charges of smuggling drugs to the Brooklyn Mafia – it would be a late embarrassment during Windsor's stay – could be as offensive as the fact that de Marigny liked young women and frequently said so to their face, even to the face of their parents if the young woman was not alone. De Marigny was sardonic, witty, civilized, and none too scrupulous. He was easy with his black friends – most of Nassau observed a rigid

153

social segregation – and his style offended the whites even more. Sometimes, they said, citing his time with his wife Ruth, he seemed just like a gigolo.

Of all the men to marry a pretty girl who would be one of the heirs to a fortune which, the gossips said, was at least $200,000,000, de Marigny was the one least likely to meet with anyone's approval. He was tolerable, barely, as an amusing single man. Marrying Nancy Oakes, though, was serious business.

The Oakes family had not always disapproved of him. Since 1938 Lady Oakes had invited him to her parties, even tried some mild match-making – but not with Nancy. In March of 1942 de Marigny went to New York to see doctors about his chronic stomach troubles. Nancy was there, and they began to see each other often. A friend of Nancy's, Georgina Rapp, proposed a trip to California; de Marigny went along, respectably confined to a hotel while Nancy stayed with the Rapps. After only three weeks of West Coast sun, his stomach began to bother him again, and he returned to New York. Nancy followed. She comforted him and cared for him. While he was in hospital, they agreed to get married – if he got well again.

Nancy had to follow family duty north to Canada. She had meant to discuss her marriage with her mother, but somehow the subject never arose. Instead, she returned to New York, newly eighteen and legally of marriageable age. De Marigny and Nancy never did explain why they married so quickly and why they married before talking to the Oakeses. It is a fairly safe assumption that they expected fierce parental disapproval.

'We were frightfully upset,' Lady Oakes said. 'We did not break with her. We had to make the best of a bad situation. After all, she was our daughter.' De Marigny and Nancy went to the Oakeses' house at Bar Harbor in Maine for two weeks, at the suggestion of Lady Oakes. De Marigny was utterly charming. Nancy's brothers and sister adored him, and he took them sailing. But the Oakeses watched with bitterly mixed feelings. 'Nancy was only a child, she was still at school,' Lady Oakes said. 'We knew that Alfred was

divorced and was still living with his former wife – or whatever you call a wife that's divorced – but we decided to make
the best of the situation and put up a brave front.'

They thought the situation like a nightmare. Later, they
would be convinced it held the seeds of murder.

The Windsors proposed another Washington trip, part
social, as an escape from the stifling summer, part business,
and part a kind of glorious affirmation of Anglo-American
relations. This last intention fooled nobody. The Duke had
asked for British Embassy help in preparing his trip, and the
Embassy sent Rene McColl, a press attaché who had been
active in a series of meetings designed to neutralize the activities of those – official and unofficial – who had given
Britain an embarrassing image in America. The Duke wanted
McColl for a week; McColl was sent for a day. In that time,
he had to assess and control one of Britain's greatest and
most awkward negative assets in America.

McColl came with a list of questions prepared with the
help of John Foster of the Embassy. They were questions
that anticipated the main attacks of the American press. If
Windsor was prepared to answer them, Foster had reckoned,
he might also be prepared to mend his ways. McColl asked
the Duke if all his luggage was strictly necessary, if he found
it essential to take a whole floor of a major Manhattan hotel.
He also asked if the Duke still advocated a negotiated peace.

The Duke coughed and produced his usual answer: that
he had indeed favoured a negotiated peace during the period
of phoney war, 'before Hitler lost his head'. Now, he did
not. McColl went to bed reasonably sure that the Duke
would behave himself.

Next morning, his confidence was shattered. 'I've been
thinking about the question about negotiated peace,' Windsor said. 'I've been talking to the Duchess. I think we'll play
that one by ear.'

Everything about the Windsors' trip – not least the public
statements about the war that they might choose to 'play by
ear' – made both London and Washington nervous. The
Windsors left Nassau in high spirits. The Duke broadcast

before leaving, to tell the Bahamas that a 'certain extensive Project' was coming to the island. He could say no more. Indeed, American forces were still sworn to secrecy about 'the Project', and keeping all related papers in a bulging safe, long after their British colleagues were freely using and talking about the finished airfields. For Oakes Field was to be extended, and a new field built out west to be called Windsor Field, and there would be work. 'We should not,' Windsor said, 'regard any wartime project solely in terms of what we can get out of it.' But clearly there would be fewer men out of work, more money circulating, at least a temporary respite from what had seemed like total economic collapse. Bay Street would gain, too; such a palliative would remove pressure for more fundamental reform.

Windsor ended his speech in splendid form. 'All,' he said, 'is well on the Bahamian front.'

Bay Street lay broken – shards of glass in the roadway, shops stripped of everything that a man could carry on his back, the remains of bottles and, in places, blood. The hurricane shutters were up, as though in preparation for a storm. The unthinkable had happened: black Bahamians had rioted in the very centre of white Nassau. The Duke, in Washington, occupied himself with the practical problem of getting home to see what the breaking of Bay Street signified.

The fury of the attack, its suddenness, created real fear among the whites. They talked of shootings, barricaded their homes and checked their shotguns. They had so long gone unchallenged, been able to say that their way of life was threatened only by the machinations of London. Now, they had felt the full force of anger that lived over the hill in Grants Town, along with the long sorrow of oppression. They had never guessed that there was anger.

It was an infuriating interruption to Windsor's trip to Washington. He held a fine line between impatience and petulance and this time he almost crossed it. He felt the wretched blacks had ruined his careful schemes for their own benefit. He knew they could not be trusted. But he also saw that the riots were an opportunity, a crisis. If he could understand what had happened, play on the aspirations and fears it revealed, he might yet win his political battles. For that, he first had to discover the order of events. He did not know if there were labour leaders who could bring men onto the streets in the numbers needed for riot. He did not know what the issues might be, except that in his mind he was sure many of them were racial. He had to sort out the order of the riot in order to see its causes and its meaning. Bay Street was broken on Monday, 1 June, but the trouble had begun on the previous Saturday.

The Project was the building of two major airfields. It gave work to thousands. Out Islanders who had become resigned to staying in Nassau without jobs or hope now found themselves in demand. Windsor had been optimistic about the results. Bay Street thought the Project was salvation.

That Saturday, though, there had been a distinct air of unrest out at Main Field in the west. The men were hard to handle. There was talk that white men were blocking higher wages for Bahamians. There were minor grievances too – problems with transport for the eight-mile journey from Nassau itself to the site, problems with food at midday. The system of paying wages – paid out on Saturday, but only for days worked up to Wednesday – made the labourers think they were being short-changed in their first weeks. It also left them without money in their pockets to buy evening meals for the first ten days of work.

Everybody on the site knew the huge gaps between the wages paid to American workers on the Project, and the money Bahamians took home. Thaddeus Johnson, at the Palm Tree Inn on Bank Lane that day, heard talk on the lines of: 'Boss man tell me he would like to pay bigger wages but he ain't got nothing to do with it because wages is fixed by Nassau Government and the Nassau people.' Most men had all too vivid memories of the booms and busts that Nassau had known in the twenty years past, and what those wild swerves had done to their pay packets. Their labour had been worth 6s to 10s a day during the rum days, but only 1s a day, if they were lucky, in the 1930s. Nothing else had

157

seemed real about the Depression in the Bahamas, except the sudden slump in wages. On the Project, the minimum wage for unskilled labour was 4s a day. It was not so wonderful, although it was well above what Wenner-Gren paid over at Paradise Town. But it was not the unskilled men who saw the great divide between Bahamian and American – largely, between black and white. A Bahamian truck driver earned 1s an hour. An American driver – same truck, same loads, same hours – earned $1.50 an hour, or 6s.

If the men had not noticed for themselves, the American foremen told them. They went drinking down in the Front Pub or the other black bars and they told the men to stick up for their rights. Government Hill would always suspect the foremen were sinister agitators. They were not. They were genuinely outraged at the way Bahamian workers were treated. It did not fit their self-image as the generous Americans.

Over the unskilled workers, the American contractors put local supervisors. Karl Claridge was one – a sharp-tongued white Bahamian who had done reasonably well for himself. He had the unlovely job of dismissing the workers who came out to the Field and refused to work seriously. The work was much harder than Bahamians were used to doing, both longer and physically tougher. Island construction paid due respect to sun and heat; the bases were built to a more northerly timetable. Claridge could not allow himself to be concerned with that. His job was to keep discipline. He answered to Morton Turtle, the top civilian on the Project, who was a long-established contractor in Nassau. Turtle knew what his workers thought of him. At the first sign of trouble he abandoned his house and his wife, fled to his schooner and stayed offshore until the riot had been cauterized and finished.

The weekend talk, the disgruntlement and the growing realization that black Bahamians had again been unfairly treated, began to turn from a general feeling to specific allegations. Leonard Storr from Andros was among the workers who had newly signed on. He heard the story that the white bosses had come to pay better wages, but Nassau people had stopped them. By the time the story reached him, it had been embroidered. Now, it was Karl Claridge, the overseer, who had told the Americans not to pay the men for time when it was raining and they could not work, and to stretch the working day on Sunday by an hour so that the men were at the field from eight to four. Storr did not know whom to believe. All he knew was that he was hard put to make ends meet on the money he had. He drove off for a load of stones and returned to find the men beginning to cluster, hot and fierce, around the administration buildings. The talk was loud and the mood was ominous.

Storr could hear the shouts of the men as he drove up: 'We strike!' A stone caught him above the eye and left a raw bruise. The police came screeching into the field, led by Captain Edward de Witt Sears, a white Bahamian who had been a sponge merchant until 1939 when the red rust destroyed his livelihood and he took to police work. He carried a gun. Sears chose to single out Storr – on the site he called himself Green, for his own reasons – and asked him the story. Storr explained in simple terms: the Americans had dollars for the workers, and the Nassau merchants were stopping them from paying out. Sears said the men should get a committee, should have it all looked into. Storr went with the labour officer, John Hughes, to a high window of the administration building and Hughes, in his official capacity, addressed the crowd.

Below, the trucks began to pull out of the field, taking men back to the other airport, closer to town. It seemed for a while that the crowd was thinning, but there was a group who refused to go. Hughes, who, as labour officer, fancied himself the only neutral on the scene, asked the contractors to get the drivers to break through the crowd and set them moving. The crowd felt hemmed and attacked. Sears was escorting Storr off the field, and the crowd saw the bruise above Storr's eye and leapt to the conclusion that it was the work of the policeman – the white, the 'Conchy Joe' policeman. They thought Storr had been arrested. They found the cars of the American foremen and began to jump on the fenders. Karl Claridge drove up and demanded to be let pass.

The crowd rocked his car, first mockingly and then force-fully, and then they took it and turned it over bodily. Clar-idge saw the faces. He thought the trouble-makers were young, maybe sixteen to twenty.

And Sears drew his revolver, and fired in the air. Now, there was real fear. Sears had a way of asking too loudly if the men wanted to get themselves killed. Storr, by his side, seemed wounded. The men scattered, very fast, and ran for the shelter of the trucks or the bush. The police and the contractors held the field, and the last of the trucks rumbled out east towards Nassau.

As labour officer, Hughes now had to determine what course of action would calm the men and keep work rolling. He did not think the trouble would spread. He considered the events of the afternoon, and thought he had not been in danger. He talked with the contractors, and he had the impression they would make up the wages for the time lost through rain. All seemed quiet. The Commissioner of Police, Erskine Lindop, taking tea with the Baron Georg af Trolle, was interrupted at five to be told of the incident, but he decided he had no need to intervene. It was enough that Hughes planned to go to Government House.

Hughes called a meeting of representatives of labour. The phrase was barely appropriate to the men who came. There was A. F. Adderley, the stiff-necked black lawyer who had distinguished himself in Britain and returned to Nassau as the island's finest trial lawyer, but who kept a stringent distance between himself and working-class blacks. There was Dr Walker, who talked in moral terms and had a wider view, but who finally saw himself as a teacher of his people, not a representative. And there was Charles Rhodriguez, a dry-goods merchant from Grants Town, over the hill. None of them was clear about what had happened out at Main Field that day, whether it was the start of revolt or merely a communal grumble.

'I did not dream,' A. F. Adderley said, 'of riotous conduct on the part of Bahamian labour.' At 6.30 the next morning, he was down at the Guns, the old and rusting fortifications where the men met the trucks that would take them to work. He prepared a speech, delivered it to an unreceptive audience of 400 and drove quickly away. The men did not move. They would not board the trucks and they would not head for work. They had no leader. Leonard Storr, still with his bruise from yesterday and trailing the glory of a sort of martyr, filled that gap. He stood and he spoke, and the men decided to strike.

Adderley drove to Main Field. The men there were refusing to check their numbers for work – a kind of clocking-on device. They were murmurous and sullen. They opened straw lunch baskets and showed him the contents, and asked how they were expected to work on such rations.

At 7.45 the Colonial Secretary, Heape, called the Commissioner of Police. He said that they would need a policeman out at Main Field. The unlucky Sears was sent, and he arrived in time to see the men rush a truck and turn it over. He went for the phone to call the Commissioner and ask for reinforcements. As he did so, another thousand men began to march onto the field, carrying clubs and sticks and machetes, singing and shouting with a fierce, determined beat as they passed the administration building. The men were marching on Nassau.

The authorities were in a state of indecision. The Commissioner of Police kept his men in barracks – he had only thirty-five available – because he thought the march was an ordinary labour demonstration and would need tact. Heape, meanwhile, had decided on a tougher line. He tried to raise the Bahamian Defence Force to set a cordon along the ridge, to stop the workers coming into the white areas of Nassau. The force's commander, an amiable water-ski champion who was said to be the magnet for stray ladies in the Emerald Beach, told Heape that would be difficult, if not impossible. His only way to assemble his soldiers quickly was to sound the siren. The Commissioner of Police was consulted and gave his opinion that sounding the siren would cause panic, that people would assume a German attack and the whole situation, still peaceful, would become chaotic. The streets were packed, and sudden fear would be disastrous. The men were still marching without incident, singing patriotic songs at the tops of their voices. The Defence Force was slowly assembled, with steel helmets and rifles and ammunition. The police decided to wait.

The procession came past the verandahs of Government House. The marchers were in Nassau. Their mood was loud and almost surprised at their own daring. Nothing like this had happened before. Nobody knew where it led.

They carried machetes, but that was no cause for alarm. As in most old plantation countries, a man could walk the streets with a terrifying cutlass, honed sharp, and everyone would assume he was going to work or to cut coconuts or simply returning home from digging a richer man's garden. The cutlass was a basic tool.

But as the crowd marched down the hill, into the colonial heart of the town, the cutlasses looked like menace and the noise began to drum. A few cars were turned or damaged, their glass beaten with sticks. Milo Butler, making a morning trip to the market, caught up with the men and was chaired to Rawson Square. He arrived in time to see the Attorney General speaking to the crowd from the steps of the Colonial Secretary's Office. Official Nassau was speaking for the first time.

Later, the Attorney General claimed he said this: 'Look here, boys. If you have a grievance, put it in the proper way. There are two ways of doing a thing – the right way and the wrong way – and you have chosen the wrong way.' He told them the truth: that the Americans had been reluctant to use Bahamian labour at all – as they were reluctant to use local labour anywhere in the Caribbean – and only the Governor's personal intervention had brought them jobs above the level of pick-axe and cutlass and muscles.

The crowd heard something different. They heard the Attorney General say that if they did not disperse, the authorities would have to bring in American labour to replace them.

The men milled in Rawson Square, seeming orderly enough to the Commissioner. When he asked, several of them threw down their sticks in a heap. They did not seem determined rioters. Yet there was something darker and

162

blood-boiling under the directionless, leaderless noise of the crowd. Morton Turtle of the Project caught it. 'For God's sake, Mr Turtle, don't go down there,' a friend warned. 'They'll kill you!'

In the crowd, Captain Sears caught up again with Leonard Storr. He was furious. 'You're looking to get killed,' he said, and Storr remembered bawling back: 'If you kill me, you'll kill me for my rights.' 'After this,' Sears said, 'we'll see that you go back to Turks Island.' Storr was bold with the rush of the crowd. 'If you send me back to Turks,' he said, 'I'll send you back to Abaco.' They stood against each other like furious lizards, engorged for fight.

Godfrey Higgs heard the crowd were looking for him – and Kenneth Solomon, and the visible, political Bay Street Boys – and he took refuge in the Prince George hotel. He called the Colonial Secretary's office to report he could hear the first sounds of glass breaking on Bay Street.

There had been a Coca-Cola truck parked on the street. Twenty cases were empty, eight full. One man wanted a drink, or a weapon. He snatched a bottle and broke it. He threw the empty bottle. The loud mob became a riot mob.

The police tried to push the crowd to the west, along Bay Street towards the British Colonial hotel. They had no training in handling crowds. They simply tried to push, in wide formation.

On the street, the men were shouting for the Bay Street Boys – for Morton Turtle, secure on his schooner; for Godfrey Higgs, hiding in the Prince George hotel; for Kenneth Solomon. Some shops had protection. Nine men kept the mob away from the shop of Percy Christie, brother to Harold; they linked arms and made a barrier. The porter at the Prince George talked the crowd into passing. Little Mary Moseley, editor of the *Guardian*, bustled along the street, urging the police to do something, telling them to turn fire-hoses on the crowd because, she said, the crowd would find that 'humorous'. Bert Cambridge, a musician and soon to be a black Member of the House of Assembly, took a club from a friend and told him he did not need it to make his point; he was seen, and the white merchants assumed that he had

163

armed himself to join the revolution. Milo Butler was out on the street, his grand bombastic personality undermining the force of his peace-making words. The crowd swept along the street, sparing shops with the heaviest hurricane shutters, or a gas station where a man in the crowd knew the owners. It was capricious, frightening. In a matter of minutes, it had gone beyond control.

Storr tried to merge into the crowd, but he could not resist one gesture. The crowd was at the West End Fruit Store and he picked an apple from the display and handed it to a bystander. The police stepped forward. They had no handcuffs, and they tried to hold Storr bodily while the crowd surged around them. Storr was one of them; the crowd remembered him, and protected him. He was lifted out of custody, literally, and he ran for the sidewalk, crawled under the Jaeger shop where there was still a gap between floorboards and the unsettled fill beneath and out to the Sponge Exchange, which had become a refuge for anyone who needed to avoid the police, gather more stones, rest for a moment.

The men on Bay Street were lifting bales of cloth from the windows, preening in clothes they had taken, throwing dog food around in Damianos' store. Captain Sears was hit in the mouth by an American foreman from the Project. The looters seemed to go west to the Red Cross headquarters. Oswald Moseley, an insurance agent and a pillar of the Nassau ascendancy, spluttered at Bert Cambridge: 'Cambridge, my God! Of all places, the Red Cross!' and Cambridge turned to him and said, with quiet reason: 'Here you are, and you've got a gun in your pocket and you won't go – and you expect me to go?'

Mrs Morton Turtle, abandoned by her husband, worried that damage might be done to Suzy's, her shop. To find out, she sent her butler.

At ten, the Camerons came and began to show rifles in the street. They worked with the police to clear Bay Street itself, to force men off the road into side streets, to drive those on the wharves onto any of the ships tied up there.

At 10.10, the inner establishment met – Heape as Acting Governor, the Leader of the Government in the House, the

Receiver General. At 10.20 they were joined by the deputation for labour, supplemented this time by Milo Butler and Bert Cambridge. All urged Government Hill that wages must rise immediately. That alone would stop the riot. Heape refused to negotiate under duress. He would make no concessions until there was order. With the police distracted by false reports that Godfrey Higg's house out east was under siege, and the Bahamian Defence Force straggling into action, it was hard enough to assemble the forces of law and order, let alone deploy them. Heape would give no special orders – neither orders to fire on the crowd, nor orders to avoid firing.

As the black spokesmen left, Bay Street stormed into Heape's office, full of purple fury, wrangling and cursing. Asa Pritchard was one of them, and he told Heape to 'take steps'; when Heape said he would consult the military, Pritchard became furious. He told Heape not to be a damn fool. He was commander-in-chief and he knew it. Pritchard fumed as the Attorney General discussed whether it was time to read the Riot Act. Heape himself could hardly get a word into the discussion. Somebody asked why machine guns had not been turned on the crowd. The same person – precisely who was later forgotten, conveniently – added: 'If the Government doesn't intend to do any shooting, we will!'

From Government House, the next sounds were crisp and distinct: firing in Grants Town, in the black quarters over the hill. It was almost noon. The soldiers and police had driven the rioters back to their own areas. They were continuing the war, at home.

Somebody said, at the first shots: 'That's the stuff to give them.' Later, nobody wanted to remember who had spoken.

Stafford Sands always thought it might have been necessary to shoot a few of the ringleaders. But nobody knew who the ringleaders were. The riot had come like a storm, something long repressed which returned in appalling, destructive form. Bay Street lay as though a hurricane had passed, and still the streets over the hill were full of rum and revolution; liquor stores had been battered open, and bars raided, especially

165

those owned by whites. This wave of anger had to have a cause, preferably a set of causes who could be hanged, for if it did not have leaders and subversives, then Bay Street had wholly misjudged the mood of the black majority for years. That was unthinkable: 'black' lived over the hill, out of the sight and the minds of white Nassau. Its irruption was brutal. It made it necessary to think about black people and it made a little change thinkable. Bay Street could not and would not think that way.

Trouble over the hill was intractable. The crowd would not listen to official speakers. When the Commissioner of Police arrived with police and soldiers, the crowd jumped the trucks and hurled stones. The Commissioner leapt down from his truck and shouted: 'Come on, now's the time!'

The crowd assumed he meant the soldiers to open fire. There was a stampede, a mêlée of flying stones; one man came within fifteen feet of the Commissioner, rock in hand, menacing. The Commissioner pointed his revolver; a Cameron levelled his rifle; the man ran. The Commissioner had to cry out: 'For God's sake, don't shoot him in the back.'

The Riot Act was read. It requires all persons to return to shelter. It allows firing in the streets if they refuse.

By one o'clock the forces had been taken out of Grants Town. Their presence was considered provoking, especially with the high-wine the men had been drinking. In the afternoon, Milo Butler and Percy Christie did the rounds of clubs and bars, trying to persuade them all to stay closed that night. But there was already drink enough in circulation. Bay Street had been broken. Now Grants Town was ready to burn.

The merchants, aware that they were not being given the attention their panic demanded, drafted a stiff telegram to the Duke. They had begun to think it odd that trouble had broken out while he was away. They were searching for conspiracies to explain away the riot. They stayed away from Grants Town and they did not know that the riot was continuing.

More was stirring than anger about wages. Down Bay

Street the men had been shouting 'Burma Road declare war on Conchy Joe' – blacks from the field declare war on Bahamian whites. 'Do, nigger, do, don't you lick nobody, don't you lick nobody.' Napoleon McPhee, a stonemason with a limp, set fire to a Union Jack: 'I am willing to fight under this flag. I willing even to die under this flag. But I ain't gwine starve under this flag!' Down in Grants Town Alfred 'Sweet Potato' Stubbs took a portrait of the royal family from a book in the library and set it ablaze. It was as though fire would purge the place of whiteness and suffering. The targets would be anything that spoke of white authority.

Grants Town police station was one of the few two-storey buildings over the hill, conspicuous and accessible. Lance Corporal MacDonald Gooding had been there since early morning, with three other men. He had heard talk of the Sunday troubles at the field, but the worst he expected was a strike.

Around eight in the morning, the men came marching out of the south, up the hill to Nassau and Bay Street and Government Hill. One carried the banner – white cloth tied to a stick; the men sang, as they went, 'We'll Never Let the Old Flag Fall'. Gooding saw the tail of the procession pass, and then, twenty minutes later, another thousand men came with a roar of noise along the street. Gooding tried to contact the Commissioner, but the noise of the crowd drowned out the telephone. He heard the crowd bellow to the black policemen: 'We don't want to see you all. We're going to Government Hill.'

All morning, he heard the rumours. He had nobody to check them. He did not dare leave his post. Four men could do nothing. It was said that on the Southern Recreation Ground the black politician Walton Young and Samuel White, proprietor of Weary Willie's hotel – that 'glimpse of Africa in the Bahamas' – had tried to calm the crowd and been beaten for their efforts. From the police station, Gooding could see the unconscious body of White being carried into his bar. By eleven o'clock, bars had been burgled, and the crowd's mood seemed to Gooding vicious and surly. At 11.15, the manager of the Cotton Tree Inn came to the police

167

station to report that his bar was under siege; the crowd was trying to smash down the doors. Gooding said he was sorry. There was nobody he could spare.

At 12.00 he heard shots. From the police station, he saw soldiers and police coming fast over the hill. He saw stones and bottles in the air. He saw a drunk man outside the police station, his fingers shot away, bloody. The crowd had surrounded the ambulance, and would not part to let it take the man to hospital. A cab-driver, Randolph Rahming, told Gooding he had no licence to drive a motor vehicle, but he would try to get the man through. He set off, men clinging still to the ambulance; he drove blind, ignoring the soldiers' challenges, ignoring the shots that pierced two men still clinging to the ambulance.

The crowd had the police station surrounded. For two hours, Gooding and his men sat out the siege. At 2.00, the mood changed again. A rumour came down from Nassau that Captain Sears – white Sears, a Conchy Joe – had shot a man dead. The crowd remembered Sears with his revolver drawn at the main field. Gooding tried to explain that Sears had been out of range when the shots were fired, that it could not possibly have been Sears. The crowd did not listen. Harold Thurston, a burly man who had regularly done time since 1917 for larceny and once for wounding a policeman, became the loud spokesman. 'You people stand there talking to these goddamned policemen,' he screamed, 'and they are in there with the Conchy Joes. Sears is a Conchy Joe. Whatever he says the police has got to do.'

The police bolted up the doors and heard the crowd break against them, like a high sea in rage. Outside, the ambulance was pushed diagonally across the street. Fire was lit with trash and gasoline. The ambulance was overturned and the seats set afire, and when they were blazing, they were taken to the fire engine in the garage and the fire was set again. The crowd was bellowing for the police killers. The fire was building in the garage which was part of the police station. Through a back window, Gooding and his men made their escape.

When the official inquiry gave its report, it said that the

events of 1 June 1942 were in no way racial. That was a lie, and Windsor ordered it.

It was the first day in Washington for the Duke and Duchess, 1 June, and it had been splendidly successful – informal lunch with the President and Mrs Roosevelt; guests at the British Embassy, which was only proper attention for a colonial governor; a sense of ease. They had business to do, but social matters came first. In Miami, the Duke had talked defence. In Washington, he talked transport, and problems of assuring essential supplies to the islands in wartime. It was solid, constructive stuff.

The cable arrived during dinner – the Duke, the Duchess, Lord and Lady Halifax and friends. Windsor was summoned by the Ambassador's secretary and returned to say that he must leave immediately. Rioting had broken out. Soon after, Windsor was called to the phone and talked with Roosevelt, who offered transport back to the island. 'H.R.H. had certain discussions last night with the President,' the official dispatch to London said, 'and U.S. authorities, as a result of which the latter agreed to send some 100 U.S. Marines to Bahamas ostensibly [*sic*] to act as a military police to protect U.S. installations on the island.' The real mission of the troops, actually US Cavalry out of Fort Blanding, Florida, was to do anything necessary to protect the airstrips.

Windsor had a foul flight to Nassau the next morning. His plane broke down, and he had to change to another. He arrived exhausted, to find the British troops had stayed on duty from 7 a.m. on Monday until midday on Tuesday. The American troops might well be needed. But their presence was an extraordinary event. The Colonial Office noted: 'The fact that we have had to ask for the assistance of U.S. Marines will lead to comparisons with Nicaragua and Hayti [*sic*] and other countries where the Marines have in the past been called in to restore order. . . .' Across the file, a senior diplomat wrote: 'All very unfortunate.' Worse, when the American troops arrived, their commander inspected the situation and announced that he had, in part, been sent to defend a Bahamian plantation and he wanted none of it. The Cavalry were exchanged for military police. Windsor needed those men. When the trouble finally subsided, he told the US consul: 'I only wish I had a reason to keep them here.'

He asked the State Department to muzzle the American press – as he had done on the occasion of his trips to America, and as the Office of Censorship had then refused to do. The *New York Times* picked up the story on 3 June, and suggested that Axis powers had caused the trouble. This rumour had already flashed by telegraph the length of the US Army's Eastern Command. The military told each other horrid stories of Japanese subversion in the Caribbean. The Duke had been clear in his reports to the US Army: it was racial rioting.

The fury continued even on the day of his return, 2 June. Chester Bethell, a white man from Abaco, had been construction superintendent at Main Field. On the day of the riot, he had been by a window, where the crowd could see his face. He had heard them crying: 'See him there! Let's kill him!' On the Tuesday, he boarded up his house and sent his family away. He took refuge in the deep rooms of his home, heard the crowd approach, could do nothing but wait. They saw the shutters and passed by, marching west, still loud and menacing.

Windsor told Roosevelt that day: 'Situation quietened and will report to you on my return to Washington.' The merchants tried to see him, but he pleaded exhaustion; he stayed with ExCo until the early hours of the morning. The Duchess would claim later that he held out for a tough line. It seems highly unlikely that any member of ExCo would have wanted action less decisive than what happened. He decided to continue the curfew Heape had imposed, and to insist, as Heape had done, that perfect order be restored before serious talking could begin. After the compromises during the riot – the failure to sound the siren, the first hour of gentle treatment before the Coca-Cola truck and the start of the wrecking – it was rather simple for the Duke to appear firm. There were no more shooting decisions to take.

The Duke, however, was ready to make compromises beyond what London or Bay Street or Washington either expected or feared. On the issue of money, he seemed already to have decided that the appropriate minimum daily wage would be 5s – an increase of 25 per cent. He wanted decent midday meals for the men. He let it be known that the labour leaders had promised no more trouble; and the merchants, meanwhile, grumbled that something – something stinging, something punitive – must be done.

Bay Street's attitudes sound clearest in letters written to Eric Solomon, the tobacco merchant, who was in his Out Island retreat throughout the riot. Nobody had reason to mince their words with Solomon; his views on labour were well known. 'If the right people had got shot accidentally,' Mary Moseley told Solomon, 'it would have been a good thing, because the big question is not one of wages but of agitation.' His brother Kenneth Solomon wrote: 'Will have nothing to say about the riot save that it should never have happened and after it did happen was very badly handled. I shall be glad when all the elections are over so that we can try and become normal again.'

There was some feeling that the riots might never have happened if the Duke had been on the island at the time. 'The powers that be,' Mary Moseley wrote, 'made no attempt to stop it until the damage was done. . . . Of course, trouble has been brewing for a long time and this was just the opportunity for which the crowd was waiting.'

More than anything, Bay Street was concerned to telegraph its fury that Heape had not done something – anything – to prevent damage. On Wednesday, 3 June, Stafford Sands, along with Harold Christie and Sidney Farrington, stomped to Government House to demand audience. The meeting was first postponed, and then permitted. The Duke was firm. He had no intention of allowing a compromise. Bay Street's men went away more content.

On 3 June, also, the Duke took to radio to make his points. He wanted to appeal to public sentiment as well as announce change. It was startlingly modern use of radio by a colonial governor, and one that Windsor's microphone manner – light and rather American, informal and not ponderous – made powerful. 'As you know,' he said, 'I left

Nassau last week to go to Washington to carry on certain conversations which would assist not only in the war effort but also the question of employment in the Bahamas. It was with surprise and indeed mortification that these conversations were interrupted in Washington by the news of the disorders that broke out here on Monday.'

He told the story – from the letter to the Acting Governor, sent after Windsor had left the islands, in which the Bahamian Federation of Labour asked for action on wages. He warned that: 'Before I can take up the question of increasing wages, my first duty must be to see that order is restored and that both the persons and the property of every citizen is freed from the threat of violence. When these rights are secured, the question of increasing wages will receive my immediate and careful consideration. I am not yet satisfied that the threat of violence is removed. Meanwhile, what is the position? A project which is of great and more than Bahamian importance has already been delayed three days. I cannot but feel that many, if not indeed the great majority, of the men who have been employed on the Project are ready to resume work. The most tangible evidence that I can have that law and order are firmly re-established is to have work on the Project started again and voluntary workers left alone, unmolested by any disorderly element in the community.'

He risked a great deal on that broadcast. If it had failed, his personal authority would have been broken. He knew in advance that there was near peace in the town, except for some isolated breaking of the night-time curfew which may have had more to do with Bahamian contempt for irrelevant regulations than any real malice. Yet he made a personal appeal with some doubt – necessary doubt – of its effect.

By Saturday, 6 June, Windsor could cable London that 'This morning about 1500 workers have returned to work, representing about sixty per cent of workers previously employed, but work cannot yet be said to be normal and workers are being guarded by American soldiers.' He acknowledged that 'racial feelings have been aroused on both sides'.

His charisma, his charm were still available, along with

172

the sheer authority of an ex-king. He overwhelmed the situation in the Bahamas because of who he had been. But he was now a questionable force in the minds of many black Bahamians. The one-time hero, the descendant of Queen Wikki who freed the slaves, listened on 4 June to the extraordinary rhetoric of Dr Walker, the street-teacher from Grants Town who came in blue serge to join a deputation of labour.

'I wish to conclude,' Walker said, 'with a personal word to His Royal Highness, the Duke of Windsor himself. Two years ago, when the radio waves broadcast the news of Your Royal Highness's appointment as Governor of the Bahamas, the deaf heard and the dumb spoke, the blind saw and the crippled leapt for joy. Your reputation as a humanitarian and King had preceded you. "Surely," we said to ourselves, "the Duke of Windsor will not allow us to continue to live amidst social inequalities that sap our self-respect and prevent us from attaining our full status as first-class citizens." Fifty-four Governors have preceded your Excellency, but not one ever brought a ray of hope to the poor and oppressed. We believe that you are not just another Governor for one class of people, but the Governor for all colours and classes of the people.

'In faith, believing, I ask on behalf of all my brothers and sisters: "Art thou he that cometh – or must we look for another?"'

It was a dazzle of chapel rhetoric, the likes of which Windsor would find quite alien, in its style and in its passion. He answered like a good committee man. 'We shall consider your recommendations,' he said, 'and report back as soon as possible.'

On Friday, 5 June, Windsor and the Executive Council discussed the Duke's talks with the contractors. He wanted the men to have a midday meal – it had been a major issue in the strike. On 6 June, there was more talk of the need for 'alleviating the condition of coloured workers'. The Duke did not say what he intended. If he was to organize a rise in wages, it would have to be done with the consent of Washington. He could not yet announce it, he thought. He could hint. More, although he seemed certain in all his dis-

173

patches of the racial basis of the riots, he still wanted an inquiry. He had heard the violence of the attacks on Heape's competence. For the sake of Government Hill, someone official and independent should ask and answer the basic questions about the days of breaking.

He discussed with the Executive Council a broadcast he planned to make. He went over the text with them and, finally, they approved it, after long talks. With the Duchess in Baltimore, he lacked the final polishing hand to which he had become accustomed. Its text was settled only hours before he went to the ZNS studios to broadcast. He reported to the islanders that work had been resumed on the Project, that there had been welcome days without violence. 'The community is slowly recovering from the terrible shock of recent events.'

He was conciliatory, this time. He saw the trouble that the curfew must bring. 'On these hot summer nights, it is uncomfortable, especially for the people who live in small houses, to be confined indoors from 8 p.m. and it has been my intention to lift the restrictions imposed by the curfew as soon as this could be done with reasonable safety.' Even the remaining limits on processions and meetings were not extreme. 'This does not mean that meetings cannot be held on private premises, but it does mean that I give the Commissioner of Police complete discretion in controlling assemblies which might give rise to civil disturbance.'

He tried to use the broadcast to reverse the reality he had reported to London and Washington. He talked of his inquiries hampered by 'what may be the work of agitators who are, I believe, in great measure responsible for the mob violence which everyone now so unanimously deplores.' He deplored, also, 'certain actions and statements which have tended to turn what is purely a labour question into an attempt to stir up racial animosity. . . . The subtle efforts of these agitators are directed towards replacing the normal atmosphere of Nassau by strife and bloodshed and by heeding them you are playing into the hands of the enemy. We are all of us members of the British Commonwealth of Nations, whatever our race or creed.'

He did not believe that. He thought it politically wise to talk to the Bahamas in this way. It was arguably the only course open to him, and it shows political sense. By blaming unspecified 'agitators', he at once avoided reminding Bay Street of the racial realities, made it possible that the House of Assembly might in the future agree to reforms, and did not alienate black opinion. It was cleverly done, but he took his line too far. In this speech, it made sense; in the eventual official report of the inquiry into the riots, it did not.

He handed out reprimands, said that the Project with work for 2000 men at 4s a day had seemed 'too good to be true ... yet the advent of your good fortune has been made the occasion of an outburst unprecedented in the history of the Bahamas in our time.' Wages, he said, were 'a matter of high policy, far beyond the power of this Government to control.' They were subject to the prevailing local minimum wage, and the same wage policy had been applied elsewhere – contrary to rumour. But he admitted the need for a midday meal because the work was more arduous than Bahamians were used to doing – Stafford Sands, it seems, began the idea as a device to avoid increasing pay. He noticed that 'the greater part of an unskilled worker's income is spent on food and he will now be able to spend on the support of his family the money he would ordinarily spend on providing a dinner for himself.'

His speech was unexceptionable. It no longer rested the argument on his own authority, but on reason, and the concessions were sensible. It was in the next paragraphs that he went wrong.

He said that 'the possibility of departing in some respect from the local rates of wages is in my mind . . . if the position here enables me to return to Washington to resume my discussions, so abruptly interrupted by the serious news of last Monday's riots, I will make it my business to consult with the Authorities as to these rates of wages and I have good reason to believe I will not return empty-handed.'

He promised 'a close inspection, not by a local committee, but by a commission of one or more persons from outside the colony who will be able to pass impartial and unbiased judgement based on the evidence I know we shall all be willing to give.'

The minor problem was the reference to 'not by a local committee,' which was clearly addressed to the possibility that the House of Assembly, once it reconvened after the election, would devise just such a committee and make fearful trouble with it.

The major problem was the cable from London which arrived when Windsor's speech appeared there in the evening papers. It was marked 'Most Immediate: Private and Personal'. It was from the Secretary of State himself, and he was furious.

'I had assumed,' Moyne wrote, 'that your broadcast would not be delivered until you had received my approval of proposed policy. I was about to telegraph to you in the following terms when I learnt from evening papers that you had already broadcast.' Colonial Office thinking was that no inquiry was needed into the riot, since Windsor himself had so succinctly explained it – in an early cable on 4 June he had said 'strong racial feeling on both sides . . . no evidence that riots were inspired from foreign sources or local Fifth Column. . . .' London also did not want mention of a rise in wages.

Nassau took all the blame for refusing to increase wages on the Project. It is true that American policy was to pay as much as local conditions would allow; which meant paying the prevailing minimum rate in most cases, since Roosevelt had already been criticized in other colonies for paying too high. It is also true that the minimum wage being by law 4s in Nassau, that was what the Bay Street merchants wanted paid on the Project. But Windsor did not. He was the advocate of higher pay against his local advisors and his London bosses.

On 10 June, Windsor replied to Moyne's criticism. He was clearly stung. He had relied, as he did now more and more, on the Americans to provide what he needed – armed men ready to take on police duties, to spare him dealing with a Bahamian force for which he had no great regard. London had done nothing. 'The handling of recent disturbances in Nassau has been greatly a question of timing and psycholoogy,' he cabled back. He justified all he had done, except for the failure to tell Moyne in advance what his broadcast would contain. He said the curfew could not have gone beyond Monday without explanation, and that meant he had to speak on Monday evening. As for the inquiry, 'I must point out,' he wrote, 'that merchants who have suffered financial loss and dominate the House of Assembly have rightly or wrongly aroused in the white population acute criticism of the Acting Governor for lack of precaution and weakness in handling of rioters. Demand for an enquiry is insistent and owing to racial feelings which have been aroused, am certain no unprejudiced board could be appointed locally.'

London still demanded consultation. Moyne agreed Windsor could talk wages in Washington, but tried to limit the increases he could negotiate. For the first time on a social matter, London was actually more conservative than the Nassau Governor. Moyne doubted 'whether such a large flat increase as one shilling a day would be consistent with that principle [i.e. Anglo-American agreement on bases] and it would be preferable that increase should not exceed sixpence a day.'

Windsor's political sense, in retrospect, seems more acute than London's. The objections to the leap of 1s in wages would have been better based on the difficulty of persuading Bay Street to swallow such a rise. Windsor thought he could manage that. Bay Street was frightened, even hysterical, and vindictive, but wages for labourers was not their immediate concern. More than anything they wanted compensation for the damage they had suffered. Windsor could certainly appease the black fury by paying high, and he would certainly have Roosevelt's backing. After the first bright burning of black anger, there was a quick dying away, but Windsor himself seems to have handled his part very neatly. It was what he knew so well from Imperial progresses, from the times in India, in Canada and in Australia, even in Scotland with the unemployed. He would use his presence, his charm, the fact that people often would trust him instinctively, to

177

calm troubled situations and to persuade crowds to leave anger behind. He was good at that special skill.

But he had not been fully tested in the riots. He had returned to find the toughest decisions already made. He had no need even to set policy, except on the concessions that were now to be made. And he defied London. He never did understand that the deference required of him – in 1936 to the new moral standards hanging around monarchy, in 1942 to the professional obligations of a colonial governor – was real and strong and necessary. He was wilful, liable to take initiatives and not be deflected from them, an unpredictable man, whose position demanded what he lacked: a respect for authority.

He did not lack courage. He took his fights, after his Washington trip was completed, to the House of Assembly. He was not always tactful – a king must always be tactful – but he was effective. He stirred real hostility.

Gossip had caches of arms in hidden places on the islands and stories of violence yet to come; the prissy John McAndrew, from his consular office, told Washington all he heard. Worse, on one afternoon, a wife heard from her husband on Eleuthera that a great storm was heading towards Nassau. She began to shutter their shop, and the rest of Bay Street saw her. The woman herself was uncertain of the story, since an over-zealous telephone operator, mindful of what under wartime regulations was information useful to the enemy, broke off the conversation when the weather was mentioned. As she hammered the shutters into place, she heard the sound of the other merchants doing the same. They, though with no better reason than her example, were convinced the rioters were coming back, that they would march on Nassau that night. The town sweltered in its own anxiety.

On 14 June, two weeks after the riot, the Duke was again on his way to Washington. He had reached the Roney Plaza hotel in Miami. Early in the morning, he called Heape to ask what had been happening. It was obvious that he did not think trouble was at an end.

A full record of the conversation survives. This is the voice

178

of Windsor at work, trying to make sense for himself of the Bay Street incidents and worrying that they were not yet over. It also shows how complicated were his attitudes, even when he seemed to have decided on a course of action.

'I've got to the bottom of it,' Heape said. 'I've just been talking with Hayes' – the senior American officer on the Project. 'Can you hear me all right?' Heape launched into his explanation. 'Hayes tells me there were some new men on the job . . . and that they didn't understand that they were paid up until Wednesday only. They get their pay on Saturdays – in other words, they worked five days and they are only paid for three. They are dissatisfied about that,' (the line went obscure for a moment) '. . . tells me that the dissatisfaction is not widespread but there is definitely talk in the town. The American foremen were seen in large numbers with the coloured workers drinking after 12 o'clock last night in the Front Street Pub, one of the coloured pubs. I told Major Hayes I think it's very undesirable.'

'Very undesirable,' Windsor said.

'I think,' said Heape, 'it's getting very definite that a lot of trouble is due to this influence.' Windsor agreed, and asked if the Colonial Secretary thought he had better delay his departure for a while. 'But it's terribly inconvenient,' Windsor said, 'and of course I think it's very bad not to go to Washington, because that's what we said.'

He tried to rally his deputy. 'Now, listen, Heape,' he said. 'Of course you couldn't give them any more wages because it would happen again – it's just the system – but they are so dumb and they will snatch at anything for a complaint.' The Duke was rarely complimentary in private on the subject of black intelligence. 'You should tell,' he suggested, 'you should have it put about that if they do make any disturbance I cannot do anything for them in Washington. That's the line I should take. Be very firm, because any sign of a disturbance at all and then my visit to Washington will be washed out. Do you see?' He wanted 'the police to spread it around, too, and the troops if necessary if any of them come around'.

'What a damn nuisance this is,' he said. He thought about

179

the ill-explained system of when wages were paid on the Project and said: 'It's always these little tiny slips, you see.'

'Yes,' said Heape. 'But I think it's very sinister that it always starts at the Windsor Field, and I'm not at all sure it isn't deliberate.'

Windsor considered, and then launched into another scheme – for the foremen on the base, the Americans, to be given 'such a dickens of a talking to', to be told that the Duke was 'extremely surprised and annoyed to think that the foremen would mix down in Grants Town. You can tell them anything you like and you can tell them the Governor is extremely annoyed. You can say to them that these men must not go down and mingle – in fact, if necessary, they must be put in curfew in the hotel. I told you they are a nasty lot, some of them. . . .' In annoyance, he added, 'These people could be anything, they could be in the pay of anybody. They could be in the pay of labour agitators here, and other people.'

Heape reported that he had been out to the fields with Harold Christie to see the men at lunch. They had complained bitterly about rotten fish in their Friday meal.

'Oh God!' said the Duke.

'Well, naturally I don't believe them,' Heape said, 'and the lunch when we were there was damn good.'

'Well, I know. I have seen it,' the Duke said. 'Of course, I haven't tasted it at all.'

Heape recited the string of complaints from the men – not enough bread, water that made their guts run – and said he had decided not to go so often to the fields, since it was too much like an official looking for complaints. Both turned to the matter of discovering scapegoats, someone to blame. Windsor wanted charges against some of the foremen, 'but it's a frightful thing to do'. When Heape said he had a 'very, very bad charge against one foreman' Windsor said, complacently, 'Oh. That would be marvellous – if you can.'

He would be available, he said, at the British Embassy in Washington if he was needed. 'I do hope,' he said, 'there won't be anything.'

One last message reached him from Nassau, this time from

ExCo's meeting on Wednesday, 17 June. Council were distinctly uneasy about what Windsor might concede during talks in Washington. He was nothing like as hard line as they wanted. 'Council unanimous that in view of Your Royal Highness' broadcast, some increase should be granted,' the cable said. 'Majority desire increase of sixpence only if Your Royal Highness considers that such grant will be regarded as a genuine effort to realize the hope that you would not return home empty-handed. Council are unanimous that they will support any decision that Your Royal Highness reaches.'

Windsor successfully arranged a pay rise – it was not hard to negotiate since the onus was always on Nassau to say what wages were acceptable. He did so by overriding all his advisors, steam-rollering them by the broadcast of which London had so fiercely disapproved. Windsor got one reform at least by exploiting his sheer obstinacy.

The courts – coroner's and criminal – heard the aftermath. There had been deaths: Roy Johnson, shot in the heart when soldiers fired on the crowd; David Smith, shot in the left thigh, who died in hospital of loss of blood while his leg was being amputated; Donald Johnson, shot dead by Clifford Holbert who was defending his father's shop against a crowd of two hundred intent on looting; and Harold McIntosh, who had been halted by British troops, tried to escape, was knocked down and ordered into a truck, was terrified and scrambled round the truck, ran for the steeps of Hawkins Hill, was challenged but kept running, and fell with a bullet in his back.

The courts heard the criminal charges – against 128 men of whom 114 were convicted. The prosecution had terrible difficulties in finding witnesses. Apart from a handful of employees at a single business – City Lumber Yard – the Attorney General complained that 'not a single person on Bay Street has come forward to help the Police in their task'. Neither black nor white would speak against the rioters. The Attorney General gave the reason for himself, without admitting it. 'If a man after years of decent labour could suddenly lose all sense of decency,' he said in court, 'then the

181

citizens of this colony are skating on thin ice which might crack at the slightest provocation.'

In Washington, the Windsors had met again with Herman and Katherine Rogers, those old friends, and those neighbours of Roosevelt. The Rogers were glad to come to Nassau, despite the season, and on the night of Saturday, 27 June, they dined late and strolled out onto the verandah to look down at Nassau. Night skies in the Bahamas have a glorious clearness, as though endless gauze has been drawn away from the familiar northern stars.

On Bay Street, Glen Rogers gave a party. He liked to have people for drinks in his store – Rogers' Junior Shop. They would talk and drink among the bales and boxes of children's clothes and stay until late if they wanted. His last guests cleared the shop at midnight and left him alone. He had things to do.

According to evidence at his trial, he took kerosene and matches and he set fire to Bay Street.

From the high verandah, the Windsors and their guests could see heavy smoke pouring out of Rogers' shop. Down below, the streets were almost deserted. Bars shut at midnight, as a gesture to control of drink after the riots. A couple of drunks lolled, unsteady under the full moon. A policeman went on his patrol.

Flames enveloped Rogers' store and neighbour buildings, almost touching, took the fire from roof to roof. Fire engines began to arrive – the police force did double duty as firemen. There were no sirens for fear of alarming people, only the sound of motors in the night, and the sound of fire.

The Duke and the Duchess ran down the hill into town. The Duke took temporary command of the firemen, frustrated by the ancient engines and the sudden problems. The nearest fire hydrant was too far from Rogers' shop to carry water. One engine clogged with sand and went out of commission; another broke down. By the time the firemen had five or six jets of water trained on the blaze, other buildings had caught. The fire was drifting down Bay Street, inexorably.

The Duke stood down by the engines, soot-blackened and drenched from the spray of the water, directing the volunteer groups who were trying to salvage anything possible from the track of the fire. He seemed what he always should have been: prince–hero, battling odds, silhouetted against rising fire. Merchants could not even retrieve books and records before the flames reached their shops. The George Street Department Store lost everything but one pair of trousers, and saved those only because they had been stolen three hours before the blaze and were later recovered by the police. Fire threatened the cathedral; an anxious dean carried out piles of chalices and records and altar dishes. At five in the morning, a slight shower dampened the blaze and stopped stray sparks from doing worse than catching the roof of the cathedral.

The Duchess made her way to Red Cross headquarters. The fire, as it came up George Street and touched the cathedral, was dangerously close to the Red Cross building. She organized a line of helpers to take out all the bandages, and clothes knitted in the Out Islands and the paraphernalia of Red Cross charity. All the work – all her work – was strewn in piles, safe from the fire.

In dawn light, the Duke had to decide if the contractors from the Project should use dynamite, to stop the fire jumping the next street, Market Street, along Bay. He gave the order. The men from the Project dynamited two buildings, cracked windows streets away, broke up the fabric of nearby buildings. But the fire was contained.

What remained was a Cyclopean landscape – big, square quarry blocks set in soot and water, soldiers guarding the remains. Two hotels had gone, and the island bookstore, and the oldest block on Bay Street, two hundred years old; and the shop where doughnuts were introduced to Nassau – square doughnuts. Most merchants were under-insured, if they were insured at all.

The exception was Glen Rogers. His shop was well covered. He was a Harbor Island man who had made his money in the rum days and come to Nassau to enjoy it. His shop was opened in 1939 – on money from the insurance company's pay-out when a house he owned, out east, had also burned down. On 22 April 1942 Rogers had taken out an extra £1350 insurance on stock and £200 on fixtures – enough to double his protection against fire. It was telling evidence when his case came to court.

The new House of Assembly came roaring back to Nassau, its days of island gala and rum and bribery complete, its seven-year chore performed. Etienne Dupuch of the *Tribune* lost his seat; Bert Cambridge, the black musician, entered the house for the first time.

The Dupuch defeat had been expected. Bay Street had marshalled all its forces against him. Local politicans led by Stafford Sands, Asa Pritchard, Percy Christie, the Bethell brothers, all deserted their own island constituencies and went south to Inagua on the yachts *Content* and *Niya*, banners flying. Their slogan was 'Vote for Bethell, the Precious Jewel'. They talked of the land of milk and honey in Nassau, all the riches of the town. They excited the islanders hugely, and Peter Bethell was elected virtually by acclamation. But the excitement did not stop with the voting. When the time came for the yachts to leave, droves of men and women tried to force their way on board, thinking they had been promised free passage out of Inagua. They reckoned Bethell owed them that favour: elections, while corrupt, ran on a strict honour system which made sure the candidate paid up. Most, but not all, the islanders were put ashore with little ceremony, but the crew of the yachts could not deal with their luggage. *Content* and *Niya* sailed into Nassau harbour, groaning under the weight of boxes and carpet bags and stray, ancient suitcases.

Early in the new House, the white merchants tried to unseat two black Members – Bert Cambridge and Milo Butler. To be an MHA required property and £200 in cash or collateral. Butler, the merchant, certainly had that. Cambridge, the musician, was more vulnerable.

'When they found I was too vocal, and opposing the powers-that-be on legislation that was not in the best interests of the place as a whole – that was when they took me before the qualifications committee,' Cambridge remembers. 'I gave them a lot of trouble. Stafford Sands would not support a motion for the secret ballot on the Out Islands – until the islanders requested it. Now, I had an old typewriter, and I typed out seventy-one petitions and sent them to influential people in the various districts and got back fifty-nine. The people had spoken, and I had challenged Mr Sands. It was only a couple of days later that the Secretary of the House told me to get my affairs in order because the qualifications committee was after me.'

Bert Cambridge considered his bank account, listed his engagements, and decided he needed help. He went to the lawyer A. F. Adderley, who had sponsored him before.

'It's my understanding that the qualifications committee is getting after me,' he told Adderley. 'And I haven't got £200 in the clear. Now, I'll ask you to lend me £200. I'm not going to spend one penny of it but just to put into my account so that when they come I'll be all right.'

Adderley was brusque at the best of times. Now, he was fierce. 'No,' he said. 'Emphatically.'

Cambridge was shocked. 'But you supported me. . . .'

Adderley shouted Cambridge down, and handed him the rules of the House to read. Cambridge pondered. He had to have £200 – but over and above all encumbrances. A loan from Adderley – or anyone else – would be an encumbrance.

For all Adderley's lofty attitudes to his black brothers, he had no intention of handing Bay Street an easy victory.

'Let's see,' he said. 'When I was to your house recently, I saw a piano. How much did you pay for that piano?'

'£400.'

'I'll put that down for £200. Your front room suite, now, how much did you pay for that?'

When Adderley had finished his sums, Cambridge had something like £2000 in unexpected collateral. 'I tell you,' the lawyer said, 'when that committee comes, you put a bottle of whisky on the table and say, "Gentlemen, have a drink. . . ." '

In the House, Bert Cambridge was always the Honourable Member for the South – he had been elected on a secret ballot, allowed on New Providence for the first time at a general election in 1942. Outside, he was either Bert or Cambridge. Mr Cambridge was not a title whites knew how to use.

He learned some quiet in his time. He still thinks that Bahamians are a peace-loving people. Even after the war, when he had chaired committees and helped find doctors and architects for a new hospital, he stood in the crowd when the Princess Margaret Hospital was opened. He had fought for the scheme, started it and nursed it. 'The powers-that-be invited all their personal friends, but the man who started the matter didn't even have a chair to sit in. I was standing among the crowd. They didn't even invite me to sit down. I tell you, I cried that day.'

Kenneth Solomon took his seat as Speaker of the House in full court dress. He liked the formality. His deputy would be Asa Pritchard, the sharp-tongued merchant who had defeated Roland Symonette for the job.

Windsor had pulled one of his astounding coups. He had taken the leader of the opposition, appointed him to Executive Council and made him *de facto* leader of the Government. Godfrey Higgs, at thirty-three, had suddenly to defend everything that months back he would have vigorously attacked. Bay Street never quite forgave him. He was too young for ExCo, they thought, and Kenneth Solomon, having been removed from ExCo so abruptly, thought it with particular venom. Higgs should not have crossed the lines. The House fumed, and sometimes patronized: Higgs remembers he could get help when he had no supporters simply by appearing 'the poor little bugger, all on his own'.

Windsor needed real authority in the House because he had decided to go on the attack. On 1 September, at that first assembling of the island politicians, he promised again a commission of inquiry, with a suitable legal officer 'who has experience of West Indian conditions and who has, if possible, never held an appointment in the Bahamas.' He called the riot unpardonable, and promised to be ruthless in preventing its recurrence.

And then he said the unsayable, the unthinkable, the unacceptable. 'Island communities,' he told the House in his speech as Governor at the opening, 'must perforce possess a different psychology to that of their continental counterparts in that their comparative isolation deprives them to some degree of the vital contacts which enable them to keep up with the trend of the times with regard to social development and welfare.' The Duke called for 'a drastic change in the psychology, both of the legislators and of the people to whom they are responsible.'

He talked of his 'frustration' – 'a feeling that is shared by many others who are working for the good of the colony.' He wanted new energy among the commissioners for the Out Islands, the local rulers who answered first to the House. He attacked 'the temptation to hold on to an economic system that was once extremely profitable in the hope and expectation that it may one day prove itself again.' He called for an end to self-interest. His frustration, it was clear, came from the fact that the House would not vote the money and pass the bills needed for reform.

The House quivered with a mixture of rage and uncertainty. They formed a committee to consider ways of increasing the colony's revenue, which actually meant ways to avoid the introduction of income tax. And Stafford Sands went for the jugular. If the Governor wished to criticize the House, the House would have its revenge on Government Hill. He called for a select committee of the House on compensation for merchants who had suffered in the riot with the power to call for persons and papers. The issues involved money, he argued, therefore the House had a right to debate them. But the committee would have to decide whether compensation was due. It would have to examine whether the Government could have stopped the riots and, if so, who was to blame.

It was a masterly Sands performance, hitting every demagogic note proper to his audience. 'There have been rumours of agitation due to Fifth Columnists,' he said, 'and other disaffected persons. If the House found that one of the main causes was seditious action, this fact should be made clear

187

in order to remove to some extent the blot on the colony's reputation.'

Higgs pleaded for time, for the House to delay its investigation until the official commission had pronounced. Sands countered scornfully. He said any Royal Commission would whitewash the facts, that Government officers would do anything in their power to avoid being brought to book, that the House wanted to discover skeletons in the closet and secrets hidden behind smug faces. As for progress, he called it like P. T. Barnum's circus trick – the sign among the animals saying 'This Way To The Egress'. Progress could be the death of the House.

Sir Alison Russell, one-time Attorney General and Chief Justice in Uganda and Cyprus, legal advisor to Malta, investigator of disturbances in Northern Rhodesia and a member of the Palestine Partition Committee, was employed to lead the Nassau inquiry at the going rate of £250 plus two guineas a day for subsistence and the use of a police car and chauffeur. He was employed to tell a lie.

In Windsor's dispatches at the time, and in the reports that reached London and Washington from other sources, there was no doubt about the racial basis of the riot. The crowd's chants about Conchy Joes, the fact that only blacks were allowed to pass freely through the town during the riot, all made the point. Nobody doubted it until Sir Alison began his work. But it was not a diplomatic or political explanation. London was already concerned that Americans might see what had happened in the Bahamas – there had also, earlier, been trouble in Bermuda – and decide to put in their own labour force to avoid more trouble. The effect would have been disastrous; it would have put high-paid American workmen on volatile islands alongside a hungry and unemployed local workforce. The Nassau riots had to be seen as something wholly exceptional, a product not of the 'colour line' that so much worried Roosevelt, but of the bizarre local conditions of the islands.

Russell admitted the point to John Dye, the American consul, in a confidential conversation which was reported to

188

Washington in January 1943. 'He stated,' Dye reported, 'that while he was convinced the colour question had much to do with the uprising, he felt he had to avoid any reference, in the matter of real evidence, to that subject.'

It was almost the only gap in Russell's questions. He did not simply ask about particular decisions made by the Commissioner of Police. He asked about the very structure of politics in the Bahamas. He elicited, along with his two white Bahamian assessors, an extraordinary picture of the white mind under siege.

Roland Symonette told the inquiry that 'sound-thinking men' would be discouraged from standing for the House if there were a secret ballot – presumably because they might lose – and that in any case the masses were 'not interested in the affairs of the colony'. Etienne Dupuch, smarting from his defeat in Inagua, said that 'under the present system of open voting it is difficult to get into the House without breaking some of the election laws of the colony and it is almost impossible to stay in the House for a long time without breaking some or all of them.' Mary Moseley could think of only two Out Islands that might be ready for the secret ballot – (white) Harbour Island, and (mainly white) Abaco. And A. F. Adderley insisted that 'the people of the Bahamas would not riot on a question of colour. There are differences but no hostile feeling. I deprecate any suggestion that this was a colour riot.'

Some merchants became alarmed at giving evidence, and turned truculent like schoolyard bullies faced with adult authority. They asked for legal opinion on whether they should give answers to questions on politics. They gave evidence in private. They refused to answer. They found themselves claiming that one visit a year to their island constituencies was quite enough, that it was reasonable the islands should almost all be represented by Nassau merchants.

The inquiry also gave a voice to the labourers on the Project. After the official voices and the grand voices, Russell heard Harold Forbes from Andros simply say that he would prefer to record his vote on a piece of paper. Wilfred Forbes from Andros told them he could get better food in Nassau

189

than at home, but if there was no more work he would have to go back. Fritz Austin, labourer, said he was paid 4s a day and he was satisfied – as he had been out of work for nine months before that and he would, he said, do anything to secure employment. He had never done any farming but he would be prepared to go to the Windsor Farm to learn, if his grandmother was agreeable.

Russell was stirring too much for the taste of the House. They wanted cash for the merchants and some formula which would absolve the Bay Street group of a responsibility they half felt. Their own committee on the riots provided them with a marvellous diversionary tactic, and they exploited it.

The committee had the power to call 'for persons and papers'. It had called, and the persons – civil servants of Government Hill – had refused to come.

Specifically, Sands had asked the labour officer Hughes to attend a committee meeting, and Hughes had said he did not think he would need an official summons. Hughes talked to Heape, who scented an issue of protocol, and wanted time to ask the opinion of the Secretary of State for the Colonies. Heape wrote to Sands and said the Duke would prefer not to compel any civil servants to talk to the House until Alison Russell's work was completed. Sands asked on whose advice the decision was made but Windsor told him, in effect (the letter was 'private and personal'), that it was none of his business.

The Duke's position was entirely reasonable. The House wanted to crucify officials and embarrass the official inquiry that they had already contemptuously dismissed. There was no reason why the Governor should cooperate in his own humiliation. Sands, though, was handed a perfect excuse for grand rhetoric. 'Not conducive to the maintenance of those harmonious relations which ought to exist between His Majesty's representatives and the representatives of the people,' he said, and 'an attempt to interfere not only with the rights of the House but with the duties entrusted to your committee.' It was a speech made for parliamentarians to chime 'Shame!' or 'Hear, hear!' on cue. They did.

While the House was still digesting this excellent excuse

for constitutional wrangling, with much consulting of authorities, the Duke sent down Alison Russell's report. Its final terms were unanimous, with the two Bahamian assessors agreeing to the whole text. Some of it was welcome to the House and to Bay Street. The report said the Commissioner of Police had indeed failed to judge the position correctly, especially when the rioters first moved to Bay Street and the police were still lined in Rawson Square. It said the siren should have sounded to summon the Bahamian Defence Force, whatever the risk of alarming the civilian population, and the police should have had more military support. Patrols should have covered Grants Town later in the day. But those tactical criticisms – which did not amount to saying what Bay Street believed, that Government Hill had been soft on the rioters – were not at all the main thrust of the report.

'It is fortunate,' Russell wrote, 'that the disturbances seem to be regarded by all classes with surprise and humiliation.' It would offer a chance of reform. He wanted policy and cash to develop the Out Islands. He wanted laws to allow trade unions, death duties and income tax. He wanted import duties adjusted so that there would be less pressure on the price of essentials. He regretted that so much of the land of New Providence, which might have been farms, had now fallen into the hands of realtors.

It sounded like the basis for the kind of programme Windsor had already discussed. It came just as the House had whipped itself into a frenzy of mistrust and suspicion and downright hatred of Government Hill. The Duke of Windsor, Governor, would need all his determination.

Moral feeling ran high after the riot. In August, with no tourists and no new vulgarians, the police and the Chamber of Commerce asked ladies to wear shorts no more than two inches above the knee, to wear no halter which 'exposed the back to any considerable extent' and to wear no 'inflammatory' bathing costumes in town. Police constables threatened to travel with foot-rules to enforce the order, and the Commissioner, on reflection, decided the matter was best not pursued.

191

There had been, also, a great ecclesiastical event, and one which the Duke, at least nominally an Anglican, could not avoid. There was a new Bishop of Nassau, a new social figure.

Bishop John Dauglish had returned to London, to the Society for the Propagation of the Gospel. He had once been the chaplain on the battle cruiser *Indomitable,* which had taken George V to Canada, and Wallis Windsor knew he was likely to have an audience with Queen Mary. She took her chance. It seemed time for an attempt at reconciliation; David had done most of his duty, as it turned out, and she had done what she could. She wrote to Queen Mary that Dauglish could give an account of David's work in the Bahamas, since Wallis feared the Queen might lack such news; and she wrote with great dignity that she regretted being the cause of separation between mother and son. Her letter had a proper patriotic tone, and much grace.

No direct answer came, but Wallis Windsor had expected none. Dauglish did see Queen Mary; she did discover the news of the islands; and weeks later the Queen shocked Windsor by including in a letter, 'I send a kind message to your wife.'

It was fifteen years before the Duchess told him what she had done, and why the flinty Queen Mary, most deeply hurt by the betrayal of duty at the abdication, had softened for a moment towards her old *bête noire.*

The new Bishop came with eight wirehair terriers, and the kind of American pedigree which delighted the complex Baltimore snobbery of Wallis Windsor. He was rich, although wedded to poverty as a monk; and he was linked by marriage or acquaintance to several of the more splendid American residents. He had even a family link with the Earl of Sandwich. He presided over a diocese notorious throughout the Church of England for its saints and incense, its ritual and manners.

The heady mixture of theatrical liturgy and social style — so different from the stone-faced Archbishop Lang who had fretted over Windsor's loss of faith — brought Windsor to church more in Nassau than at other times of his life. He was a notorious agnostic, unwilling to admit the almost mystical link between Church and King which he had been meant to represent in his brief months on the throne. But in Nassau he was diverted at the very least by religious practice, by the Spanish gilt and the wonderful candles and the ebullient slogans. 'Exalting the Divine,' was written over one church, 'since 1929.' 'I think,' one local priest says, 'the Duke really rather enjoyed it.'

By summer's end the troops had settled. The streets were full of uniforms, Royal Air Force men and soldiers, often using the bars and the surreys that the tourists had now deserted. Hot summer and a flood of unattached males created predictable problems: with drink, so that the more notorious cafés were made to shut at 10.30 and lost their liquor licences 'with a view to reducing crime among military forces and maintaining a high standard of fitness and morale among the troops stationed in the colony'; and with venereal disease, so that the police were under constant pressure to sweep the more obvious ladies from the main streets. Nassau had become a garrison town.

Airmen trained in the Bahamas because the weather was perfect. Not a flying day was lost. Conditions proved too perfect in practice: airmen lost over the Ruhr on a smoky, smoggy night, with a load of bombs, were ill prepared by their flights over calm water through clear air. Nassau also acted as a staging post for transport command, taking planes newly built in California and delivering them to Accra on the Gold Coast, from where other units could take them to active service in North Africa. Neither the men training nor the men flying had an over-strenuous schedule. Only officers went to the yacht clubs; the hotels had, for the most part, been converted already to barracks; for most other ranks, social life had to be created out of anything available. A horde of healthy, unattached young men invaded every level of social life. Bahamian matrons fell for dashing officers. Girls from over the hill fell for airmen. Blue-blond British was added to the Bahamian gene pool. The white Bahamian euphemism was 'going wild in the bush'.

193

For a terrible brief moment in May 1942 it had seemed that even cinemas might have to close because of the war, and the aircrews would have nothing official in their lives except work, sun and sea. But John Dye at the consulate told Washington: 'The movies are the only form of evening amusement left in Nassau and are really necessary. This will be especially true when the thousands of young American and British air trainees arrive in the near future.' The protests worked, and the supply of movies was saved – half for Bay Street, half, with 'all coloured cast', for over the hill.

The Forces were the making of Wallis Windsor. 'I never worked so hard,' she said. 'I never felt better used.' She had taken her duties as Governor's wife seriously – run the Red Cross, been titular head of the Dundas Civic Centre which trained domestic servants, graced the proper dances and cocktail parties for war work. Sometimes, the ladies of the town detected a certain distance: she belonged, with enthusiasm, to the Nassau Garden Club, a snobbish enclave, and she would sometimes submit arrangements of exquisite flowers that had been done by ADCs. She would see that her contribution was made, but not always make it herself.

That sense of remoteness had begun to crumble with the infant welfare clinics. She was not especially talented with children, but she divided up her mornings between the clinics and the Red Cross and she made sure that both worked – paying out of her own pocket, if necessary. She was still essentially an administrator – which was her single most useful contribution, since dozens of other women could do the work, but she was peculiarly well placed to animate it. Yet at the infant welfare clinics, she stayed to see the children, not just the books. A sense of caring had been obviously stirred in her. Her emotions were engaged. For perhaps the first time in her life, she was allowed to work constructively and to see the product of her work: which was, in part, the survival of children who might not have survived without her. In her class and her time, she could hardly have hoped for such achievement; when the chance was offered, she took it brilliantly.

All this work was a preparation. She founded a canteen

194

for the black members of the Bahamian Defence Force. She would have had no choice but to segregate the canteen, even if her personal inclinations had been for mixing; in the Second World War, both American and British forces were rigorously segregated, to the point of separate regiments and separate shower facilities on active service. It is more to the point to admire Wallis Windsor for seeing the need and filling it.

When the troops came in large numbers, she was ready. The Imperial Order of the Daughters of Empire set up a canteen in the Masonic Building on Bay Street. Wallis Windsor demanded necessities like suits from the British War Relief Society in New York, and she cajoled playing cards and teaspoons and ping-pong balls from them and from anyone else who would give. A dragon lady sat at the canteen door selling tickets between sweeps of ornamental palm; once inside, there were games and bingo and billiards, ping-pong and quiet rooms for reading and writing, weekly dances and occasional movie shows. The Duchess found the girls for the dances, the volunteers to be waitresses, the equipment they all needed. She also played hostess – at cocktail parties for each batch of new arrivals, and at the dances in the evenings. She brought the place to life, turned a barn of good intentions into a lively club.

She had already engineered the conversion of the annex to the Royal Victoria hotel – a wooden building in the high style which once housed the imported hotel staff in the winter season, and now was empty – to a hostel for survivors of shipwreck. She had worked there assiduously, even breaking off from writing letters to friends because another shipload had arrived, weak from the peculiarly vicious exposure of being cast adrift on a sparkling, tropical sea. She now had the hostel, and the Bay Street canteen. But the numbers of troops were growing. She needed still more space.

She persuaded Frederick Sigrist, whose house they had used in the first months in the Bahamas, to give her the shell of the Bahamian Club on West Bay Street, which he had newly bought. It was an ugly, white-stucco building, unprepossessing and deserted; no more tourists came, and its gaming licence had been suspended for the duration of the war. Wallis Windsor took it over. With the help of Lord Nuffield's money she made that, too, into a canteen. Her afternoons were spent being a short-order cook, making bacon and eggs for airmen who could say they had eaten lunch cooked by the Duchess. Military censorship said it was the single most common topic in letters home.

Her work was now hard and gruelling – physically hard, since the Bahamian Club kitchen was badly ventilated and furiously hot. It was a full day, since her administrative chores started in the morning, the canteens absorbed her in the afternoons, the dances might keep her busy in the evening. She had a full mind: she was careful to know the histories of her children in the clinics, her soldiers at the bases. She was beginning to acquire the habit of public speaking, the chores of representing as well as running such a network of good works. She spoke from filing cards propped behind her handbag so that nobody would be quite sure that she was reading. She took the Duke's advice on the fine points of delivery – the grand gestures with the arms, the survival technique of always having the last sentence on each card retyped as the first sentence on the next, to avoid awkward pauses. She claimed her audiences understood her more through telepathy than through her speaking technique. But she had mastered that technique. She was becoming a skilled public person.

The Duke had to accept that her time was public. Sequestered mornings were no longer possible. As she became more and more effective, he had to face his near impotence, unable to persuade or kick the Bay Street Boys into any of the reforms he wanted. His aspect on the golf course in the afternoons was melancholy – that old refrain of 'When I was King . . .' had returned. While the Duchess worked furiously, he had time for bone-fishing trips to Andros, or other amusements. The Duchess seemed to acquire energy from the demands she put on herself, although she was still losing weight and feeling the pain of the stomach ulcer which her Baltimore doctors had wanted to operate on more than a year before. She was working, and her time was full; he felt useless, and his time was hard to fill. They both had reason to feel deserted in exile; they also felt that their lives were growing separate.

Of course, the Duke would accept, tolerate, even encourage whatever made Wallis happy. He always did. His private feelings as he stomped the golf course could be read only in his sad eyes.

The Duke of Windsor had a cause: the rehabilitation of the Out Islands. But every time he came close to forcing change, some miracle distracted the House of Assembly. The miracle of the bases, first, gave employment in Nassau, attracted Out Islanders who could send money home and gave a brief prosperity to the distant islands. The coming of the airmen was a second miracle. It meant economic activity in Nassau almost like a winter season.

His problems in the distant islands started with the commissioners. They were government and law and life and death on their islands – courts, gatherers of taxes and duties, able to decide if public money should be spent on saving a life by sending the sick to doctors and hospital in Nassau. They answered to the House of Assembly, if they answered to anyone. They were corrupt and honest, bright and hopeless. But when they were a scandal, neither Duke nor Government could shift them.

J. Z. Bethell was the Commissioner on San Salvador, the island to the east of the archipelago where Columbus first landed in the New World. J. Z. Bethell was a problem.

In six months he had raised only two criminal cases although, as the Attorney General noted, 'I doubt whether the people of San Salvador are more law-abiding than elsewhere.' His methods of accounting for customs duties became so bizarre that Clarence Town on San Salvador had to be shut down as a port of entry. As a commissioner his power to intimidate was freely used. An island wife, Amy Gay, wrote to the Secretary of the Board of Agriculture in 1941: 'I have the honour to acknowledge that in the absent [*sic*] of my husband the Commissioner had constantly been visiting our home trying to get me to be his sweetheart and when Mr

Gay returned I related the matter to him and ever since then the Commissioner began to get against my husband and that is what he is doing all through the Island trying to get mens wifes [sic] and young girls to go his way and when you refuse then he gets against you and I myself have no more respect for him than a little play boy.'

Such a man was clearly not the engine of reform on an island. Windsor's problem was how he could be sacked. The corps of colonial civil servants recruited locally was small, and dismissing any one of them, especially on black testimony, was very difficult. In Bethell's case, the Nassau authorities themselves thought he was fiddling the customs books and dropping criminal charges improperly. They also had the evidence of his lechery. The best they could do, astonishingly, was to organize a transfer to some other Bahamian island. It was hard to see which island deserved him, but the Colonial Secretary, for reasons not recorded, thought Andros.

When even the necessary personnel could not easily be shifted, Windsor's frustration is easy to understand. The House of Assembly would only vote money for the islands as a sort of dole. Specific schemes gave a few men money for a while, but nothing fundamental was changed.

He warned the specially assembled commissioners and teachers of the Out Islands that 'unfortunately, the good times have failed, temporarily at any rate, the easy money has vanished and to a great extent the employment it provided.' He talked of drought and hurricane, sparse earth and difficulties with mailboats – all the practical burdens of Out Island life. 'I want you to know,' he said, 'that I do understand your many difficulties and what you are up against; besides which, it will serve to bring out in stark relief some of the long term remedies that will be required and the measures that must be adopted if we are – one and all – determined to create a NEW ORDER for the islands.' (The capital letters are in the official published version of the speech.)

He wanted administrative change – an Out Island commissioner 'to effectively plan and carry out a long term policy of Out Island rehabilitation and development.' The same commissioner would check spending and 'in this way, it is hoped that the legislature can be confidently invited to approve each year in the immediate future of a substantial sum for the rehabilitation of the Out Islands.'

He knew the dangers of his public statements. 'If I have been accused of being too frank in my last public utterances,' he said, 'it is an accusation I in no way resent.' But he was asking active help for a group regarded in Nassau – by blacks and whites alike – as country cousins at best, and idle, drunken, stupid country cousins at worst. The House of Assembly, already full of its constitutional crises and its ancient rights, was in any case in no mood to cede a penny to the Government.

'The House,' Stafford Sands said, 'is expected to write a blank cheque.' Other Members concentrated their attack on what the money already voted had bought by way of public benefit. Alvin Braynen announced that he had been to inspect the Windsor Farm. He said it had raised £20 worth of food for the £3000 the House had invested. 'I joined three games of Whoopee there,' he said, 'and I was fleeced. At least I learned to gamble at Windsor Farm.'

Bay Street took no interest whatsoever in preventing abuses of labour. Even the simple issue of limiting the hours a shop assistant worked was, according to Stafford Sands, a restriction of liberty found 'only in Axis countries and crown colonies'.

The eventual Act on the subject was 'unsatisfactory', Windsor admitted to London, and the Trade Union Bill 'imperfect . . . but [it is] impolitic to introduce any amendments at this stage. . . . Although the Act leaves something to be desired, its enactment has established important principles.' Windsor was over-optimistic. The bill on shop hours cut working hours (excluding mealtimes and breaks) to eight on most weekdays but to eleven on Saturdays. A man could be required to stay on his boss's premises for nine hours a day and twelve on Saturdays, and then, thanks to the Act, he could be required to work indefinite overtime, although at time-and-a-half. Shopkeepers lost little.

As for speculation in land – criticized harshly in Alison Russell's riot inquiry report – the Duke simply brushed it aside and said that he could see nothing wrong. He was not allowed to introduce even the idea of income tax, since the House was set against it and the House alone could change money law. Even on matters like birth control, he procrastinated: 'in view of local opinion in this matter, it is felt that it would not be wise to take any action.'

His frustration promised a painful Christmas.

The Duke and Duchess flew to Miami on a Christmas spending trip. They came unannounced and quietly – the Duke dressed in a manner no colonial governor would usually choose: wide flowered tie, straw hat, country flannels. He was rather between tailors since links with London were impossible. New trousers came from Harris in New York, who was London-trained; his old coats were still good. He got the habit of separate tailors for top and bottom of a suit. The Duchess called it 'Pants Across the Sea'.

Their official reason for the trip was a rest – 'I have,' the Duke said, 'been working pretty hard.' The Duchess had shed six pounds from a frame which rarely carried more than 100 pounds.

There was a period at Palm Beach, but this time it was brief. Wallis Windsor had other plans. They spent time with Herbert Pulitzer, son of the newspaper magnate, a one-eyed pilot whose disability had ruled him out of United States forces but whose skills had won him a commission in the RAF. They left for Miami, and the Duchess announced: 'I am going to give them a Christmas party.' She would will a Christmas, full of presents and glitter, for the soldiers and airmen in Nassau. 'I am not giving any presents to friends this year,' she said, 'and we both said we wouldn't give each other any. We have all made a sort of pact that everything should be for the men in the armed forces this Christmas.'

She went to the stores, mobbed by salesgirls and shoppers, looking for Kodak cameras, shaving kits, diaries and billfolds and pipes and rubber-lined beach bags. The search for the pipes took days; on the first expedition, she could only find fifty. She planned a lucky dip for the men; those who pulled pieces of paper from the bran-tub would have presents from the huge tree, and the rest would get razor blades and shaving cream. She ordered eighteen turkeys and twelve hams – 'things you just can't get in Nassau' – and heaped up the front of the car with parcels. She went shopping for the Christmas tree, an eighteen-foot giant; 'I've been telling him he ought to make me a very good price,' she said in earshot of the shopkeeper, 'because it's for soldiers.'

Her best help was the new friendliness between Nassau and the Forces, a sense of settling in. There were dances for the men, night after night, in settings like the Nassau Yacht Club, and the Windsors led and performed. There was an airmen's party for town children on Christmas Eve; 250 were invited and 500 came. Trucks took them out to the air base; they fed hugely, watched Mickey Mouse movies, took home a bottle of Coca-Cola, a half-pint of ice cream, a bag of sweets and a new shilling, all bought by the airmen and aircrew. One corporal sat solemn and straight, a three-year-old black child on his knee, feeding assorted Christmas treats by the spoonful. All the time the child stared into the corporal's eyes, unable to look away from unfamiliar kindness.

The Forces saved the Bahamas. The collapse expected in January 1942 did not occur. A. F. Adderley had told Legislative Council that 'necessary revenue could not be found in the manner in which the colony had been fortunate enough to collect it in the past.' One official had even said 'no rational person could object to income tax'. Now, the Receiver General, the colony's treasurer, announced a £18,000 surplus on the year in place of the £76,000 deficit that the colony had budgeted. The single greatest factor in the change was an improvisation by Stafford Sands, who had suggested the colony overprint its stamps to celebrate the four hundred and fiftieth anniversary of the coming of Columbus, and had raised an extra £30,000 to £40,000. Bay Street's lawyer had delivered the surplus, and the surplus meant Bay Street did not have to consider seriously the list of anathemas like income tax and death duties and labour reform. Windsor now realized that his main bargaining card – the coming crisis – had been taken from him.

The Duke called the bank and demanded: 'What is all this about arresting the Air Vice-Marshal's plane?'

He had been given the startling news that his distinguished house-guest's plane was under armed guard at Oakes Field, and the Air Vice-Marshal himself under orders not to leave the colony. The atmosphere at Government House was understandably strained.

John Gaffney had patiently to explain why the plane was under arrest.

Every person who arrived in the islands – military, civilian, even royal – had to fill out a form for exchange control, declaring how much foreign currency he or she was carrying. Should they buy pounds in Nassau at the bank with any of that cash, the amount would be shown on the form. When they left the colony, every note had to be accounted for.

Gaffney explained patiently: 'You go out from time to time, sir, and you always fill in a declaration of what foreign currency you are carrying.'

'I do?' Windsor sounded uncertain.

Gaffney played carefully on the royal ego. If even His Royal Highness, the Duke of Windsor, Governor of the Bahamas, had to complete the forms, then surely a mere Air Vice-Marshal should not be exempt.

'Absolutely,' said the Duke.

The officer commanding at Oakes Field, who had spent his early morning pink with rage on the doorstep of Gaffney's bank, slowly calmed down. The Air Vice-Marshal retreated from his position of dignity, and his plane was freed.

There were solid reasons for what might otherwise seem a bizarre arrest – a colony's secretary for exchange control arresting the plane of a senior British officer. Nassau had once again become one of the clearing houses for Nazi currency coming from South America. This time, $50,000,000 of US currency in the hands of Axis couriers – a wave of money which could have been disastrous to the delicate balance of trust and bankruptcy on which the British war effort was based – was finding its way north through the best protected channels of all. The British Royal Air Force was flying money for the Nazis.

Planes from transport command left Nassau without official cargo. The point of the flight was to deliver the plane itself for active service in North Africa. Enterprising officers filled the bellies of planes with cut-price alcohol and took off either for Recife in Brazil or for Ascension Island. The cargo was strictly illegal.

At Recife, where drink was expensive, or at Ascension Island, where drink was the only consolation on a ragged Atlantic rock, the RAF aircrew would sell their cargo, usually for American dollars. Those dollar bills were often recycled from occupied Europe, the notes that had been in the bank vaults that the Nazis had stormed in 1940. The airmen either held them, and brought them back to Nassau, which seemed an easy spot to change them for sterling – thus building the active street market in American currency – or took the cash to Accra, where there was a lively market in diamonds, which could be resold in Recife on the return journey. The diamond run changed two batches of Axis currency – the money from Recife going out, the money from Recife on the return journey. In Nassau, some was presented to the bank, and the story of the rum runs and the diamond business began to emerge. More, though, disappeared into the float which hotels and shops were allowed to maintain. It was impossible to check each day how much US currency was circulating in the colony, and a black market was hard to police.

Into that black market the RAF was injecting quantities of the dollar bills that American and British security were desperately trying to corral in South America.

Nancy Oakes, now Nancy de Marigny, lay in a Palm Beach hospital with gangrene of the mouth, preparing for an abortion. She had always been the protected, favoured child, but now, to her loving parents, she seemed more like a victim.

After the marriage, and the uneasy truce at Bar Harbor, the de Marignys had gone to Mexico City. There, Nancy's health had collapsed. She caught typhoid fever, and needed seven blood transfusions. 'She was desperately ill,' Lady Oakes said. 'It was awful.' She had to have parts of her upper jaw and some teeth removed; and over long and painful months, the chronic mouth trouble had turned to trench mouth and then to gangrene. She struggled to what social life she could manage – occasional cocktails, dances, parties – but she felt increasingly gloomy.

In December, she discovered she was pregnant. Her parents were horrified. They bristled with euphemisms. They said Alfred de Marigny should have 'taken more care' of her, although doctors had said they could resume sexual relations. They thought him wholly responsible for the sight of their baby, mouth strapped, smile deadened. They never forgave. Sweet Lady Oakes was still trying to have de Marigny hanged in 1945.

De Marigny took a room in the same suite at the Palm Beach hospital. He needed a tonsil operation. Sir Harry discovered him there and reacted with fury. He bellowed and shouted. De Marigny resented Oakes's intrusion; he was in his own wife's room during daylight hours, and he was not prepared to deal with Sir Harry's tangle of crude, protective emotion toward his daughter. Oakes had threatened to 'kick him out of his room'. De Marigny cancelled his operation and told a doctor he would like to 'crack Sir Harry's head'.

When Nancy left hospital, there was a kind of cold truce. De Marigny could leave his clothes at the Oakeses' house, but not stay there. The Oakeses accepted a dinner invitation from him, but Sir Harry studiously ignored him throughout the meal. Tempers ran high enough for Sir Harry to redraw his will. All of his children would now have to wait for their inheritances. None of them could touch the principal until they were thirty, although they were free to will the whole sum to anyone in the event of their death before that birthday.

Nancy insisted on returning to Nassau, although Lady Oakes was terrified that she would become pregnant again, and knew her daughter still needed two operations to set her mouth right. The separation was cruel for everyone. Alfred de Marigny tried to mend it by seeing Walter Foskett, lawyer to the Oakeses in Palm Beach. Foskett refused to help him to restore relations. Instead, he said he held a letter about de Marigny – written by his ex-wife Ruth. He had not yet shown the letter to Lady Oakes, and he would not release it to de Marigny or to his lawyer, Godfrey Higgs. He simply told de Marigny he was 'a crook, and about to go to jail'.

When the de Marignys returned to Nassau, Alfred tried to discover more. Lady Oakes would send only a brisk acknowledgement to a letter from her son-in-law's lawyer. 'Sir Harry didn't want to carry on any further correspondence because we had done as much as we could for Nancy at that time, and it was then beyond us.' Estrangement now had a heavy tinge of hatred. The Oakeses became convinced that de Marigny was wickedly turning their eldest son Sydney against them. They were furious that de Marigny refused the offer of some property, so distant from Nassau that neither servants nor friends could easily reach it. More, they thought that de Marigny would never amount to anything, and his failure to move in the right circles was best evidence of that.

On 27 March 1943 Oakes accepted a dinner invitation to see the de Marignys after a reception at Government House. Nancy and Alfred had been invited, but they had not gone. Oakes told them they were asses. 'If you don't go out and meet people,' he said, 'you don't get anywhere.' Through the evening Oakes drank heavily. By the time dinner was utterly finished, he was in a state of temper. 'You have written a filthy letter to Lady Oakes,' he said, apparently of de Marigny's attempt to discover precisely what his ex-wife was writing about him. 'Your lawyer has done the same thing, too. And if ever any of you two repeat such things, I will have both of you whipped.' Oakes was beyond control now, a rough man slapping words on the air. 'As far as that girl in the house is concerned' – his Nancy, his beloved Nancy – 'she has caused enough trouble to her mother and I don't want to have anything to do with you.'

Oakes had always thought de Marigny an adventurer. Now he forced his point. 'As far as I'm concerned,' he shouted, 'Nancy's going to get nothing from me at any time. N-o-t-h-i-n-g.'

Days later, de Marigny had a birthday party and invited Nancy's brother, Sydney Oakes. It grew late, and Sydney took to a bed in the guest-room. At four in the morning, the door buckled under strenuous pounding. 'Open the door,' a voice bellowed, 'or I'm going to break it down.' De Marigny opened the door. Sir Harry stood there, his fury absolute. It was as though his children had deserted him to the enemy camp – first Nancy, now Sydney. He would horsewhip de Marigny if he did not leave the Oakes family alone. De Marigny was nothing but a sex maniac. Oakes stormed to the guest-room and bodily heaved Sydney out of bed. 'Get your clothes on,' he shouted, 'and get to hell out of this house.'

The breach seemed almost complete. But Nancy de Marigny did not want to be separated from her parents. She would not consider herself apart from them. 'I wouldn't say that we were cut off,' she said, 'we just never had occasion to see them. There was a misunderstanding between two generations, but it wasn't serious.' Yet she returned a gift of £2000 in war bonds that arrived unheralded in her bank account; it looked too much like charity to poor relations. And she wrote, in the high moral tone of adolescence, to both her parents. If they could not overcome their prejudice against de Marigny and give him the respect and trust he deserved, she could have no love for them and she could accept no help from them. 'I pray God,' she wrote, 'that you may also see the truth and justice of these statements.'

The Windsors clung to privilege, even when they later abandoned duty. The Duke had always wanted Wallis Windsor's letters to be exempt from censorship, just as his were because of his diplomatic status. He called on the American Secretary of State in May 1943. 'He said while it was a very little matter, he would be exceedingly glad if she could be put in his class in this respect. He added that the British Embassy had made an effort to get this done but failed on the presentation that the Duchess did not fall within the purview of the statute on the subject.'

Windsor was turned down without too great embarrassment; his letters continued to sail through the Miami postal censorship office, with strict orders that they go untouched while hers were delayed. He was not told the real reasons why the Duchess of Windsor would continue to be censored. Adolf Berle, coordinator of intelligence, was determined that she should be kept under watch. He wrote:

> I believe that the Duchess of Windsor should emphatically be denied exemption from censorship. Quite aside from the shadowy reports about the activities of this family, it is to be recalled that both the Duke and Duchess of Windsor were in contact with Mr James Mooney of General Motors, who attempted to act as mediator of a negotiated peace in the early winter of 1940; that they have maintained correspondence with Bédaux, now in prison under charges of trading with the enemy and possibly of treasonous correspondence with the enemy; that they have been in constant contact with Axel Wenner-Gren, presently on our blacklist for suspicious activity, etc. The Duke of Windsor has been finding many excuses to attend to 'private business' in the United States, which he is doing at present.

The Windsors had so far fallen from grace that their simplest actions became suspect. The State Department index had a neat card: 'Windsor, Duke of: suspected subversive activities of.' Whether through dogged conviction or sheer insensitivity to the political implications, they would not drop their suspect contacts. Charles Bédaux, for example, who had already caused them enough personal pain through the humiliation of their cancelled tour to America in 1938, was now in Allied custody. He stood accused of exchanging military information about the Persian Gulf for the return of his company's Amsterdam files which had fallen into Nazi hands. It later became clear that he had acted as economic advisor to the German administration in France. Meanwhile, Fern Bédaux, the graceful mid-Western lady to whom Wallis Windsor had felt so close in the days of the Windsor wedding, was at liberty. The Windsors might have fooled themselves that Fern Bédaux was a proper friend for a royal governor and his wife, but only if they had been so stupid that they did not ask how the lady was surviving in occupied

207

Europe. In fact, she was surviving scandalously well. She was running her husband's business for him – not just the French part, which had never been put under direct Nazi control, but also the 'international' companies, which were wholly German.

The Duke could not afford to be sensitive to the chill that official Washington exuded. He was still ambitious to escape the Bahamas, to use the old contacts which had supported and nurtured him during the abdication. He pursued old friends ruthlessly, hoping they could intervene for him. Poor Lord Beaverbrook found himself in the Waldorf Towers, trapped between the Duke and Duchess two floors up and Madame Chiang Kai-shek two floors down. He had no wish to listen to the Duke asking for his support with Churchill, since he was already decided to offer no such thing and he would have been acutely embarrassed to tell the Duke to his face. The only solution was an elaborate game of hide-and-seek. Every time the Duke called, Beaverbrook had 'gone for a walk'. Days of evasion ended with Beaverbrook cracking, and asking his secretary David Farrer to call the Duke's equerry and fix a meeting. Farrer duly called, and the Duke himself answered. Utterly confused, Farrer could only think to say, 'Oh, God!' and slam down the telephone.

That summer, more than 2600 men left the Bahamas for work in the fruit and vegetable fields of Florida. It was Windsor's doing – the product of his negotiations in Washington to find work for the islanders once the Project was complete. It meant wages of two to four times the going rate in Nassau paid to men who had to send a third home for the support of their families, and save another third. It suited everybody, but it had taken hard argument in America. The Miami City Commission, for example, had been violently opposed to bringing Bahamians to Florida. They wanted a government subsidy to American farmers to employ Americans, apparently believing that the free market would then birth, grow and train labourers instantly. Such an American labour force was simply not there to be tapped, and the case against importing labour began to weaken when

Californian farmers were allowed to bring Mexican labour into the USA in the early 1940s. The Duke won his case.

Bahamians had the habit of finding promise in America. Some had slept rough in Central Park and known the Harlem of the 1920s. Some remembered the Flagler days in Florida, when one in five Bahamians was working off the islands. Even in wartime, the fortune-seeking run north to New York could still exert a powerful attraction. A boy called Sidney Poitier, for example, had set out from Cat Island to take his chances in Miami and Manhattan.

The men for Florida were chosen from the registered unemployed. Government refused to allow the American teams any space in the heart of Nassau; they feared the trouble that might follow large crowds assembling there. Instead, they provided a rough examining room outside the main town, with no piped water or lavatory, where the examining doctors from the US public health authorities had to scrub their hands in a basin with a pitcher of rain water. Six American ladies, wives of US employees in Nassau looking for something to fill their time, volunteered to help US Immigration handle the forms and applications for thousands of mostly illiterate labourers. After two weeks they quit. They said they could not stand the lack of toilets and the terrible prevalence of venereal disease among the men. One doctor, with one nurse, struggled on with the examinations and reported of the Bahamians that 'most . . . compare very favourably with the American Negroes of this class.'

The migration brightened the streets. The new money went, in part, on clothes – 'co-respondent shoes and suiting delirious in both colour and price', according to Rosita Forbes. Nassau wages rose slightly and so, observers said, did the rate of drunkenness. The new American consul, Henry M. Wolcott, reported 'a more restless spirit among domestic workers in Nassau and many of those working on the Base'. The deprivations of war were also beginning to cut into life. Food was not plentiful. Gasoline was rationed, and buses simply stopped running for a while, leaving most islanders stranded far from work or shops. Pellagra and other diseases of malnutrition actually became more obvious and more common even as the migration money returned. The rash of petty crime across the island increased. Rationing of food, slowly introduced, became a political point; Asa Pritchard, the white grocer, was put in charge of the system, and black politicians instantly assumed he would weight it to the benefit of whites.

Beneath at least some of the restlessness was the feeling that the American scheme had created a new and privileged group of black labourers. Unlike Flagler's men, these workers had proper contracts, proper agreements, relatively comfortable work camps. Their diet in Nassau was limited by poverty and war; in Florida, they had bacon and egg for breakfast, fruit juices and enriched bread, meat and fresh vegetables. Once they had worked on the bean and sugar cane harvests in Florida, there were special trains to take them north to dig potatoes and cut vegetables in Maryland, Virginia and North Carolina. They were not a second-rate class, as they had been when working on the airfields in the Bahamas, and they had a chance to see a way of life which had been closed to them in the islands. For the first time since Flagler, a large number of black Bahamians were seeing an alternative to the way the Bahamas was run. Simply because they worked together, and moved together, they were insulated from the worst shocks of American racism. It began to seem there really was a promised land. It began to seem that there could be change in the Bahamas.

Summer scalds the islands and leaves tempers raw. Flowers flare out – blazing poinciana trees, suddenly all scarlet and coral-pink; bougainvillaea in a new excess of russet and mauve and red and purple; the yellow puoi, the spikes of yucca. The colours shimmer in a light that becomes lurid with damp and rain and thunder. Summer is claustrophobic and still, except for the balls and forks of lightning. It is the proper, limelight setting for a melodrama.

PART THREE

MURDER

In the morning, mosquitoes teased at the body of Sir Harry Oakes. He slept with the windows and screens open to the sea air, and biting insects came to trouble him. That night, the mosquito net was gone, burned away, hanging charred from the ceiling. The door to the hallway was open, and between hall and room was a trail of soot and flame. The walls were marked with hand prints that seemed to be in blood. The body of Sir Harry Oakes was still.

Someone had taken a blunt instrument with a triangular edge and had brought it down four times on his head, crushing blows that filled his skull with blood. While he was still alive and struggling, someone set fire to his body, doused it and the room in something like gasoline. As he lay dying, the fire took hold. His body was charred and blistered. Feathers from a pillow were caught in the draught of the electric fan at the foot of his bed. The feathers stuck to the sour discharge of his burn blisters.

The body lay like a timber taken from a fire, a blackened thing. The night had been violent – storm, thunder, rain. It was as though some stray force, some lightning bolt, had caught at Harry Oakes and levelled him. A little flame still played on the mattress of his damp bed when the doctors came.

Harold Christie found the body. Christie had slept the night, he said, at Oakes's home at Westbourne. He was a bachelor, who did not need to account too closely for which beds he occupied; when it was convenient, he would spend the night in one of the Oakeses' guest-rooms, which were always ready for such strays. Oakes himself had all his family in the States, in the summer cool of Bar Harbor. Caves Point, his huge house further to the west of Nassau, was not practical for such a time. He preferred the seaside breeze at Westbourne.

Oakes had been on the point of leaving Nassau for Bar Harbor, free at last to spend summer in the comfort of the north, his business affairs organized. Nassau had begun to seem only one of his homes. He had spent so much time in Mexico – looking after little Nancy, arranging the start of Banco Continental, talking investment – that the Bahamas seemed a haven from tax rather than a place to live. He had begun to feel, so he told de Marigny in the days when they were talking, that he was surrounded by sharks, that he could make no proper use of his capital in the islands. Mexico seemed bright and shining, with the promise of oil and profit. He had the political contacts. He had the channel for funds. In the Bahamas, what Harry Oakes did amounted to philanthropy – enjoyable because Oakes liked the immediacy of hard physical work on clearing bush or building roads, but still without a return.

He did not like to be guarded. There were no dogs. The nightwatchmen were off duty. The doors to the whole house were left open and the servants had gone by eleven each evening. Lights burnt late at Westbourne to show that Oakes was staying there. Anyone could have come into the house at any time. Bougainvillaea vines, old and established and knotted, curled up to the first-floor balconies. The doors from balconies to bedrooms were left open. Harry Oakes was supposed to sleep with a pistol, to live in fear; the island rumour had him pursued by ill-used partners from his mining days who wanted revenge. Yet he seemed to use Westbourne with no thought of security. He did not even put a door between himself and the night and the man who killed him.

Christie's story was this: for the morning of 8 July 1943, Oakes had organized a press trip to look at his sheep, newly introduced to the Bahamas and bringing the screw-worm fly and other pests with them. Christie was to accompany the trip. The evening before, Oakes and Christie had played tennis; had taken drinks and dinner with Christie's friend Mrs Henneage, a young woman whose husband was at war,

214

and with a neighbour; had talked a little when the guests had gone, played checkers and then retired to bed. Christie had taken a guest-room which had not been formally prepared; the maid, it seemed, did not know he planned to stay the night. Oakes had gone to bed taking a copy of *Time* magazine.

The night was busy with lightning. Christie said he had woken several times, closed a window against the teeming rain, killed a mosquito that was troubling him. Oakes's room was two doors from the one Christie used — a bathroom and another bedroom were between. Christie heard nothing, he said, except the roar of thunder and the hiss of rain.

He woke and, after a pause, went to wake Oakes for breakfast. The stairs were grimed with soot. There was the spoor of fire on the carpet outside Oakes's room, and marks from hands. Through the door, past an ornate and decorated screen, Christie could see Oakes's body. He thought his friend was still alive. He ran to the bed, took up the head and turned the body, pressed water from a vacuum flask to Oakes's lips, wiped the face of the corpse with a towel. Between Oakes's room and his own, he left splashes and handprints of blood.

Harold Christie held the body, and realized that it was still, and let it gently down onto the pillow. He was wild-eyed. He called for the next-door neighbour, Mrs Kelly, wife of Oakes's business manager. He called Etienne Dupuch to say that Harry was dead. He called Government House.

The Duke and Duchess were still in bed when the amiable Gray Phillips knocked at their door. It was early, far too early for such interruptions. The Duke talked to Phillips in the doorway, and the Duchess, drowsy, heard scattered words and phrases in their talk. She heard the word 'murder'.

The Duke came back to the bed and told her that Sir Harry Oakes had been murdered. She had thought him such a good man, she would say later, and the Duke had admired his pioneer spirit. He had been an ally, a doer of good works, a dinner guest. For the past three years, his life had involved the Windsors, and theirs was tangled with his. He had been sympathetic to German needs, and to the Duke's often re-

215

peated line that peace should be negotiated. He had been a financial engine of the Bahamas, when the Duke needed him. He had also been a founder of Banco Continental, an associate of Wenner-Gren, a breaker of exchange control regulations, a defiant architect of the illegal channels through which the Windsors had passed the $2,500,000 held by Wenner-Gren largely for their benefit. Windsor had been a conspirator in the Mexican business, and Oakes had been a prime mover.

And now Oakes was dead. The press had wind of the story immediately. Etienne Dupuch cabled out the bare details. The Duke imposed censorship too late, in an attempt to give himself time to think. Even the little that Dupuch had sent was enough to whet the appetite of the press. They could imagine a seashore mansion on a tropical island on a stormy night and a brutal intruder who did to death the richest baronet in the British Empire. There was money and mystery, a grief-struck family, a royal governor in charge.

If they asked questions – the right questions – the Windsors' long haul back to respectability was at an end. The chances of lobbying a Beaverbrook for some special, suitable position for the Duke would be over. The story went too far back, had too many roots to be allowed to surface yet: it involved the Bédaux links, the times with Mooney and Wenner-Gren, and all the political mistakes of the Windsors, for Oakes was at least on the fringes of all of those. The Oakes murder meant questions about Oakes's money – where it had gone, how it had gone, who else had been involved in the economic network Wenner-Gren had instigated. The Windsors would at the very least appear greedy and amoral – sending money illegally from a struggling Empire to invest alongside blacklisted neutrals in a country ripe for sabotage. All the half-told stories about treason and risk and possible defections, the determined support for anti-British factions in America, would be out in the open, in the courtroom.

All they had done, and wanted to redeem by their work in the Bahamas, would be on front pages if press or police began to ask the simplest questions about Oakes's money or Oakes's friends.

'For Lady Oakes's sake, I hope it turns out to be murder,' the Duke said in the presence of the first doctor to see the body, Dr Quackenbush. 'For the colony's sake, I hope it is suicide.' Quackenbush said he first thought suicide was possible – if the holes in the skull were caused by gunshot wounds. But probes through the bone showed that there were no bullets. No man could fracture his own skull with a blunt instrument in four different places. Quackenbush's comforting theory that the ineffective fire might have been a device to make suicide look like murder – he never explained why – was very soon exploded. Harold Christie telephoned Walter Foskett, the Oakeses' lawyer in Palm Beach, and told him only that Sir Harry had died. There was a pitiful, general wish that the death should never have happened, that body and blood and ash could be explained away. Only in official channels did the euphemisms die down. Heape, the Colonial Secretary, called Lord Halifax in Washington to say that Oakes had been 'killed'. He wanted help in allowing Foskett to travel to the Bahamas without a passport.

The wild rumours began as soon as news of the death spread across the island, phone call by phone call. The black population mourned Oakes sincerely. Unlike most charitable gentlemen, he made sense – he would buy the land of a hungry widow and lease it back for nothing, so that she could farm; and he would pay labourers on the night so that they went home with food for their families. He liked to run bulldozers, to slash at undergrowth, to work alongside the men. He lacked the spurious polish of the Nassau bourgeoisie. But the whites had no reason to love him. He was coarse and vulgar and his great wealth and his crassness made him both inescapable and a pain to the delicate sensibilities of the white rulers. Nassau held many people who might have considered the murder of Sir Harry Oakes.

Only one white man professed great regard for Oakes in public, in those first days. 'In addition to being one of my best friends,' Harold Christie said, 'he was also my best client. He purchased more property from me than any other six persons.'

There were a dozen spites and grudges which could, in some humid and stagnant night, have ended in killing. The islands had so much to hide – dubious financial deals, a political morality which had allowed Wenner-Gren free rein, the defeatists and collaborationists, the legacy of rum-running and drug-dealing, the half-century in which the islands had lived on the lam.

It became clear, as the details were added to the rumour, that Oakes had died around three on a stormy morning. He had been killed deliberately – not in a sudden passion, not as the result of an argument gone wrong – since the murderer must have entered the house with the weapon ready. No instrument able to inflict those strange triangular wounds was found in the house, although there was a pile of balustrades outside. Whoever entered expected either to face Sir Harry's violence – Sir Harry, while strong, was sixty-eight – or else to do him violence; and the weight and power of the weapon ruled out a subtle defence or a warning. Sir Harry had been killed with malice aforethought.

It could have been some Canadian prospector, or some Australian, from the days before Oakes was rich; someone crossed by Oakes, and turned jealous and vengeful. There was talk of a man seen on Rawson Square who had asked in rough accents where he could find the bastard Oakes. Yet anyone with an ancient grudge would have had to struggle south through wartime controls on cash and travel, to pass through immigration not only on entering the Bahamas, but also on leaving the United States; or else, if he came illegally, to risk crossing from America in the early weeks of the worst storm season and in defiance of submarine attacks. Nobody could say why a grudge should have flared up into murder so suddenly that Oakes had to be killed in July 1943 and at no other time.

There was talk of Mafia involvement, that the body was burned and feathered as a warning to other people with power in the Bahamas – perhaps even the Duke and Duchess. Meyer Lansky's Hotel Nacional in Havana was running into trouble because of the uncertain position of Batista, the Cuban dictator; Lansky might have wanted to expand into the Bahamas for his gaming. He was certainly known to several senior Bahamians – Harold Christie among them – from the rum-running days in Nassau. Almost thirty years later, informants did come forward to say that Lansky had ordered Oakes's death. But they muddled their story. They thought Oakes sat on Executive Council, which would have considered applications for gaming licences; he did not. He sat only on the Legislative Council, which was not nearly so important. The same informants muddled details of Harold Christie's movements on the night of the murder. And their story did not make sense. The law had been changed in the Bahamas to allow gaming in 1939, but all licences were suspended after America entered the war. No further applications were made until 1945, and the best evidence is that Lansky did not consider the Bahamas for his base until 1946. Batista was by that time re-established in Havana, and Lansky's need was not pressing. Without tourists, gaming was illegal; the law forbade Bahamas residents to gamble. Tourists could not return until the war ended. Why should Lansky have felt that the issue was so urgent that Oakes had to be killed? If it was indeed a Mob killing – which depends on everybody knowing who pulled the trigger or threw the knife, so that the killing conveys the right message – why did it take thirty years for the story to surface at all? It should have been in the interests of the Mob to have it widely and immediately known that they had the power to kill the richest baronet in the British Empire if they wanted. The story made more sense in the 1960s, when British investigators were trying to unravel the corruption surrounding casino gambling in the Bahamas. Then, it was useful for Lansky's men to claim credit for a spectacular, brutal killing. It reinforced their authority at a time when their associates were under close scrutiny. The 'confessions' were actually a warning.

Yet on that first morning after Oakes's death, people wondered about the Mafia – about the past of the islands, about how it could return to haunt them.

There were rumours, also, of a voodoo killing. Before

photographs of the body were ever released, it was whispered that Oakes had been castrated. It was said that some black man had taken ritual revenge for Oakes's seduction of his woman. When Evalyn Walsh Maclean, one of the richest women in the world and the owner of the cursed Hope Diamond, became fascinated by the mystery, she laid out thousands of dollars on an investigation and was presented with the voodoo theory.

There are stronger rumours of a white man's jealousy. Some said a husband returned early from a fishing trip and found his wife with Oakes; that she had jumped from the house balcony and escaped; that the husband, with Harold Christie's help, had beaten Oakes as a warning, and had gone too far. The fire had been the product of panic.

The stories were cruel speculation. Most of them involved Christie – either as participant or as witness to the actual killing. Christie was assumed by many islanders to have had a hand in the murder. Their feelings were confirmed when other murders followed, over the years, as those who came too close to the truth simply died. A groundsman at Lyford Cay, who claimed to have seen a boat come ashore that evening, was found dead; a woman from Washington who talked indiscreetly of her theories was found at the bottom of a well; Harold Christie's own secretary was murdered. Asking about the Oakes murder meant asking about the islands – the tangle of intrigue and corruption and scandal. It was clear on that first morning that even the most seemingly hysterical and unreasonable theories about the death could not be discounted. Nassau politicians did know the Mob well. The islands had been a centre for rum-running and drug-smuggling – even into 1941, as we shall see. Nazi money did run through Nassau. Political leanings that were close to treason were openly discussed, in a British colony, while Britain was at war.

Almost the most extraordinary fact about the Oakes murder is this: that none of the theories, from death by obeah to death at the orders of Meyer Lansky, could be discounted. They all seem plausible in islands with a history of living at right angles to the law.

Windsor banned reporting of the murder too late, but he did so as a reflex action. He had banned stories from the dance of Sally Rand to the memorial service for the Duke of Kent, his brother, killed in an air crash – the latter on the grounds that if the Germans knew he was to be at the cathedral at a certain time, they might somehow contrive to bomb the service. His actions were resisted by Etienne Dupuch, but not felt outrageous by others in Nassau. They were used to threatening to expel foreigners who criticized the islands in any way, to managing news.

Windsor's real mistake, made later that morning, was a phone call. He rang Edward L. Melchen of the Miami police force and told him Oakes had died 'under extraordinary circumstances'. He said it was 'very, very urgent' and asked if any rule would prevent Melchen 'and one or two of his men' from coming to Nassau for a 'special investigation'. The twelve o'clock Pan Am plane would be held for Melchen and his colleagues.

Later, that phone call was made to seem extraordinarily sinister. It was certainly a terrible failure of judgement, but it is consistent with Windsor's earlier attitudes and conduct. He would not call Scotland Yard. Temperamentally, he had come to rely on American help – Roosevelt's cavalry and military police during the riots, for example; and, besides, transport problems were such that a London detective would have taken days or possibly weeks to reach Nassau. The Duke, in any case, had no high regard for Scotland Yard; he had sent his own bodyguard, Sergeant Harry Holder, home to Britain a year before without giving any reason, and he chose not to replace him from London. He should have sent for the FBI, given all the circumstances, since they were the most accessible national police force; there is no evidence on how much he knew of the Bureau's interest in his activities, and the file they kept on his contacts. But he chose to call the one American policeman he knew, who had acted on occasions as his bodyguard in Miami. Humidity was blotting away any possible clues, fingerprints and footprints, and he needed help urgently. He snatched at Melchen.

He could not have done much worse. Miami police had

been under investigation for several years. They were accused of excessive tolerance to gaming, and high-handed, brutal tactics with suspects in custody. Their reputation was very low. Melchen arrived with a fingerprint expert called Barker – a motorcycle officer who spent five months in the Bureau of Criminal Investigation as a clerk, was appointed its superintendent for want of other candidates, and was busted to the ranks in 1939 for insubordination. Worse, Windsor decided to take personal charge of the investigation, to make it a matter of his ego and his reputation. His only professional helpers would be Melchen and Barker. He discounted the local police. He thought they did not have the proper fingerprint equipment – in fact, the local RAF station did – and he thought them pompous and ineffectual; he still remembered the performance during the riot, the failure of toughness in his view, and he thought the force altogether too black.

He wanted a quick solution. Melchen and Barker understood the urgency. They had their ways of rushing to an arrest.

The room had been absurdly tousled by hurried policemen, scratching for clues. Nobody seemed to find it strange that there were no fingerprints of either Oakes or Christie in the room – although Christie said he had sat for a while with Oakes the night before, and that he had tried to give water to the body. The bloody handprints, rusting now, at the height of a man standing, were neither measured nor checked. There was no precision. Instead, there were the general outlines of the crime. There were firemarks in the hall, as though fire had dripped down the stairway and the stairwell. There were bloodmarks on the door to the room where Christie said he had slept. That bed was rumpled, but not deeply – as though a man had lain there briefly, rather than spent the disturbed night that Christie reported.

Christie insisted he had slept at Westbourne. From the start, his claim was mystifying. He must have slept through the murder of his best friend; through the savage beating, the attempts to set fire to the hallway – outside Christie's room as well as Oakes's; and what seemed to have been a struggle on the stairway. Although he said he had been restive, he had heard nobody pass his door, much less, as the handprints suggested, try the handle of his door. He could not be sure if the doors that led from his room into Oakes's bedroom – through two other rooms – were shut or not; since he had suffered from the mosquitoes on previous nights, and since Oakes would not sleep behind a screen to keep the insects out, Christie supposed that the doors must have been shut. Summer storms do have a violence which can blot out noise and light, but still Christie's story seemed bizarre.

Because he was a local grandee, a member of Executive Council and a friend of Windsor's, nobody wanted to say he was lying. But the evidence grew. The single most damning statement came from Captain Sears of the police force – the same Captain Sears whose gun had caused so much trouble during the riot. Sears said flatly that he had seen Christie in a station wagon driving along Bay Street that night.

Christie's lies complicated the issues terribly. It was hard to see why a man should insist that he had been on the scene of a crime if he had not. Oakes was such a friend of Christie's, and such a source of income; there had even been talk, which Christie encouraged, that Oakes wanted him to quit the real estate business and manage the Oakes fortune. It seemed unthinkable that Christie should be connected with the crime. It seemed bizarre that he should risk such a connection.

The house was open, the way from the road and from the sea was unobserved. Marks of a small craft on the beach by the Westbourne jetty were allegedly found that morning; but they were not analysed or reported. Policemen trampled the stairs until there was no hope of discovering sand or mud or wet footprints from the night before. On such a foul night, anyone entering from outside must have left tracks of some sort. If they did, they were obscured by the well-meaning police. Even the time of death was in question, since a little fire was still smouldering when the first doctor saw the body. A line of blood across Sir Harry's face ran distinctly from ear to nose, yet the body had been found, Christie said,

223

facing upwards. It made no sense. The body must have lain face down after the blows were struck. Even Christie wiping the face in his little act of mercy could not obscure that fact.

Into this chaos came Melchen and Barker. They added their own complications: although the only point of bringing Barker was his expertise in fingerprinting, he had amazingly forgotten his fingerprint camera. He seemed assiduous in his examination of the room, but confusion and humidity would have made it hard for him to discover much. He did not claim to have found – and identified – any particular fingerprints.

Early in the investigations, Melchen and Barker had been told the story of Nancy Oakes and Alfred de Marigny. De Marigny was the outsider, the trouble-maker, and the policemen seem to have liked the idea of him.

De Marigny had heard the story of Oakes's death in garbled form from J. H. Anderson, that pillar of the Bahamas General Trust and bagman for Axel Wenner-Gren. He hardly believed it. He was not even sure which house Oakes was using, but he suggested that Anderson might like to come with him to Westbourne, which seemed a likely starting place. The knot of police cars around the house showed that he was right. Mrs Kelly told him what had happened, and he said only: 'This is terrible. I think I'm going to be ill.' He tried to offer friendly help, as a member of the family. He said he would contact Walter Foskett in Palm Beach, would contact the Governor for help in flying the body to Bar Harbor. He spoke briefly with Lady Oakes when she called Nassau that afternoon, mainly to talk with Harold Christie.

That evening, Colonel Erskine Lindop, Commissioner of Police, called at de Marigny's house on Victoria Avenue and asked him to return to Westbourne. Melchen and Barker this time wanted to make a body examination of de Marigny – moustache, beard, hands, forearms; they peered at the hair with the help of a small standing light, and later with a flashlamp. They were looking for evidence of burning – marks which might suggest a man had been in Oakes's room when the fire was started. After ten minutes' rudimentary inspection, they challenged de Marigny: they had found

224

burning – could he account for it? They returned to Victoria Avenue with him and searched his wardrobe, asking about his laundry, checking shirts and ties. The police left a rather reluctant Lieutenant Douglas at the house to keep an eye on de Marigny. Douglas complained he had lost his night off, and considered the fuss was only because 'Sir Harry has plenty of money. If it was some poor coloured fellow in Grants Town, I just would be asked to go and take information about it and that's all there would be to it.'

Inevitably next morning, de Marigny had to go again to Westbourne. He walked on the beach with Douglas, among the stinging sandflies, to stand away from the confusion in the house. He wondered out loud if the police had yet found the weapon which killed Sir Harry and if the case could continue if it were not found. He chatted about circumstantial evidence and said in French law it was not enough to convict a man. He thought he was making casual, if macabre, conversation. The police thought he was giving a voice to his fears.

Melchen asked to see him. At first, he was gentle and insinuating. He wanted to know if Harold Christie had been in debt to Oakes, or held some grudge against him. De Marigny said Christie was a friend of his and he had no intention of answering Melchen's question. Melchen said that he knew de Marigny had dinner guests the night of the murder, and that he had driven them home close to Westbourne, close to the time the doctors had fixed for Sir Harry's death. 'Did you see any light at Westbourne last night?' he asked. 'Did you see any cars?'

His tone changed abruptly. 'Are you sure you didn't come to Westbourne last night?' he asked. He stabbed his finger at de Marigny. 'Didn't you want to get quits with Sir Harry and came here to see him and had an argument with him and hit him?'

De Marigny denied it. He said, reasonably, that he would pay calls on Sir Harry during daylight hours, if at all. He could have added that he would have been taking a terrible risk in walking unannounced into Westbourne with intent to murder: anybody might be staying there overnight besides

225

Oakes. Melchen began to menace, to bully. He told de Marigny there were witnesses who had seen him walk into Westbourne in the early morning. De Marigny said, with considerable dignity, 'I defy you or anybody in Nassau to say any such thing.'

Melchen asked de Marigny to pour him a glass of water. At the time, that did not seem significant.

That afternoon, the Duke of Windsor went to Westbourne. He spent two hours in private conversation with Barker. Immediately after their talk, Barker ordered the arrest of Alfred de Marigny. He was charged with the murder of Sir Harry Oakes.

Melchen wanted a private talk with de Marigny, he said. Policeman and suspect went into the western drawing-room of the house. Melchen asked if de Marigny had anything more to say, but started speaking himself before de Marigny could make any proper reply. 'I want to warn you about one thing,' Melchen said. 'In this case, nobody is too big or too small to be arrested. Even after we've gone away, we'll come back and keep investigating the case.' It was the start of a classic third-degree interrogation – making the suspect feel there is no escape, that his pursuers are relentless, that somehow they know such things as he has hidden even from himself. It was the way Melchen and Barker were used to making a case stick; it was Miami police procedure, long before the Miranda case gave suspects in American police custody some limited rights.

But it went wrong. 'When Barker said to our police, "Arrest de Marigny", they arrested him,' Eugene Dupuch remembers from covering the trial. 'Melchen and Barker said to themselves, "Now we'll get the true story." But Major Pemberton of the Bahamas police said: "Oh no, you don't. You've told us to arrest the man and now you can't ask him a single question. You have to caution him and he is entitled to keep quiet." '

At 6.30 Colonel Erskine Lindop told the press de Marigny was under arrest. Barker and Melchen did not have the confession they expected, or the chance to win one. They barely had evidence that de Marigny had been near Westbourne, let alone inside the house. They had the town talk about de Marigny and his strained relations with Oakes. They had nothing else. Their case was still to make.

Official London was not happy. 'The Governor is at some pains to explain why he took the rather unusual step of calling in men from outside, which I must confess I don't very much like,' the Colonial Office noted on the file. 'But in the circumstances, I would not rush to judgement.'

Windsor's first cables to London reported the death 'under circumstances which are not yet known. Hope to obtain expert advice of Chief of Miami detectives immediately to assist local police.' The Colonial Office was embarrassed by Oakes. His baronetcy was for services rendered in London – the financing of a hospital – and not in the Bahamas. The Secretary of State first drafted a message of condolence to Lady Oakes, then took advice on Oakes's career and decided to send none at all.

Windsor justified the invitation to Melchen 'who,' he cabled, 'has been known to me for three years.' He said that Erskine Lindop, Commissioner of Police, had agreed since his 'local police force lacks detectives with the requisite experience and equipment for investigating the death of a person possessing such widespread international business interests.'

He reported de Marigny's arrest and a day later asked again for some official message of condolence from London for Lady Oakes. And again, London refused.

If de Marigny had been tried in July, his own counsel Godfrey Higgs believes that he would have been hanged. 'Strung up in the streets, practically,' he says, 'the feeling ran so high.' He seemed noisy and flamboyant and a braggart – Higgs had once had to put him out of his club – and the marriage had left the town furious at him rather than at Nancy Oakes. He made an excellent scapegoat.

His first nights in jail were restless and troubled. The fact was reported and Nassau deduced a bad conscience. Actually, the roaches of Nassau jail were hardly conducive to a

227

good night's sleep. In the little fevers that brewed around the case, it seemed significant that Stafford Sands came to visit de Marigny and then withdrew from the case. It was not. Godfrey Higgs had always been de Marigny's lawyer, and would defend him at his trial; the only reason that Higgs was not present after the arrest was the breakdown of the train on which he was travelling through Florida. He was left sweltering on the track, utterly out of touch with the world, hoping desperately for the return of movement and air-conditioning.

But 'Nassau was a very moral and proper little place', as Higgs said, and the prospect of a wicked man being punished was exciting. The politics were already complex. Much of the Crown case would be entrusted to A. F. Adderley, a man the Duke refused to tolerate on ExCo; the defence would be led by Godfrey Higgs, leader of the Government in the House of Assembly and a member of the Duke's inner councils. The Duke was clearly disturbed by the sense of rot that came from the case, and the political troubles that might follow it. 'The whole circumstances of the case are sordid beyond description,' he wrote, 'and I will be glad when the trial is over and done with.' It was, he said, 'no ordinary crime'. He sensed the partisan divisions in the town. 'The older and more conservative elements and the whole Negro population suspect de Marigny's guilt,' he wrote. 'On the other hand de Marigny, who is a despicable character and has the worst possible record, morally and financially, since his adolescence, has insidiously bought his way with his ex-wife's money into the leadership of a quite influential, fast and depraved set of the younger generation, born of bootlegging days, and for whom they have an admiration bordering on hero worship.'

London took advice and agreed that 'in view of the sordid circumstances of which you have told me, you are wise in arranging to be away from the Colony at the time when the accused, if committed for trial, will appear before the Supreme Court.'

If only it could be so simple for the Windsors, if only they could simply be away. Yet if for any reason the proper, selected villain, de Marigny, failed to hang, there would still be the questions.

Nancy de Marigny heard of her father's death on 8 July. She had been in America escaping the heat of Nassau; the doctors had ordered her north. She wanted to know more than the speculation of the newspapers, and she reckoned her best chance was to go to her mother at Bar Harbor. On her way, she called Barker. He told her there would be no question who the guilty party was. He offered telephone numbers – office and home – where she could contact him if she wanted to know more when she passed through Miami.

She was tempted by the offer, but she still wanted to go to Bar Harbor first. There, she found Melchen and Barker already installed. Lady Oakes had gone straight to bed after her husband's funeral. Barker and Melchen still insisted on telling their story. Nancy was told to leave the room.

When she returned, Lady Oakes had moved from the exhaustion of grief to something close to hysteria. The policemen were told to repeat their story; Lady Oakes wanted to be sure that Nancy heard it. Melchen and Barker said the killer had found a stick from a pile of balustrades, had climbed the outside stairs to Oakes's bedroom and struck him down. While he was still unconscious, the killer doused Sir Harry with insecticide and set the bed on fire. The flames must have revived Sir Harry, the policemen said. He tried to fight off his attacker.

Lady Oakes could take no more. With a rare tact, the police left the room with Nancy. Their brutal recital continued.

They told her that Sir Harry must have been in terrible agony, that he had finally been overcome, struck again on the head and the fire started a second time. In the struggle, the ornate screen in the bedroom must have been knocked over; the killer had replaced it to mask the fire from the roadway. They said they had no doubt that Alfred de Marigny was the killer.

Barker added that he had found fingerprints and handprints on the screen. At best, de Marigny had been there

229

when the crime was committed. More likely, he did it himself.

Melchen was startled. It was the first time his colleague had mentioned these fingerprints, so essential to making a rather weak and circumstantial case conclusive. In a two-day journey from Nassau to Bar Harbor, he had not even mentioned the recovery of a single decent print of anyone.

The terrible and graphic account of Oakes's death stayed with Lady Oakes, and with Nancy. It was enough to turn the mind of any listener against any suspect. The police were asking the Oakes family about de Marigny's possible motives, about curious things he might have said or done which would bear sinister construction; but they asked the questions only after they had told their horror story and promised they could prove that de Marigny was the killer. It was clearly a highly prejudicial and improper form of questioning – Miami procedure, perhaps. It almost seemed that Barker might have some other motive for the story and his casual offer of a home telephone number so that Nancy could contact him in Miami to discover more. He would have done the same if he planned extortion, or to demand payment for suppressing evidence that could only lead to pain and hurt in court.

But he underestimated Nancy de Marigny. 'One thing that is more or less unpredictable,' she said, 'is human nature – and I cannot say that I have made a study of it – but from my knowledge of Freddie during the year since our marriage, the situation seems fantastic to me.' She flew to Nassau to visit him in prison, to comfort him as best she could. She seemed a heroine: a girl of nineteen, dressed in stark white, a countess whose husband faced the rope for the murder of her father, a wife who would not let her husband stand alone. 'My mother thought it was perfectly natural that I should come to my husband,' she said. 'I am told that people did not expect me to come back – but I can't imagine why this should be.' She said she would have come immediately, but she felt she must attend to her mother in her state of shock. 'I don't think,' she said, 'my father would have wanted me to do otherwise.'

From early July until 31 August, the case against de Marigny rambled through the magistrates' court, adjourned from week to week, the evidence presented in scattered and muddled form. The magistrate had to determine only whether there was a *prima facie* case against de Marigny, but the prosecution stalled, week by week, over defence objections. The technical evidence against de Marigny was complex to assemble. The defence was happy enough to see the proceedings prolonged. Every day saved was a greater chance that Alfred de Marigny would not hang. It allowed time for the hysteria of the town to diffuse. In the last week, the defence sprung surprise witnesses simply to continue the case.

The court heard that de Marigny's financial position was none too secure; his sole means of support was the chicken farm which he was operating without benefit of the essential Government permit. They heard of the family tensions and arguments within the Oakes family, of de Marigny's dinner party on the night of the murder and his trip in the early morning to take dinner guests to their home near Westbourne, of what de Marigny had said to Lieutenant Douglas about circumstantial evidence and where his fingerprints had been found. While this dark picture was being assembled, Nancy de Marigny deployed a fashionable New York investigator called Raymond Schindler, a man with a sense of drama and of public relations, whose cases had made the *New Yorker* as well as the yellow press. Schindler would hint at new clues – never specified; and he would express resentment at the lack of official cooperation, and even at occasional official harassment. He gave the impression that brave Nancy de Marigny had told him to uncover anything – and therefore that she was confident he would find nothing to incriminate her husband. Around the court and the inquiries the press hovered. The little local awkwardness for the Windsors had been inflated, even in wartime, to the crime of the century.

When finally the trial opened on 13 October, the press benches were jammed. Hearst sent Erle Stanley Gardner, creator of Perry Mason, on his first newspaper assignment. He led a press expedition to the sunroom of Westbourne, swept an arm at a card table and proclaimed, 'Well, Colonel, there's the Chinese checker board just as it was left on the fateful evening.' Colonel F. G. Lancaster, acting Commissioner of Police, had to explain that various police officers had been playing at the table for three months.

'Don't let it worry you,' said Gardner, expansively. 'Facts will never spoil a Hearst story!'

Alfred de Marigny stood in the dock, clean-shaven and without the raffish Van Dyck beard he had once sported. He seemed elegant and still gaudy, an exotic figure. His French accent, his taste in ties, his manner marked him out as different. The jury, assembled with difficulty in such a small town to try so notorious a crime, seemed lumpish and dull beside him. They had come to judge whether the outsider, the scapegoat, could be hanged for the unthinkable crime. The murder of Harry Oakes had become an offence against the established order of things, an act which presaged anarchy. It served to focus all the rumours, the self-doubts of a community which sensed that change would be its ruin. The respectable, proper façade that de Marigny had broached by marrying Nancy Oakes had crumbled totally in face of the murder. Nassau's image of itself as a proper place dissolved before the warring rumours and theories.

Nancy de Marigny, loyal throughout the magistrates' court proceedings, would be called as a witness for the defence; she was therefore excluded from the court proceedings until her turn to speak. Her mother would speak for the prosecution. Family and town divided over de Marigny's guilt.

Harold Christie was called to give evidence on the second day. His position was now extraordinary. Prosecution counsel invited the jury to discount what he said – although Christie was a prosecution witness. Counsel pointed out that nothing in Christie's version of events implicated de Marigny – or, indeed, anyone – and that it would be challenged by the defence. Adderley told the court the prosecution's case would stand without Christie.

It would have to. From the start, it was obvious that Harold Christie was lying on oath. He said he had slept at

232

Westbourne that night. He said he had heard nothing of the killer, nor of the struggle and the fire and the beating that had taken place only two doors from his bedroom. He admitted that he had given a press conference for foreign reporters and said to them that he was not lying to shelter a woman; American papers had suggested that he was. He tied himself into his evidence and struggled there. Godfrey Higgs pursued him. It was a moment of acute embarrassment: Higgs and Christie were colleagues on ExCo and old political associates. Yet Higgs had to throw doubt on as much of the prosecution's case as possible. Higgs pursued Christie on the matter of the towel he used to wipe Oakes's face – even asking which side Christie had used, forcing Christie to an exasperated 'For God's sake, Higgs!' Christie could not explain why blood should have run from ear to nose in a corpse lying on its back. He denied that he had left Westbourne at all that night. 'If Captain Sears said he saw me out that night, I would say that he was very seriously mistaken and should be more careful in his observations.'

Christie's performance gave an edge of melodrama to the trial's start. It was not, however, the real issue. The jury were left to wonder why on earth Christie should insist he was on the scene of the crime if he was not, what significance sleeping in Westbourne could have for him. But they had now to turn their minds to the crux of the case against de Marigny.

The prosecution could easily establish the bad blood between Oakes and de Marigny; it was admitted that de Marigny had been close to Westbourne on the night of the murder; it was admitted also that de Marigny's finances could have been in better order. The prosecution argued that Oakes had been about to leave for America, that he would have seen Nancy de Marigny, and that the accused was afraid that Oakes would turn his wife against him. If Oakes had done that, they suggested, de Marigny's financial position would have become disastrous. The motive always seemed a little tenuous, since on the prosecution's own account, Oakes and de Marigny had not been in touch since Oakes had instigated the flaming row with de Marigny months before. It was never clear why de Marigny should suddenly take it into his head to prosecute a feud which had been largely on Sir Harry's part. When Oakes left for America, it was actually not at all certain that he would even see Nancy, let alone that he would be able to persuade her against de Marigny. Nor did the prosecution suggest how de Marigny – who apparently did not even know which house Oakes was using – could have known when Oakes planned to leave for America.

The prosecution, of course, did not have to prove motive. It was enough that they prove de Marigny had been in Oakes's bedroom on the night of the murder. Fingerprints have a brief life in the tropics; they waste with the high humidity. If de Marigny's prints were in Oakes's bedroom, they could not be much more than twenty-four hours old. If the police could prove they found the fingerprints before de Marigny had gone officially to Oakes's room to be questioned, then it would follow that de Marigny had been in the room unofficially – and very recently. Since he denied that he had even entered Westbourne, the fingerprint evidence could prove him a liar and put him on the scene of the crime.

Constables of the Nassau force trooped through the witness box in the magistrates' court to swear that de Marigny had been taken upstairs for questioning between three and four in the afternoon on the day after the murder. The time was significant; it was after Barker had done his first fingerprint work, after he had taken Scotch tape and India rubber and produced a perfect de Marigny print from, he said, the Chinese screen that stood in the bedroom. If de Marigny had been legitimately upstairs before two that afternoon, it would introduce a fatal ambiguity into the evidence. He might have touched the screen accidentally while talking with Melchen.

Three police constables, and Melchen, swore to the time. They lied. The official police log in Nassau showed that de Marigny was questioned between 1.30 and 2.00, that he had not even been at Westbourne at the time the police said he was under questioning.

Higgs, and his junior counsel Ernest Callendar, made much of the curious fact that the fingerprint expert Barker had not even told his superior Melchen of the perfect de Marigny print until the interview with Lady Oakes at Bar Harbor. There began to be a great suspicion about the fingerprint evidence. Higgs, who had taken a course in fingerprinting to prepare himself for the trial, had identified a real and deep flaw in the prosecution case. He would pursue it relentlessly, handicapped only by the fact that no court in the Bahamas had ever before dealt with disputed fingerprint evidence. This was a new technology of crime detection, and the courts and the police seemed equally uncertain about what it meant.

The fingerprint most damning to de Marigny came from the screen in Oakes's bedroom. It was Exhibit J. It was the one piece of evidence which the defence had to explode in order to win.

Barker in the witness box was truculent and bright. Higgs attacked him first on the evidence he had given that de Marigny's hair was singed. Such burning might have happened while setting the body of Sir Harry alight, or else it might be due to one of de Marigny's more mundane explanations – lighting a cigar, lighting a lamp through the funnel of a hurricane shelter, working around the cauldrons used for scalding chickens at his farm and the open fires under the cauldrons. Barker was vague about what a 'considerable amount' of burns on de Marigny actually meant; he said it was not 'the actual number of hairs but rather the fact that a large area of the Accused's hands and arms were burnt.' The evidence had never been shown to Pemberton, head of the Bahamas Criminal Investigation Department. Barker said he had followed usual practice in Miami; the evidence had been shown only to the Commissioner of Police, Erskine Lindop. From the prosecution's point of view, this was worse than useless. Barker was already suspect and Erskine Lindop was not available to back up his evidence, for between the magistrates' court and the Supreme Court hearings, Erskine Lindop had been promoted out of the Bahamas to Trinidad. He was not available to give evidence at the de Marigny trial, and he was the only witness who could have confirmed or denied the statements that de Marigny's hair had been extensively burned.

235

It was a bad start for Barker. Exhibit J made things worse. As evidence, it was not ideal, for it was not the fingerprint in its original place, but a lift – a version made by putting adhesive tape over the original and lifting it. There was no supporting photograph to show where it had come from and it carried two curious moisture marks in the background. There had been a delay in making a positive identification, strange for so good and clear a print. Barker knew it was legible when he left Nassau for Miami on his first visit, yet he claimed in court he had not positively identified it until 19 July, ten days later. He made it seem that the Miami policemen had decided to arrest de Marigny before they had the crucial piece of evidence.

On the witness stand, Barker appeared less expert than he had seemed to Windsor in the first days of the inquiry. He admitted that humidity might have destroyed all fingerprints of Christie and Oakes from the night before the murder, but could not explain why one print of de Marigny, supposedly made a few hours later, should have survived in perfect condition. Higgs talked of coincidence. He insisted that Barker identify precisely which section of the screen had yielded the print, and Barker could not say. Pressed harder, he suggested a section with a distinct scroll pattern. No such pattern appeared on the background to the print which Barker brought to court. Higgs reminded Barker of the two circles of moisture on the print. He suggested that a fingerprint on a damp surface should have broken those perfect circles; or else that, if the moisture had condensed after the print was made, it should have broken the ridge marks in the print and made it illegible. The print might have come, for example, from the glass Melchen asked de Marigny to fill during his interrogation.

'Can you find anything on the background of that screen,' Higgs asked, 'to resemble these circles?'

'No, sir.'

'Is that another coincidence, Captain Barker?'

'I have to believe it is.'

The finer points of fingerprint technique might be lost, but the jury could watch Barker's credibility evaporate before them.

'This is the most outstanding case in which your expert assistance has been required, is it not?'

'Well, it's developed into that.'

'And I suggest,' Higgs said, his detailed cross-examination now coming to its moment of kill, 'that in your desire for personal gain and notoriety, you have swept away truth and substituted fabricated evidence.'

The prosecution case was in terrible disarray. A police corporal and a police constable repeated the magistrates' court story of when de Marigny had been interviewed at Westbourne; but Melchen changed his story, and the police from Nassau had to follow suit. Higgs and Callendar now had perfect licence to emphasize how odd it was that the police had admitted their error on time only after members of the force had read their colleagues' testimony in a local newspaper and found discrepancies. The prosecution did not tell the defence the evidence would change. The Chief Justice called the mistakes 'a gross error'.

It had been a polite trial. The Attorney General had insisted it was somehow improper for the defence to attack Harold Christie. The fact that de Marigny was the accused limited evidence to a succession of domestic details – money, abortion, health, marriage – instead of the financial detail which Melchen and Barker had, according to Windsor, been imported to examine. Beyond the fact of the murder, and the fact of the trial, Nassau had been spared embarrassment to a remarkable degree.

De Marigny was acquitted of murder by a majority verdict. One point remained as the crowd rose to cheer him from the court. Alfred de Marigny had been framed. It had taken perjury by two Miami policemen, and also by members of the local force. 'The Solomon gang', as Heape called them, were ready to call for an inquiry into police conduct, and their voice, the *Guardian*, talked of 'Laxity displayed at the scene of the crime, when the whole premises from the entrance gates should have been placed under guard for the purpose of searching for every possible clue, before or after the detectives arrived.' Such laxity, the *Guardian* shrilled, was 'beyond comprehension'.

The jury, almost unheard through the cheering that greeted their verdict, unanimously demanded the deportation of de Marigny as an undesirable. Even the little peace that the acquittal brought would produce new embarrassments for Windsor. His errors of judgement, perhaps even his own intervention on the afternoon before the arrest, had produced a near travesty of justice – the fabrication of a case of murder against an innocent man. Now he needed that man out of his territory, for ever. If de Marigny stayed in the Bahamas, the tatters of Windsor's authority would be quite blown away.

On Saturday, 15 November, Alfred de Marigny and his friend Georges de Visdelou were asked to leave the colony. Heape was Acting Governor; Windsor had taken Colonial Office advice and stayed far from the islands, mostly in New York, until the case was complete. Heape, on 17 November, warned London that 'retention of these men will create discord in the community and demonstrate the impotence of the local government.' Windsor cabled his support from New York on 19 November: 'failure to deport them would constitute deplorable evidence of the impotence of the local government and have very serious effect on the colony's reputation throughout the world.' The Secretary of State in London wrote: 'We must do our best.'

Neither War Office nor Foreign Office was in the slightest bit sympathetic. The Foreign Office told the Colonial Office that it was not possible to deport somebody for being undesirable, and since the pair had been labelled undesirable by a court, the War Office was not prepared to offer them transport. American authorities refused transit visas for them, which made travel by way of Miami impossible, and the Mauritian authorities demanded evidence that the 'undesirables' had really been born there. Reasonably, they wanted to be absolutely sure that they could not avoid responsibility for a rather exotic problem.

Windsor became frantic. On 26 November he tried to pull

rank with London. 'The relation of the Government with the local people is strained to breaking point,' he cabled. He threatened to go straight to Churchill with the problem if nothing was done. He also spelt out his objections to de Marigny, a list of libels which went far beyond the evidence at the trial. 'His matrimonial history shows him to be an unscrupulous adventurer,' he cabled. 'Twice divorced and three times married since 1937. Despoiled second wife of £25,000 and then married daughter of millionaire. Has evil reputation for immoral conduct with young girls. Is gambler and spendthrift. Suspected drug addict. Suspected of being concerned in the unnatural death of his godfather Ernest Brohard. Evaded Finance Control Regulations by obtaining divorce from second wife.' This litany of corruptions went far beyond even the wildest Nassau rumour, so far beyond, indeed, that it seems to have been the product of a curious, obsessive fever in the Duke's own mind. It ended with two statements that were objectively true. 'Convicted of offence of being in possession of stolen gasoline and of gasoline rationing orders. Engaged in two enterprises in violation of Immigration laws.' On the subject of de Visdelou, the Duke deployed less detail. He pointed to his conviction on the same gasoline charges as de Marigny, to his 'evil reputation' and to the fact that 'he is believed to be financially dependent on de Marigny'. Such an explosion of bile and invention would have been difficult for Windsor to justify or for London to accept, but the Duke was saved by bureaucratic precedent. Under Dundas, Nassau had twice cabled London about de Marigny – in November 1939 and February 1940. Since he had already been enrolled as a suspect, further accusations carried more weight.

Still, to Windsor's great humiliation, the War Office would not budge. They needed every seat across the Atlantic to Accra, and south to Mauritius. They could not tell whether Mauritius would accept either man – indeed, whether the Gold Coast would allow them to land – and they feared perpetual custody of two stray delinquents, stateless and homeless, who could never again touch down anywhere.

De Marigny tried some optimism in the face of general,

vitriolic disapproval. His yacht had been called the *Concubine*. Now, he promised one of his defence lawyers, he would rename the boat *Exhibit J*. Its effect on Nassau's proper ladies would be much the same.

He saved further awkwardness in December by simply leaving the islands for Havana, with Nancy at his side. The 'undesirables' had ceased to be Nassau's problem.

For the Windsors, the murder and the trial were ruinous. Bay Street could now discount a Governor whose royal name was not enough to negotiate two spare seats on a bomber flight to Accra. Windsor's personal authority and personal contacts had proved valueless. It was kind to walk delicately around the fact that the Duke had taken personal charge of a murder investigation in which a man had been framed; but his name, and the name of the colony he governed, had gone round the world in open scandal. He had become conspicuous for being too close to corruption. Such atonement as his work in the Bahamas represented, such achievement as the efforts of Wallis Windsor, were now obliterated by his faulty judgement, his lack of influence, the ugly truth that he had been involved in the framing of an innocent man.

And the inconclusive end of the trial did not help matters. If the domestic tensions of the Oakes family could not explain the killing, perhaps the money could. And the money led to Windsor, again and again.

It was truly Elba, now. Nobody could believe the Duke was fit for a wartime post of prominence. The Duke himself seems to have stopped his more direct lobbying. He had become a compromised extra in a classic mystery. Such men do not make ambassadors or rulers.

There never was an official solution to the mystery of who killed Harry Oakes. A Scotland Yard investigation in 1947 saw no reason or means to re-open the case. Assorted informants claimed to know the solution and troubled Lady Oakes with demands for money, time and favour in return for some part-digested, dubious 'truth'.

There are, however, quite clear clues which may lead to a

proper answer – compatible with all the record. They begin with the matter of Sir Harry's will.

When the estate went to probate, it proved to be worth not the £50,000,000 of general rumour, but only £4,000,000. It is true that Nassau probate does not include real estate, of which Oakes had considerable holdings. Even so, there was a huge gap between what was generally expected, what those close to the estate thought to be at least a £10,000,000 or £20,000,000 will, and the actual bequests. Lake Shore Mines was not as successful as it had been, and it was the foundation of Oakes's fortune; the Bahamas property was still worth rather little, and would certainly be impossible to sell for the £6,000,000 minimum needed to account for the gap between will and expectations of the will. The money had gone.

If anybody had troubled to ask where, they would have discovered the links to Banco Continental and to Mexico, the whole connection with Wenner-Gren which Windsor also had tried to use. The balance of Oakes's fortune was either in Mexico, or was ready to be transmitted there.

That fact upends the conventional view of Nassau motives in the murder. Instead of a benefactor on whom all Nassau professionals might depend, Oakes was an insecure foundation for fortunes. Harold Christie was losing not just his best friend, but his best client to Mexico and he knew it. It might seem on the surface that Christie had no motive to kill Harry Oakes. Actually, he had the strongest possible. Oakes was leaving, and his trip to America might prove the moment when he left for good. Christie could not follow him. Yet Christie's living, especially in wartime, was largely 10 per cent of what Harry Oakes could be induced to spend. If Oakes died, control of his estates would pass to trustees – Lady Oakes (to whom Christie was close), Kelly, the business manager (a friend of Christie), and Walter Foskett, the Palm Beach lawyer. Those three had some interest in continuity – they lacked Oakes's more buccaneering spirit. If they had control of the Oakeses' estates, Christie would still have some say in the running of Sir Harry's fortune, would still take his commissions and give his advice.

241

Oakes had already decided against buying the Bahamas General Trust, which would have given him the core of a financial organization in the islands, in favour of Banco Continental, which would allow him to disburse his moneys in Mexico. He had spent more and more time in Mexico since 1940, starry-eyed with the investment possibilities he saw. His social life was moving toward Mexico, and his family was spending more time there. Christie, meanwhile, was quizzing the State Department about foreign investment in Mexico and finding that he would be effectively excluded; he was a prominent target already on the Office of Censorship list of those whose letters and phone calls were to be watched. Christie tried to get the State Department to say that men like Oakes would also be discouraged, but he failed.

Christie had a crisis on his hands. For months, even years, the trend of Oakes's thinking had been clear. Christie had even helped make some contacts for him. But if he actually decided to go, then Christie was in deep trouble. Christie's expertise, such as it was, consisted of an intimate knowledge of the Bahamas Islands and the amount that millionaires would pay for them. He was no financial expert, or business manager. He left the operation of his own real estate business to his brother Frank, while he made the deals. If Oakes said he was leaving, Christie would have reason to panic. He would need to stop Oakes immediately.

The killing was clumsy, its concealment inept; yet it appeared deliberate – an early morning attack on an unarmed man. The evidence was so hopelessly botched that it was impossible to say with any certainty where or when Harry Oakes was killed, or even what chemical had been used to set him afire or what comprised a dark viscous liquid found in his stomach. Yet the nature of the blows was clearly murderous.

The fire led some theorists to talk of a Mafia killing, in which the charred body was meant to be an additional element of horror. That is not likely. If fire had been set to disfigure the body hideously, and only that, the killers would have needed to control the fire, to ensure that it did not spread, bring down the house and ruin their drama. If they were Mob killers, one may assume their professionalism. In fact, the fire was still burning when the first doctor arrived on the scene. It had not been snubbed and controlled.

De Marigny as killer was always implausible. A quite separate rumour in the town had told of Oakes awaiting some vengeful figure from his mining days. Because of that, it was said, he slept with a gun. De Marigny, had he entered Westbourne, would have expected the old man to welcome him with a blast from a revolver. De Marigny was hardly a welcome guest. More, if de Marigny had spent months planning the killing – and it was months since he had had contact with Oakes – he would perhaps have done rather better than the killer did at covering his tracks. And if the killing was impetuous, nobody could suggest a good reason why it had been triggered on that particular night.

The killing was amateurish, and the fire most likely started to burn the body and obscure the crime. The wounds that killed Oakes were made by a weapon never found, and might have been misinterpreted if the body had been pulled from a smouldering house. Somebody wanted Oakes dead, but also wanted his death to be considered either an accident in a fire or, at worst, a mystery.

Christie's court evidence, with its insistence on his continuous presence at Westbourne throughout the night, makes sense only if we assume that Christie regarded his presence as having great significance. To assert it, he risked perjury since he had been seen in the town that night. If he had needed to protect a particular mistress, he could have claimed that he had spent the night with other friends. He had good reason to meet Oakes in the early morning for their press trip to the new flock of sheep. It is exceedingly odd that he felt it necessary to cause himself the great embarrassment of explaining away his failure to hear or sense the killing that happened so close to him.

Yet there was one thing which his absence from the house would guarantee, if he were indeed in league with whoever killed Harry Oakes. It would guarantee them a clear run. If Christie could promise the killers that Oakes was alone and unguarded, he would greatly simplify their task. If he did so, he would know that leaving Westbourne that night to give such information was of huge importance, would deny it at all costs, and would stick to his story. That is what he did.

Had Christie wanted murder done, he certainly had Mob figures who would help him. But he need not have turned to the Mob. The brutality and the ineptness of the killings suggest more amateur operators – from the Bahamas, perhaps, or paid to come from mainland Miami. Christie was never properly investigated. It seemed, since nobody prepared to talk knew of the Mexican connection in its full extent, that he could not possibly have a motive. The defence at de Marigny's trial particularly said they did not believe he was involved in crime. Windsor and Christie shared common interests in concealing Oakes's intentions in Mexico. They also shared the Masonic bond of loyalty; Windsor attended at least one Masonic initiation in Nassau, and came from the old royal tradition of Freemasonry.

This explanation is, of course, speculation. The evidence was simply obliterated by police incompetence, and complicated by police lies. Unlike other accounts, however, the motive is in this case amply documented and pressing; the opportunity clear; and the theory explains the more bizarre parts of the trial evidence quite satisfactorily.

After de Marigny went free, there was a sense of nightmare. Indeed, the murder still produces queasy feelings in the islands, even warnings to researchers that they would be better leaving the subject well alone.

And it ate at Lady Oakes, as did her feeling for de Marigny. She wanted him found guilty. Bancroft, then Attorney General for the Bahamas, told London in 1945 that Lady Oakes was still looking for further evidence in the case. Her search was not a general one. She still wanted to prove that Alfred de Marigny killed her husband. She wanted an answer she could endure.

PART FOUR

REFLECTION

The water runs over white marl and clouds until it seems like milk. Slow boats edge across the Bight, and then the shallows, and the old sponging grounds called 'The Mud'. There are miles of shell, left pink and derelict in whorls and spins and points and fragments. In the still evening, flat-bottomed skiffs took the party to their camp near Flamingo Island.

The Duke had come to shoot on Andros. He came with the Bethell brothers, moneyed whites from Nassau. They had invited, also, Basil McKinney, the head of the Agriculture Board, the hard-drinking brash adventurer in a distinguished family.

At five in the morning, they set out in pairs. Each white man had his 12-gauge gun, his number 5 long-range shells, and his black man to paddle the light canoe. They went with bully beef in cans and bottles of beer. It was a ritual masculine expedition – sweaty and unshaven and ebullient. They made soundless progress with the wind, the canoe only a whisper in the white water, waiting for the ducks to rise out of the current against the dawn sky and wheel and pitch into the wind. The canoe could shiver to fifty feet from the flock before the birds took fright and beat up into the air. Up went the blue-winged and the green-winged teal, the pintail and the canvasback, sometimes a whistling duck, and into the flock the men blasted their guns, a pepper-sound of flat shot in the silence.

On the River of Milk, they would tell, boat by boat, their hunting stories: how the fat grouper were known to school at full moon two months of the year, how high the count of ducks went the last time the boats took to the water. In a few days, there would be three or four hundred birds dead around the camp – a fuss of gaudy feathers to act as trophies.

What else was there for the Duke to do now, except to play the role of a gentleman of leisure, to escape to America for as long as London would allow, to shoot and fish and play golf in Nassau? He maintained his duties as Governor, but it was painfully clear he could achieve nothing. It was as though he had acquired the habits of defeat and scandal.

Basil McKinney, for example, had become a difficult companion. He was a man of some importance in the House of Assembly, a local politician of consequence, and a distinguished yachtsman. He had been to the Chicago yacht races in 1944, and was in no great hurry to return to the heat of Nassau. He was staying with friends on Long Island for Labor Day. On 7 September, his hosts showed him the morning newspaper, with a story about a grand jury indictment handed down in New York.

He would need a lawyer. Basil McKinney was on narcotics charges.

McKinney, a leading light of Nassau, was on credible charges alongside men with aliases like Charley Four Cents, The Eye and Gigolo. The chain of the indictment made him the prime dealer in morphine and liquid opium, the ultimate source. It was true his business on Bay Street was a woollen shop and not a pharmacy, but the jury had suggested the drugs came originally from Haiti by a chain of Nassau yachtsmen. They dropped some distinguished names.

McKinney loved adventure, that is sure. He drank too much and wanted to be a swashbuckler. His image was spoiled only by the fact that he still lived at home with his parents. Nobody could be sure that drugs did not pass through Nassau – it was certain that both morphine and cocaine had travelled to America with the rum-runners in earlier years. And the case against McKinney was never brought to trial. Given a choice between prosecuting on the Nassau evidence or the New York evidence, the prosecution chose New York and then fouled their own case.

There was a victim of all this: Bertram Bow in the indictment – Burton Franklyn Bowe in fact – was a Nassau sea captain and a fisherman, indicted along with the others. He did not have friends on Long Island or attorneys in New York. He went to the court, was granted bail and sent home to prepare his defence. He lived for a year in a kind of terror, fearing to stand trial in a country he did not know, whose courts dispensed a fearfully expensive justice. Even if the charges had been brought to court, he would have been accused of little more than sailing his boat out to a rendez-vous by Jupiter Light. The jury never said if they thought he knew what he was carrying. He had a year which was sour and miserable, and when the charges were dropped, his bail was still forfeit – $1000 that Burton Bowe had never owned.

On the River of Milk, such talk would have been improper. What mattered was the cloud of high-beating wings as the ducks rose from the water, the sound of shots. The Duke sat, boyish, in his skiff, the black pilot at the bow with a har-poon. In the water moved a swordfish, basking at the surface, back fin and tail exposed like bronze sickles. The men were afraid the pilot might stab at the fish and overturn the skiff.

'Don't juke him,' they shouted, and the Duke, uncertain of their meaning, joined, 'Oh, no. Don't juke him.'

The swordfish turned lazily away.

Windsor slowly lost his hopes of a fortune from oil. Standard Oil of New York had been invited to prospect on his Can-adian ranch and had declined.

But he was interested in the waters of the Bahamas as a likely source of oil. Wartime shortages made it profitable for major companies to lobby for a chance to search. In theory, Anglo-Iranian, the British combine which later became BP, had been in the game since 1937, but they had not been active. In March 1941 Windsor gave a personal interview to F. C. Panill of Standard Oil. Standard was pursuing every diplomatic means to be recognized as partners with Anglo-Iranian in the Bahamas. Windsor was pursuing every means to have Standard act as his partners in Canada.

The deals foundered, largely because some 98 per cent of the possible land and water areas for oil were Crown prop-erty, and Government and House of Assembly were predictably at each other's throats over who owned, and who controlled, the oil. The House wanted mineral rights vested in the House; Windsor, under Colonial Office pressure, wanted them for the Crown. Kenneth Solomon and Stafford Sands were implacable on the issue and London was left to fume about 'the difficulties with which we are faced in dealing with antiquated and parochially minded colonial legislature'.

Windsor still had the power to startle London. He made a sudden change from all official positions and proposed that any oil company making application would be allowed to scout for oil in the Bahamas. He argued that he could always use the Immigration Act to exclude any geologists of whom the Foreign or Colonial Offices disapproved. 'It is of course wrong for His Royal Highness to make this bright suggestion,' London noted, 'when we have told him that we want to vest in the Crown, but that if New Providence is to be thrown open for exploration, Anglo-Iranian and Standard Oil are to have the first right of refusal.'

Windsor, of course, had now lost interest in his old allies Standard Oil. They had refused to help in the search for oil in Calgary.

In November 1943 the issue became pressing. Oilfields drilled off Miami looked promising. The big oilopolies wanted rights to explore in any waters which seemed to offer the same sort of geological patterns. Windsor told London that the British Embassy in Washington was putting pressure on him to allow a Los Angeles firm, Superior Oil, to start surveys of its own. London did not check with Washington, but still cabled Windsor that 'it is usual to deal with applications for oil exploration licences in order of priority.' London was 'perturbed'. Twenty-four hours later, when they heard the Washington version of the story, their perturbation grew.

For on 29 December the Washington Embassy told London that they had made absolutely no representations to Windsor about Superior Oil, nor had they tried to put pressure on him. They had simply told him that one Arthur May, geologist, planned to visit Nassau; that he was employed by

Superior Oil; and that Superior was a respectable company. It was a routine message.

When May arrived in February 1944, Windsor was 'intensely interested' in everything he did, and allowed visits to several of the Out Islands. He was infinitely helpful. He was still, after all, looking for partners in his Canadian venture. Windsor's priorities were easy to establish, and he was bad at hiding how he sought to achieve them.

Wallis Windsor's recurrent stomach ulcer took her to New York for hospital treatment in 1944, a merciful release after two years of pain and a violent loss of weight. She had a chance to catch up with all the gossip about old friends and to prepare for the day when she could again launch herself into society.

The Duke had failed. It was not that he had been wrong. His intentions on matters of local politics had been wholly honourable. It was that he lacked the understanding of the limits and the powers of his own position. His sense of constitutionality was too vague. As Governor, he might perhaps have influenced and led. Instead, he fell into a series of crude traps which allowed the House of Assembly to discount what he was attempting to do. He would either be too brutally direct, or else refuse the brutal possibilities in his power: he could, at any point, have suspended the House of Assembly for the duration of the war and simply forced his plans on the islands. He chose not to. In part, he had himself created his lack of choice and options. By sticking to the tight inner circle of Bay Street for his advisors, by excluding all blacks, he denied himself an alternative power base. He depended on Bay Street, and Bay Street defied him; and he neither pushed hard for the reforms London demanded, which might have given him the Imperial budget that would have allowed change, nor allowed Nassau to see him as a manipulator of London, someone capable of the political game of using what London offered and still pursuing his conservative bent. He kept the wilfulness of a prince, the impetuous, wild-mouthed spirit; but he never added to it a mature understanding of his own position. As King, he would

251

have been the same. Edward VIII would have been like a boy, emotional and impulsive, attractive and eager, but not a ruler, not a man capable of understanding the limits of his power, or evaluating the forces in his way, or keeping silence or bending if circumstances demanded either course. As a royal duke, he maintained his claims of privilege – he said it was bad form in Britain for newspapers to criticize the royal family, and therefore that the Nassau press should not attack him – but he had no feeling for the newly mystical air that monarchy bore. He could not use royal charisma, even when he claimed it. He had been democratized, as the snobs had said before his abdication, and in that process he had lost the authority of the crown and its connections. He simply seemed spoiled, immature in his lack of understanding of what his actions might mean.

He did damage, too. Excluding blacks from political process during those war years when other colonies unbent had the effect of widening the racial divide in the Bahamas still further. The fury of the riot, the new riches from working in America were defining alternatives to Nassau's smug and dominant whites. Windsor did nothing to channel that evident change.

Attempts were made, though. A. F. Adderley, that stiff-necked lawyer, wanted political position. Windsor kept him from ExCo; Adderley proposed a party of his own. He was 'an aristocrat', Bert Cambridge says. 'He was imbued with prejudice, too. But class prejudice. I've seen him talking to a white woman with his hat in his hand, but I've never seen him tip his hat to a black woman, regardless of who she was. He was such a bigshot that he didn't associate with the masses.'

Adderley was a natural member of ExCo – he had, after all, been worth £1000 for the prosecution of de Marigny, when the usual defence fee handed out to barristers was three guineas. Excluded from power, he founded the Bahamas Civic and Welfare Association. It began to meet in February 1944. Its prime objective was 'to take steps to blot out ignorance wherever it may be found'.

It was a startling concept since 'there has never before

been any marked endeavour on the part of Negro Bahamians to organise a general welfare network in the interests of its [*sic*] race.' McAndrews at the US consulate added: 'There has been, for some time past, a noticeable trend towards the Negro population using its influence in matters having to do with the government of the colony. They resent the fact that few Negroes occupy any of the governmental offices and so far as this consulate is aware, there is only one Bahamian Department, the Crown Lands Office, whose director is a Negro.' There were black lawyers, and black doctors and black Members of the House of Assembly, but the gap between those achievements and the pitiful power of blacks to help themselves in face of Bay Street was ugly and obvious.

McAndrews talked with Adderley (identified in the report only as 'a leading Negro lawyer in Nassau') and was told: 'the post-war era would have to be the time that matters of policy would come to the fore; that the Negroes would then have to assert themselves and that further delay in promised, or inferred "promised", reform could not and would not be tolerated.'

Windsor did not fool the black population. They knew just how limited were his proposed reforms, how disinclined he was to change the ways of Nassau society.

It was fighting talk, and Adderley took it to the platforms – disastrously. 'He couldn't get the crowd to attend because they didn't have respect for him because he didn't have respect for them,' Bert Cambridge says. 'The last meeting I attended, the minutes were first on the agenda as usual. I was secretary and I got up to read the minutes and he stopped me. He said: "I have not seen these minutes. They must be submitted to me for my approval before the relevant meeting." I said: "I am the secretary. If I'm not capable of writing the minutes, amendments can be made – after I've read them. In plain words, you don't need me as a secretary if I've got to bring the minutes to you." ' Out of the audience stood up Harry Glinton, building contractor, who said solemnly to Cambridge: 'Who do you think you are, talking back to Mr Adderley? If Mr Adderley says bring the minutes to him, you got no alternative but to do as he says.' Cambridge says: 'I put the minutes back on the table and I never went back.

'He was a very fine man, but dictatorial as hell. He used to tell his meetings: "You people have got to learn to follow your leaders. Blindly." '

With Adderley's grand association, the immediate chances of effective black political organization died away. It was dissolved within three months of its foundation. For the moment, black voices remained rare and eccentric – the Milo Butlers, the Bert Cambridges. Blacks still cried.

The main success of Windsor's policy was also the factor which removed any hope of putting pressure on the recalcitrant House of Assembly. Each week in season, some 325 men left Nassau for work in Florida and the Southern states. Very soon, there were no more men 'of suitable types and adequate numbers' to keep the Windsor training camp open. There was some argument in February 1944 over reserving men for military recruitment – the Bahamas Defence Company and Air Service and police force lacked volunteers – but the Governor in Council agreed 'that food production in the United States was of greater importance at the present time to the war effort than the enlistment of men for the services and that even if recruitment of labour was deferred it was more than likely those who preferred going to Florida would await the re-opening of labour recruitment.' Out Islands in turn took the available jobs, and even Grand Bahama and Inagua, which then had more jobs than people, provided volunteers. The terms and the money were spectacular by Bahamian standards, and the Americans, after their initial resistance, were happy enough.

Out Island development came to nothing. The House of Assembly endorsed it 'in principle . . . but preferred that one island should be developed at a time.' Eleuthera was chosen, but before the money could be voted the House broke again into its constitutional troubles. It wanted three Bahamians, not in the public service, to be additional Out Island Commissioners. To get its way, it tried to repeal laws which the Legislative Council had already amended. The grand schemes

254

foundered in a too familiar shouting match. Nor did the islands, under Windsor, get the secret ballot on which he had set his heart.

He lost the battle for income tax, which would have been a basis for very general reform. Dundas had proposed it, and London had seconded in December 1940. Windsor warned in 1942 that the 'time has come when direct taxation should be grafted more deeply into the colony's economic structure'; and a year later he talked of 'the more important part which direct taxation should play'. Nothing happened, and since the deficits mended themselves, nothing was likely to happen. Professor Richardson from Leeds, Windsor's admirable economics advisor, proposed an income tax which would be levied solely on income arising in the colony. It was designed to avoid any shock to the rich expatriates who kept the economy afloat in return for their freedom from tax. Since the House of Assembly was by definition not expatriate, it did not take kindly to the idea.

Nor did Windsor achieve much social reform in his five years, despite the hard work of the Duchess and his own concern for housing and conditions of life. Nassau was kept sweet by the simple expedient of making Out Islanders have passes to come to New Providence, which allowed them visits of only two weeks. Seamen and travellers with occasional business in the capital were allowed red cards. Security, Immigration and Customs had to stamp passes as the islanders came and went. Between Florida labour and the pass laws, trouble could be kept far away from Bay Street.

In all his island exile, little troubles, little dishonesties continued. The ex-King of England chaired meetings of Executive Council whose main subject was whether to repair the wooden legs of Sergeant Demeritte, or whether £90 could be spent on the Government House refrigerator, which the Duchess greeted with a glorious and unhidden glee. He also helped his friends, with no great openness. In June 1944 London asked if the US Naval Air Station at Banana River could use an island called Wood Cay for target practice. Neither Air Ministry nor Admiralty raised objections. Windsor, however, cabled: 'Am advised that bombing practice in

255

this vicinity would constitute danger to and would disturb fishing activities and inter-island mail vessels, etc. There is narrow channel between Wood Cay and India Cay through which there is fairly frequent traffic. In the circumstances, much regret must advise against granting application.' Windsor left out his real interest: that Wood Cay belonged to friends. At Christmas 1940, it had been Harold Christie's spectacular present to Mrs Axel Wenner-Gren.

At the end of war, they left the islands quickly. Windsor had even asked the State Department for permission to travel on Arthur Vining Davis's *Eldarette*, a boat with no licence to carry paying passengers. He organized the shipment of his wine to the United States; the Duchess sold to the Bahamas that furniture which she had provided in Government House. There was some haggling over price.

They left exhausted, thin, defeated. Their reforms had never happened and their authority had dissolved. The Duchess was ungenerously refused proper recognition for her stalwart war work. Her politics, her fripperies, her schemes got in the way. There was a consensus that they could not have done much damage in the Bahamas, despite alarmist stories that caches of arms were on the islands ready for an uprising. The matters of treason, riot and murder were forgotten in their glossy, social life.

On a little ship, the Windsors sailed from Nassau, some months before the term of his Governorship – five years – was complete. The British Government would offer only one alternative job: Bermuda. The Duchess herself, now fifty, would only say of him: 'What a pity!' And 'I still think something could have been done.' Everything was uncertain now – where they could live, what they could do, what reception awaited them in America and in Europe and in Britain. He was humiliated, and she was tired. The prospect of their coming idleness alarmed them.

Their sweet legend – the King, his love, his sacrifice – seemed very far away.

After the summer, the first passages from America to Europe

opened, and the Windsors sailed for Paris. They were offered freedom from tax in France, and they accepted with alacrity. They recovered all the wartime gossip – who had slept with whom, who flaunted the fact, who collaborated, who made money, made enemies – and calculated the new alliances and rules.

The Windsors were properly launched on American society now, and they still had loyal friends in Europe, but paradoxically their circle began to shrink. Old friends died, or drifted away. The Windsors had so little substance to hold loyalty. Their world was café society, a publicized, limelit world of rich people running desperately from boredom. The Windsors courted publicity – both wrote their memoirs; both profited handsomely from doing so – and their style was a flak's style. Wallis Windsor would always be a part of lists of best-dressed women; but such lists reflect not taste, but conspicuous and often eccentric consumption. David Windsor's style was imitated most by the cheapest end of Carnaby Street. Their style of life, despite its scale, smacked of *Homes and Gardens.*

They became a sideshow, a little booth in a circus of spending. For a couple with all the pretensions – and the blood – of royalty, it was remarkable how little old money and how few old names were in their entourage.

David Windsor wanted work. He petitioned four times for a job – to represent the British Government in America, as a kind of ambassador-at-large, a salesman for the flag as he had been so proficiently between the wars. He begged Ernest Bevin, the obdurate trade union leader who was Foreign Secretary; Bevin would not recommend him. He tried to influence his brother, the King, but George VI would do nothing. He went to Attlee in 1948 and to Churchill when the old man returned to power in 1951. Everybody knew too much about David Windsor, and suspected worse. He might at any moment, given his panicky fear of Bolshevism, misjudge the intentions of another James Mooney or Charles Bédaux or Axel Wenner-Gren. His concept of duty had proved so elastic that nobody could predict when the royal will – so charming in a boy, so tedious and dangerous in a

257

man in late middle age – would once again derail him. He was best left in his rented apartments in Palm Beach or Newport, in the Waldorf-Astoria or the Paris Ritz. There, the artificial gossip-column glory rendered him absurd and safe, the willing help of social climbers and social promoters like Elsa Maxwell. Every day of visible indulgence took away his seriousness, his potential to harm or hurt.

For Wallis Windsor, the grand style seemed a perfect fit. True, there were moments when some powerful frustration seemed to work within her, and burst out in humiliations to the Duke or more than usually wild-eyed behaviour at great parties; but it was assumed that she was happy with the round of openings, dinners, balls. The absurdity of her interviews on style and furnishings – 'not only does such a dinner menu mean working up the menu with the chef,' she wrote, 'it also involves deciding the service to be used and the motif of the table decorations, whether the dominant colour is to be iceberg blue or pastel green' – suggested a shallow woman who saw pattern and fulfilment in a glossy domestic round.

Her position was in truth more sad. She was forced into the more feverish, more insubstantial ends of café society because of her marriage. The fact that Windsor had been King made her a magnet for a set of publicity-seekers, and made her an outcast for others. Yet she was no more outrageous or absurd, certainly no more Right-wing or pro-German, than other women of her time and class and nationality. She merely attracted attention. She was scrutinized and condemned because of her royal links for attitudes that were very common; and as such, she made a convenient scapegoat. With the years, the effect was terrifying. As a scapegoat, her every action was a half-page picture, a gossip-column lead. Once it had been decided that she was outside the rules of proper society, she was fair game. It was the Duchess, at seventy, doing the twist, whose startled, frenzied expression went round the world; and the Duchess whose face was scrutinized in column after column for signs of the rumoured face-lifts. The Duchess was never granted

258

the decent obscurity that other women of her age and class would never lack.

She was much more than the socialite; she had proved herself in the Bahamas. She had shown courage and sense and stamina. She had understood the need for birth control, clinics for syphilitics, orange juice for children; how to deal with men suffering from exposure on the seas, how to organize a social life for thousands of soldiers. She had worked hard, and she had understood problems which must have seemed infinitely remote among the extravagant unreality of their new social round. She could respond to challenge, and the only challenge allowed to her now was to make a life from suitcases – Vuitton suitcases, but still no basis for a life. It is not surprising that she became hungry for diversion, amusement; that she drank more than she had done before the war; that her stories sometimes seemed to wander off the point. She had become an elegant device for socializing. As such, she was an anachronism. The real rich were raising defences round their money, flaunting less; the Windsor set, and the few groups like them, alone kept alive the 1920s hedonism.

Wallis Windsor was wasted – a woman doing, as she always did, her duty, but doing a duty which was utterly trivial.

Once the Windsors had sold their life stories as commodities, even the pretence of royal dignity was gone. They were another upper-middle-class couple, ageing and affluent, but not close to the very rich, the unlikely survivors of a legendary romance.

The limelight which followed them in exile also illuminated strange creatures around them in the Bahamas – creatures of treason, murder, betrayal. The Windsors valued their secret schemes, but their very name and glamour were enough to draw attention to those secrets. In their island years, they accidentally exposed the seamy, graceless, brutal side of the money and the moneymen who were later their friends. Behaviour that would be buried in systems, expected by cynics, became visible and scandalous because of their involvement.

Once they had gone to Paris, their friends and associates could rest more easily.

Axel Wenner-Gren returned to Nassau at the end of the war. He sold his interests on Hog Island to the American millionaire Huntington Hartford; the island was renamed Paradise, and became the hub of gaming and tourism in Nassau. Wenner-Gren was never removed from the Allied blacklist, despite long and frequent protests from his Mexican exile, and he retained his German links. In 1953, Alfred Krupp, banned from business in Europe because of his hideous war record, approached Wenner-Gren in Nassau. As a result, Wenner-Gren became Krupp's front man once again. This time, he bought into Bochumer Verein, a major German industrial company; his holdings – first 42 per cent and then another 6 per cent – were held in Wenner-Gren's holding company until Krupp needed them. Promptly, Wenner-Gren sold to Krupp, and the house of Krupp had returned to great industrial power in Europe in defiance of Allied plans.

Harold Christie went from strength to strength. When war ended, and Britain had a Socialist government, migrants came to the Bahamas to escape what they imagined would be confiscatory taxation. Property values soared, and stayed high, and Christie's commissions made him a very rich man. He helped in the creation of Lyford Cay, the enclave of solid money at the west of Nassau; he was knighted for his services to the colony; he married, late in life, a Palm Beach divorcee. He also retained his honour through the sordid period when white Bahamian politicians took bribes and kickbacks from the developers of Grand Bahama, now a tax-free island with casinos, and became a scandal which demanded a Commission of Inquiry. Harold Christie was among the few honest men.

There was little happiness for the protagonists in the Oakes case. The Oakes Estates became hugely valuable because of the property boom, and the family did well. Personally, though, their times were hard. Alfred de Marigny and Nancy Oakes retreated to Havana without having the formal church wedding they had planned as a reaffirmation of their marriage. The couple drifted apart and were divorced in 1949.

De Marigny now lives in Texas, still painfully aware of how close he came to the gallows. Nancy Oakes made other marriages – one to von Hoyningen Heune, son of the German minister who tried to detain Windsor in Lisbon – and now lives mainly in Cuernavaca. Her mother, Lady Oakes, survives.

The Bahamian policemen have for the most part retired – Lieutenant-Colonel Erskine Lindop to the suburban life of Wimbledon, Captain Edward Sears in Nassau. It was the Miami policemen who ended in melodrama. Melchen was retired from the force and his reputation never recovered. Barker was hauled before the American Fingerprint Association and disciplined; he was later accused of links with the Mafia; he was shot down by his own son in self-defence when he went berserk at home.

James Mooney followed corporate logic and, despite his views on war in 1940 and his attempts at a negotiated peace, was by 1944 a valued advisor for the Americans on Britain's war preparedness.

Of local politicians, Sir Roland Symonette became the first Prime Minister of the Bahamas; Stafford Sands became the all-powerful Finance Minister, full of schemes and corruptions. The secret ballot and, eventually, the granting of the vote to women changed the balance of power in the House of Assembly for ever. In 1967, a black party won a narrow majority for the first time. Sands shredded and burned his papers and left the Bahamas. Milo Butler was one of the new black leaders. In 1973, when the Bahamas took independence from Britain, Sir Milo went to Government House as the first black Governor General of the new nation, living in the mansion where Windsor had once lived. Bert Cambridge remained too independent of political machines to keep power, and retired from the parliamentary game; of the riot leaders, 'Sweet Potato' Stubbs sits in the geriatric wing of the Bahamas General Hospital. He is old and very quiet now.

As for the islands, they abandoned the rich as their main source of income in the early 1950s, and settled for a species of mass tourism. Paradise Island opened for business, and the great hotel at Fort Montagu Beach shut its doors. The

261

dreamy peace of the islands was broken up and marketed. Casinos came, with attendant bribes and rumour, and the islands became a notorious entrepôt for the northward drugs trade, now in marijuana and cocaine. Income tax was never introduced, and grateful big banks channelled their schemes through the islands. On tourism and banking – both industries peculiarly sensitive to issues of confidence and trust – the Bahamas became a rich nation with a veneer of money spectacular by Third World standards.

If the Windsors left a trace – beyond a skein of scandal and a sentimental legend – it is in barely suppressed animosity between black and white on the islands. At a time when war conditions seemed to narrow the racial division in other places, and started change, Windsor's personal attitudes and political failures actually widened the gap in the Bahamas.

It was not the sort of issue which would trouble the dinner table gossip in Paris, and there was no reason why the Windsors should know of their consequences; they only returned once to the islands, for a brief visit. Their war years were better left unexamined, unexplored, for the sake of royal peace of mind. The Windsors simply went to a retirement which was comfortable and empty. They had come as suspects, and they had left ruined. The Windsor legend ended in the Bahamas.

THE SOURCES

This story was meant to go untold. British files in London have been weeded with an eye to royal embarrassment; even the Windsors' 1944 visit to New York cannot be discussed until 1994, since the files have been sealed for fifty years. When the Bahamas became independent in 1973, the Foreign Office sent officials to check through the files left in the colony, and select those worth preserving; all the others were either destroyed or left in the custody of the Nassau Cabinet Office, which insists on applying its own fifty-year rule. Files from the Nassau Development Board and the Finance Ministry were burned and shredded by anxious white politicians when the first black government of the Bahamas took power in 1967.

But the evidence is available, for anyone prepared to search. The National Archives in Washington hold a vast amount of detailed information on the Bahamas while the Windsors were there – reports from the Nassau consulate, FBI inquiries, Intelligence reports on the state of the islands, records of discussions on defence, political opinion and, every time the Windsors visited America, the detailed accounts of the special agents set to guard them. The Roosevelt Library at Hyde Park has all the available material on relations with the Roosevelts, and the papers of Henry Morgenthau and other senior American diplomats who operated in the Caribbean. Roosevelt, unfortunately, did not approve of writing memoranda of diplomatic talks, nor of having a secretary note the proceedings; it is a major gap. Where criminal proceedings are part of the story, Federal Archives around the United States have copies of the depositions, grand jury indictments and the course of the case. It is also, slowly, becoming possible to tap the files of the Office of Censorship. The one unfortunate consequence of the fall of Richard Nixon was that he did not have time to promulgate the executive order he had promised to open those files to researchers; they remain, at the behest of President Truman, sealed 'in perpetuity'. Yet diligent archivists in Washington are finding proper ways to interpret existing statutes, and Truman's order, and make some material available.

In London, the division between Foreign and Colonial Office records proved particularly important. Files which were clearly awkward to release – dispatches in which the Duke of Windsor was reprimanded by London, for example – were often filed by the Colonial Office and then sealed from public view. The Foreign Office, however, might file them under some related topic and, when those files were made public under the British thirty-year rule, not think to check what they contained. Similarly, records of the New York consulate seem to have been less closely checked than those of the Washington Embassy. In the absence of a Freedom of Information Act – indeed, with British bureaucratic nerves notoriously tender – such clues were invaluable, and revealed material which other researchers have chased in vain.

In Nassau, the Archives are well organized, but they are new. Even records from the Ministries of the 1960s are patchy. Records from the colonial period are in more disarray. Criminal records are heaped without order in a room in the central police station, among termites and cockroaches, and the police archivist confesses he had never been able to find the files on the Oakes murder, or even discover if they are there. Now that the central archives are on a proper professional basis, at least some of the basic material – Executive Council minutes, Board of Works minutes, Colonial Secretary's files – is becoming usable. Both the Archives and the Nassau Public Library have excellent collections of newspapers and magazines of the period. The Public Library also has a first-rate collection of Bahamiana, from school magazines to Government reports and including most published works which deal at all with the islands. This collection was a cornerstone of this book.

Partly as a legacy of political suspicion, Nassau Archives have been given very few collections of private papers. I was particularly grateful that Roy Solomon allowed me access to letters written to his father, Eric Solomon.

Much of my material was assembled in extensive interviews, or by correspondence. I am very grateful to all those who helped me, including those who asked that I should not use their names. My thanks to, among many others: Lady Caroline Butler, W. E. A. Callender, Father John Calnan, Bert Cambridge, Sir Etienne Dupuch, Eugene Dupuch, Dr Cleveland Eneas, C. P. Erskine Lindop, Sir Randol Fawkes, Sir John Foster, J. H. Gaffney, Godfrey Higgs, Mrs Leslie Higgs, William Sweeting, H. M. Taylor, Mrs Sally Woodruff. In Mexico City, I am grateful to the Asociación de Banqueros de Mexico, the Comisión Nacional Bancaria y de Seguros (Armando Gutierrez De Lira) and to the Centro de Estudios Historicos of the Colegio de México (Dra Josefina Zoraida Vázquez). Many correspondents helped me, including: Alcoa (Edward L. Crouse); Beaverbrook Archive (A. J. P. Taylor); Robert Simmons Ewing; Clayton Gaylord; M. Knoedler and Co. (Nancy Little); New Scotland Yard (G. J. Kellard); Pan American Airlines (Ann Whyte); Queen's Own Highlanders (Lt Col A. A. Fairrie); Swedish Embassy, Washington (Lars Ulvenstam, Margareta Paul); Yale University (George D. Vaill). I am also grateful to the staff of the Registrar General's office in Nassau for their help in tracing the often dusty and elusive files on companies and clubs which appear in this story. I owe special thanks to Mrs Eileen Dupuch Carron, Editor of the *Nassau Tribune*.

For the sake of brevity, the notes and bibliography that follow have been restricted to essential sources. Unless a note indicates the contrary, it can be assumed that: material on speeches in the House of Assembly is taken from contemporary reporting in the *Nassau Tribune*, as is the text of all broadcasts and public speeches by the Duke or Duchess of Windsor in the Bahamas; decisions of, or discussions in, Executive Council are taken from the minutes of Executive

Council; quotations from the Duke or Duchess without other specific sources are taken from contemporary reporting of their words and actions, in the *Miami Herald*, *Nassau Guardian* or *Nassau Tribune*, and in most cases represent agreed wire service copy which was nationally distributed and cannot sensibly be ascribed to any one newspaper; material on the Oakes family and on the murder of Sir Harry Oakes, where not otherwise noted, is taken from the extensive contemporary reporting of the trial of Alfred de Marigny, collected as *The Murder of Sir Harry Oakes Bt*, and published by the *Nassau Daily Tribune*, 1959; material on the course of the riots, unless otherwise stated, comes from the contemporary reporting of evidence before the Commission of Inquiry in the *Nassau Tribune* and the *Nassau Guardian*. In several cases I regret that I cannot name sources. I am aware that this arouses suspicions, but islands require a certain discretion of those who intend to continue living there.

The bibliography has been limited to titles cited in the notes, or directly used in the text. A fuller bibliography of the available Bahamiana is in the collection of the Nassau Public Library.

In the notes, citations have been limited as far as possible to the minimum information which would make the material retrievable. Thus, archives are indicated: (B) = Federal Archives, Bayonne, New Jersey; (HP) = Roosevelt Library, Hyde Park, New York; (L) = Public Records Office, London; (N) = Archives, Nassau; (W) = National Archives, Washington DC. In British citations, reference numbers are given with record group. In American citations, the group is omitted, for reasons of space, if the material is in the archives of the State Department. Other locations are indicated by conventional abbreviations for US wartime departments, where these are clear, or by the full title of the agency if there is any ambiguity.

In the bibliography, place and date of publication naturally refer to edition used.

NOTES

p. 15   *the escort destroyer:* (W) 844E.001/53
      'Darling,' said the Duke: Windsor, 1956, p. 337

p. 16   *'big news':* Dupuch, 1960

p. 17   *Previous Governors:* Clifford, 1964

p. 19   *letter from contacts:* (W) 800/20211/Wenner-Gren/
      46½, 17 February 1941
      pushy: (W) 800/20211/Wenner-Gren/211, 18 June
      1942, Swedish Minister to Berle
      hard-drinking: (W) 800/20211/WG/35
      Messersmith: (W) 800/20211/WG/12–1042, 10
      December 1942

p. 21   *American consul:* (W) 844E.001/53, 17 August 1940
      flowers: Windsor, 1956, p. 338
      afternoon: St John, 1969

p. 23   *'I shall have to work':* Airlie, 1962
      usefulness: c.f. Airlie, 1962; Legge, 1921; Turley,
      1926; Windsor, 1951
      'I like': Legge, 1921, quoting *Je Sais Tout,* 1912

p. 24   *'often I remain':* Legge, 1921, quoting *Je Sais Tout,*
      1912

p. 26   *'those vigorous people':* Windsor, 1951

p. 27   *'God's gift':* Chase and Chase, 1954

p. 28   *Cecil Beaton:* Chase and Chase, 1954

p. 29   *'Really!':* Pope-Hennessey, 1959

p. 32   *'cold-blooded act': New York Daily News,* 12
      December 1966, quoted by Birkenhead, 1969

p. 33   *a place to stay:* Channon, 1967

p. 34   *foresaw 'difficulties':* Wheeler-Bennett, 1958
      'Dowdy Duchess': St John, 1969

p. 35   *Churchill was aware:* c.f. (L) CAB 65 172 (40) 4 and
      (L) CAB 65 174 (40) 4

corrupt and unreadable: (W) 844E 001/51, 9 July
    1940
New York: (W) 844E 001/52, 20 July 1940
p. 36   'sweet morsel': (W) 844E 001/52, 20 July 1940, and
    memorandum from Truitt
    Monckton: Birkenhead, 1969
p. 37   gorged herself: c.f. Bermuda press conference
    Pan Am clipper: New Horizons, October 1940
p. 39   'middle-aged couple': Memphis Press-Scimitar, 21
    September 1940
p. 40   asked London: (L) CO23/709, 26 August 1940
    'sense of disappointment': (L) FO371/24249–556, 24
    August 1940
    'Don't you see?': St John, 1969
    she designed: Nassau Magazine, March 1941
p. 41   cost of the curtains: Godfrey Higgs, p.c.
    refusing a £10 grant: c.f. (N) Board of Works
    minutes, 28 May 1942, 17 October 1944
p. 43   'ideals of misgovernment': (L) CO 23/712
    'merchant princes': (L) CO 23/712, May 1940
p. 44   'fundamental fact': (L) CO 23/712, 27 March 1940
    a fleet: Dundas, 1938
p. 45   One in five: Department of Statistics, 1976
p. 46   'Booze Avenue': Clifford, 1964; de Winton Wigley,
    n.d.; Dupuch, 1967; Lythgoe, 1964, Messick, 1969
p. 48   'the prettiest village': Cooper, 1959
p. 49   Father Quentin Arnold Dittberner: Colinan, 1973
p. 50   'Ganymead [sic]': Clifford, 1964
    Harold Christie: McDermott, 1979
p. 51   trusts in Nassau: (N) files at Registrar General, esp.
    RoyWest Trust
p. 53   Bede Clifford: Clifford, 1964
p. 55   counting the people: St John, 1969
    fake Chippendale: Nassau Magazine, December 1940
    ADCs: (L) CO 231/701, 27 August 1940
    Executive Council: Godfrey Higgs, p.c.
    'I really think': Mrs Leslie Higgs, p.c.
p. 56   'I was once King': Forbes, 1946
    binges: c.f. (W) MID 2257–a–124, 24 April 1931
p. 57   cigars and brandy: Windsor, 1956, p. 339

p. 58 *Parcels of money:* J. H. Gaffney, p.c.
p. 61 *Moulichon:* (W) 844E 001/55, 12, 21 September, 20
       October, 1940; 58, 2 October 1940; 59, 6
       November 1940
       personal cable: (W) 844E 001/62½
p. 62 *wine from Sichel:* (W) 844E 001/121
       washing: (W) 844E 001/63, 23 October, 20
       November 1940
       a year later: (HP) Morgenthau papers, 450:79
       La Croë: (W) 844E 001/73, 5 March 1941
       scrawled on the file: (W) 844E 001/69
p. 63 *very special help:* (W) 844E 001/76½, 7 April 1941;
       844E 001/114
p. 64 *open boats:* (N) ExCo minutes: (W) US Coast Guard
       26/64, 17 October 1940
       'admission of Jews': (N) C171; (L) CO23/681
p. 65 *Frankfurt:* (L) CO23/681
p. 67 *of the first directors:* (N) Registrar General
p. 69 *no love for Britain:* (W) 800. 20210, Albert J.
       Lothian, 30 December 1941
       one Allied consul: Forbes, 1946
       radio masts high: (W) 862.20211/2641, 20 November
       1941
       direct to Roosevelt: (HP) PPF/Wenner-Gren, 6, 7
       September 1939
p. 70 *peace with Goering:* (W) OSS XL 13225, 18 July
       1945, quoting *Expressen*, Stockholm
       Krupp's front man: Manchester, 1969
p. 71 *told the Governor:* (W) 800.20211/WG 46½
       'My visit': (HP) PPF/Wenner-Gren
p. 72 *Mexico:* (L) FO371/30573, 28 November 1941
p. 73 *stateless artists: Veck.-Journalen,* 16 November 1941
       his agent Bigge: (HP) PPF/Wenner-Gren, 4 January
       1943
       Bédaux: (W) 740EW1939/1844, 5 March 1940
       Warren: (W) 800.20211/W G/44½, 25 January 1941
p. 74 *the American consul:* (W) 811.34544/202, 28
       November 1940
       A. J. Lothian: (W) 800.20210/Albert J. Lothian,
       30 December 1940

271

p. 75　*war came closer:* Pearce Jones, 1941; (L) CO 23/691
p. 76　*confined to port:* (W) 800.20211/WG/1
　　　　carried Bofors guns: (W) 800.20211/WG/1
p. 77　*'whisky and soda':* Mrs Leslie Higgs, p.c.
　　　　salary of £3000: Colonial List, 1939
　　　　expense account: (L) FO115/3453
　　　　Washington correspondent: (HP) OF48A, 13
　　　　　　December 1940, Newbold Noyes, *Washington
　　　　　　Evening Star*
p. 78　*'public figure':* c.f. Eden, 1966
　　　　'the Wennergren [sic] *yacht':* (W) 800.20211/–/
　　　　　　51½, 16 April 1941
　　　　private files: (HP) PSF/Great Britain 46
p. 79　*in German pay:* idem, 5 January 1937
　　　　Eleanor Roosevelt: (HP) ER to FDR, 4 November
　　　　　　1937
　　　　'misunderstandings': (HP) PSF/Great Britain 46
　　　　'Early in December': Wheeler Bennett, 1958 (quote
　　　　　　22 November 1940)
p. 80　*'good to see you':* (HP) PPF/7160, 31 December 1940
p. 82　*Canadian papers: Financial Post* of Toronto, quoted
　　　　　　Nassau Tribune, 3 January 1941
p. 83　*waiting at Cat Cay:* (W) 811.34544/425A, 2 January
　　　　　　1941
p. 84　*American Quisling:* (W) 862.20211/3, 14, 20 June
　　　　　　1941
　　　　'no sense whatever': (W) 862.20211/M/2, 5 March
　　　　　　1941
　　　　Case School: (W) 862.20211/M/15, 9 July 1941,
　　　　　　quoting UP, 1 June 1940
　　　　Sloan argued: (W) 862.20211/M/19, 8 August 1941,
　　　　　　quoting Sloan to Lewis, 6 April 1939
p. 85　*GM line:* (W) 862.20211/M/19
　　　　wooed by the Nazis: (W) 862.20211/M/16, 23 July
　　　　　　1941
　　　　an Opel plant: (W) 862.20211/M/16
p. 86　*at the dockside:* Etienne Dupuch, p.c.
　　　　holding $2,500,000: (W) 800.20211/271, 21 July
　　　　　　1942
p. 87　*first to warn:* (HP) PPF/WG, 4 January 1943

Rudolf Hess: (W) 740.0011 EW1939/21295
'*Little Princesses*': (L) PREM/4, 19 June 1940

p. 88 *matter in hand:* Churchill, 1951

p. 93 *Nelson Doubleday:* (N) Registrar General, file on Porcupine Club

p. 95 *secret assignations:* (W) 844E.001/70

p. 96 *Princeton arrived:* Robert Simmons Ewing, Clayton R. Gaylord, p.c.

p. 99 *de Marigny wrote:* (L) FO115 WT 1097/BB/1/44, October 1942
Oakes and Christie: (W) 800.503112/16, 22 July 1940

p.100 *introduction:* (W) 812.516/646, 15 April 1941

p.101 *sizeable stockholder:* (W) 812.516/646, 16 July 1941
officials estimated: (W) 800.20211/WG/80½, 16 December 1941

p.102 *Mobilia SA:* (W) 800/20211/WG/248, 9 June 1942
'*more "out in front"* ': (W) 740/00112A EW1939/5791
also in Nassau: (W) 812.516/646, 15 April 1941

p.103 *Embassy feared:* (W) 812.516/646, 16 July 1941
'*such proposals*': (W) 844E.12/5, transmitting report by Dr P. T. Crawford, 8 April 1944
'*We Southerners*': Forbes, 1946

p.106 *Pepsi Cola:* (L) FO 115 WT 1097/BB/1/44
abolish: (L) FO 115/4140
'*get rid of them*': (W) 844E.001/60, 1 November 1940

p.107 *way to find work:* Morison and Commager, *Growth of the American Republic*, New York, 1962, vol. II, p. 719
'*useful contribution*': (L) FO371/30640, 19 February 1942
Roosevelt anticipated: (HP) FDR OP 4101, 19 March 1941, 18 July 1941

p.109 *insensitive:* (L) CO23/691

p.115 *good reasons:* (L) PREM/4, March 1941 on

p.117 '*Matters*': (L) PREM/4, 19 July 1941

p.118 *Rosita Forbes:* Forbes, 1946

p.119 *to buy an island:* London files withdrawn

'*pal of Goering*': (W) 800.20211/WG/38, 28 May 1941

p.120 '*what it may be*': (W) 800.20211/WG/48, 22 June 1941

nominal scheme: (W) 800.20211/WG/54, 19 July 1941

British Intelligence: (W) 800.20211/WG/46½

'*defeatists*': (W) 800.20211/WG/211, 18 June 1942

p.121 *Panama Canal:* (W) 800/20211/77, 24 November 1941

'*thundered*': *New Horizons,* October 1941

'*much distressed*': (HP) PPF/7166, 24 September 1941

p.122 *grand progress:* c.f. (W) 844E.001/98–4/11, etc.

p.126 *passengers:* (W) 800/20211/271

p.129 *Cary Grant:* (W) 811/20212/34

'*political boss*': (L) FO115/34231

the firing: (N) C306A, 306, vol. 1

p.136 *Riot and reform:* (W) OPD 350.05, 2 July 1942

p.145 *A report:* (W) 844E.12/5, c.f. 844E.12/6

one in three: (W) 844E.12/5

'*untrained*': (W) 844E.12/5

p.147 *guarding the person:* Lt Col A. A. Fairrie, p.c.

great estates: (W) 800.20211/WG/278, 15 September 1942, transmits report by Hugh B. Griffith

p.148 *sad letters:* (W) 800.20211/265, intercept 1 September 1942

p.149 *his war:* (W) 800.20211/WG/209, 17 April 1942 and OSS/344152, 1 May 1943

'*as a gentleman*': (W) 800.20211/WG/138, 16 January 1942

as Adrian Alvarez: (W) 800.20211/WG/344, 11 August 1943

Bob Martin's: (L) FO 115 WT 1097/BB/1/44, 23 April 1944

expecting $750,000: (W) 800.20211/WG/138, 16 January 1942

Anderson was rumoured: (L) FO 115 WT 1097/BB/1/44

Bahamas General Trust: (N) Registrar General, see RoyWest Trust Company

p.150 *warned him:* (L) FO 115 WT 1097/BB/1/44
cabled London: (L) FO 371/30640
p.151 *startling story:* (W) OPD 381/Bahamas, 13 April 1942
bothering his contacts: (W) 800.20211/WG/267, 26
May 1942
p.153 *marriage was announced:* from testimony at trial of
Alfred de Marigny: see supra
p.155 *Rene McColl:* Sir John Foster, p.c.
series of meetings: (W) R & A report, 25 February
1942
p.156 *bulging safe:* (W) OPD 600.12, 19 August 1943
Bay Street: from testimony at Commission of Inquiry
into riot: see supra
p.163 *firehoses:* Mary Moseley to Eric Solomon (collection
of Roy Solomon)
took a club: Bert Cambridge, p.c.
p.164 *'Cambridge, my God!':* Bert Cambridge, p.c.
p.167 *'Burma Road':* Fawkes, 1978
p.169 *That was a lie:* (W) OPD 370.61, 11 January 1943;
c.f. (L) FO 371/30644, 4 June 1942
first day: Windsor, 1956, p. 341
'certain discussions': (L) FO 371/30644, 2 June 1942
'All very unfortunate': (L) FO 371/30644, 3 June
1942
plantation: (W) OPD 381/Bahamas, 24 June 1942
p.170 *'I only wish':* (W) OPD 370.61, 11 January 1943
refused to do: (W) e.g. OC 1123, 012D/8, 27
February 1942, 012C/2, 9 May 1943
This rumour: (W) OPD 370.61, 2 June 1942
'Situation quietened': (HP) PSF 49:1942, 2 June 1942
p.172 *cable London that:* (L) FO 371/30644
p.173 *'I wish to conclude':* Fawkes, 1978
p.176 *cable from London:* (L) FO 371/30644, 9 June 1942
Windsor replied: (L) FO 371/30644, 10 June 1942
p.178 *A full record:* (W) OPD 370.61, 18 July 1942,
transmitting MITP, 14 June 1942
p.182 *dined late:* Windsor, 1956, p. 342
p.184 *unseat:* Bert Cambridge, p.c.
p.186 *'poor little bugger':* Godfrey Higgs, p.c.

p.188 *confidential conversation:* (W) OPD 370.61, 11
       January 1943
p.192 *Queen Mary:* Windsor, 1956, p. 347–8
p.194 *terrible brief moment:* (W) 844 E.4061 Motion
       Pictures/6, 4 May 1942
p.195 *separate shower:* (L) CO 537/1266
p.197 *a scandal:* (N) C280
p.200 *between tailors:* Windsor, 1960
p.202 *was under arrest:* J. H. Gaffney, p.c.
p.203 *Nancy Oakes:* from de Marigny trial evidence
p.206 *'a very little matter':* (W) 844 E.001/118, 19 May
       1943
p.207 *'denied exemption':* (W) 811.711/4039, 18 June 1943
       Bédaux: (W) 862.20200/247 Bédaux, quoting *New
       York Times Herald*, 18 February 1944
       Fern Bédaux: (W) 862.504/905, 5 June 1943
p.208 *Poor Lord Beaverbrook:* Farrer, 1969
p.209 *feared the trouble:* (W) 844 E00/30, 17 May 1943
p.210 *bacon and egg: Nassau Guardian,* 1 May 1943, 18
       June 1943
p.213 *Sir Harry Oakes:* Dupuch, 1959
p.215 *still in bed:* Windsor, 1956, p. 346
p.218 *Mafia involvement:* Houtts, 1972; but also
       Commission, 1967; Messick, 1969
p.219 *voodoo killing:* Maxwell, 1955
p.221 *a phone call:* (W) Office of Censorship, 012B-XR-0/
       6C
p.227 *London was not happy:* (L) CO 23/714/68001/150,
       as dated
p.242 *prominent target:* (W) Office of Censorship, Chr box
       989
p.244 *further evidence:* (L) CO 23/714/68001/150, note
p.248 *narcotics charges:* (B) Criminal 40144, Eastern
       District of New York, 2 August 1944; (W)
       844E.114 Narcotics/9–1144, 11 September 1944
p.249 *waters of the Bahamas:* (L) FO 115/34231
       personal interview: (W) 844 E.6363/3, 6 March 1941
p.250 *'the difficulties':* (L) FO 115/34231, 16 November
       1943
       'perturbed': (L) FO 115/34231, 28 December 1943

p.251 *May arrived:* (W) 844 E 6363/9, 8 February 1944
p.252 *startling concept:* (W) 844 E 43/1, 4 March 1944
p.254 *325 men:* (L) FO 371/38536
p.255 *helped his friends:* (W) 800.20211/WG/postal
       intercept; (L) FO 370/38700
p.256 Eldarette: (W) 844E00/4–545, 5 April 1945

In the citations above, certain files in Washington whose reference numbers begin with '800.20211' are always followed by the name of the main subject. For brevity, WG stands for Wenner-Gren and M for James M. Mooney.

BIBLIOGRAPHY

Airlie, Mabell, Countess of, *Thatched with Gold*, London, 1962

Albury, Paul, *The Story of the Bahamas*, London, 1975

Birkenhead, Lord, *Walter Monckton*, London, 1969

Bocca, Geoffrey, *Life and Death of Sir Harry Oakes*, London, 1959

Bryan, J., III, and Murphy, Charles J.V., *The Windsor Story*, New York, 1979

Channon, Sir Henry, *Chips,* ed. Robert Rhodes James, London, 1967

Chase, Edna Woolman, and Chase, Ilka, *Always in Vogue*, London, 1954

Churchill, Winston, *The Second World War*, vol. IV, London, 1951

Clifford, Bede, *Proconsul*, London, 1964

Colinan, J. Barry, OSB, *Upon These Rocks*, Collegeville, Minn., 1973

Commission of Inquiry into the Organisation of the Business of Casinos in Freeport and in Nassau, London, 1967

Cooper, Diana, *The Light of Common Day*, London, 1959

Craton, Michael, *A History of the Bahamas*, London, 1962

Department of Statistics, Nassau, *Demographic Aspects of the Bahamian Population 1901–1974*, Nassau, 1976

Department of Statistics, *Monthly Newsletter #7*, Nassau, September 1971

De Winton Wigley, H., *With the Whisky Smugglers*, London, n.d. [ca. 1927]

Dundas, Charles, *Agriculture in the Bahamas*, Nassau, 1938

Dupuch, Etienne, 'Governorship of the Duke of Windsor', in *Bahamas Handbook*, Nassau, 1960

Dupuch, Etienne, *Tribune Story*, London, 1967

278

Dupuch, Eugene, *et al*, *The Murder of Sir Harry Oakes Bt*, Nassau, 1959

Eden, Anthony, *The Reckoning*, London, 1962

Eneas, Cleveland W., *Bain Town*, Nassau, 1976

Farrer, David, *G for God Almighty*, New York, 1969

Fawkes, Randol, *The Faith that Moved the Mountain*, Nassau, 1978

Forbes, Rosita, *Appointment with Destiny*, New York, 1946

Holm, John, 'African Features in White Bahamian English', in *English World Wide*, 1:1, Heidelberg, 1980

Houtts, Marshall, *Kings X*, New York, 1972

Legge, Edward, *Our Prince*, London, 1921

Lythgoe, Gertrude 'Cleo', *The Bahama Queen*, New York, 1964

McDermott, Benson, 'Harold Christie', in *Bahamas Handbook*, Nassau, 1978

Manchester, William, *The Arms of Krupp*, London, 1969

Martin, Ralph G., *The Woman He Loved*, New York, 1974

Maxwell, Elsa, *I Married the World*, London, 1955

Messick, Hank, *Syndicate Abroad*, London, 1969

Nicolson, Harold, *Diaries and Letters 1930–1939*, ed. Nigel Nicolson, London, 1966

Pearce Jones, Guy, *Two Survived*, New York, 1941

Peggs, A. Deans, 'A History of Bahamian Education', M.Ed. thesis, Durham

Pope-Hennessey, James, *Queen Mary 1867–1953*, London, 1959

St John, Adela Rogers, *The Honeycomb*, Garden City, New York, 1969

Shorer, Cyrus J., 'Population Growth of the Bahama Islands', PhD thesis, University of Michigan, 1955

Symonette, Michael C., and Canzoneri, Antonina, *Baptists in the Bahamas*, El Paso, 1977

Thompson, F. A., *A Short Geography of the Bahamas*, Nassau, 1944

Turley, Charles, *With the Prince Round the Empire*, London, 1926

Wall, E. Berry, *Neither Pest nor Puritan*, New York, 1940

Wheeler-Bennett, John W., *King George VI: His Life and Reign*, London, 1958

Windsor, Duchess of, *The Heart Has Its Reasons*, New York, 1956
Windsor, Duke of, *A King's Story*, New York, 1951
Windsor, Duke of, *A Family Album*, London, 1960